REFLECTIONS WITH MORNING COFFEE

365 Daily Devotions for Busy People

Sr. Dr. Vassa Larin
Vienna 2016

XENOPHON PRESS

Title:
Reflections with Morning Coffee: 365 Daily Devotions for Busy People

ISBN: 9783950436907
Copyright © 2016 Sister Vassa Larin.

All rights reserved. No part of this book may be reproduced, stored in a retrieval system, or transmitted in any form or by any means, electronic, mechanical, photocopying, recording, or otherwise, without the prior written permission of the author, except as provided by U.S.A. copyright law.

Published by Xenophon Press LLC
10237 Rogers Drive
Nassawadox Va 23413 USA
XenophonPress@gmail.com
1-757-442-1060

FOREWORD

This book of daily devotions is intended as an aid to anyone interested in making contemplation/meditation a part of daily life. Each reflection, based on a passage from Scripture and, occasionally, on the liturgical calendar of Byzantine-Rite Christianity, is brief, so that it can be fit into a busy schedule. The reflections are meant to be read only one per day, perhaps with one's morning-coffee, on the train-ride to work, or whenever one has five minutes. The brief daily reflection is also meant to be combined with some daily prayer and a bit of daily self-examination. That's the way these reflections were written—just one a day—throughout the course of one very busy year in Vienna, Austria.

The scriptural passages used here are based on the New Revised Standard Version, sometimes modified by the author according to her reading of the Greek text, and Old-Testament passages are translated based on the Septuagint.

JANUARY 1

BEGINNING AGAIN

"In the beginning was the Word, and the Word was with God, and the Word was God. He was in the beginning with God. All things were made through Him, and without Him nothing was made that was made." (Jn 1:1-3)

I am beginning the year, again. So let me think about the very basis for my "beginning." I do have a beginning, because I am created. I am not alone and meaningless. I have Meaning, because I am created by the eternal Word, the eternal Meaning, God, the Logos. *"In the beginning God created the heavens and the earth."* (Gen 1:1) My existence is not isolated; it is relational. I am a creature, and relate to my Creator, and to all creation.

Let me remember my Meaning, our Meaning, not as a New Year's resolution, but just for today. Because every day I begin again. I cannot build my connection with God today on yesterday's prayer or on last Sunday's church-service. Today let me say, repeatedly, *"In the beginning was the Word."* And let me fill my day with that Word, the eternal Meaning that is God. I take in a bit of Scripture in the morning, and carry it with me throughout my day.

JANUARY 2

RUNNING HIS RACE

"Therefore, since we are surrounded by so great a cloud of witnesses (the saints), let us also lay aside every weight (ὄγκον) and the sin that entangles easily, and let us run with perseverance the race that is set before us, looking to Jesus the pioneer and perfecter of our faith, who for the sake of the joy that was set before him endured the cross, disregarding its shame, and has taken his seat at the right hand of the throne of God. Consider him who endured such hostility against himself from sinners, so that you may not grow weary or lose heart. In your struggle against sin you have not yet resisted to the point of shedding your blood..." (Heb 12:1-3)

There are many worthy "causes" or struggles, which can foster my human sense of belonging, and make me want to get up in the morning. Today I am reminded in the passage from Hebrews that I have such a "cause." It is "the race that is set out before us," of the cross-carrying journey, pioneered by Christ Himself and traveled by "so great a cloud of witnesses." It is the spiritual struggle, with its quiet challenges and victories, according to the light-filled principles of His word.

As I begin this year, let me embrace my primary "cause" once again, laying aside "every weight" or secondary matter that may obscure the simple-yet-not-easy task before me. Let me put my daily growth in Christ first, and other matters second, that I may be truly, uniquely useful to Him and others close to me. I let Him in today, the "perfecter of our faith," to build with me and to do with me as He will, in the unique adventure that is "the race set out before us."

JANUARY 3

FROM THE STEM OF JESSE

"And there shall come forth a rod from the stem of Jesse, and a Branch shall grow out of his roots: And the spirit of the Lord shall rest upon him, the spirit of wisdom and understanding, the spirit of counsel and might, the spirit of knowledge and of the fear of the Lord; And shall make him of quick understanding in the fear of the Lord: and he shall not judge after the sight of his eyes, neither reprove after the hearing of his ears... The wolf also shall dwell with the lamb, and the leopard shall lie down with the kid; and the calf and the young lion and the fatling together; and a little child shall lead them." (Is 11:1-3, 6)

How immediately recognizable is the "character" described in these prophetic words. Centuries before His appearance to us in a manger in Bethlehem, our Lord Jesus Christ is called here "a rod out of the stem of Jesse,"—of the wealthy Jesse who lived in Bethlehem and had eight sons, the youngest of whom was David. The prophet Isaiah "sees" so vividly the "Spirit" of the God-Man, Who was to be a descendant of David: Isaiah "sees" Christ's wisdom, might, quick understanding, abstinence from superficial judgment ("he shall not judge after the sight of his eyes"). The prophet also "sees" the unifying, conciliatory effects of our Lord's coming to us in His humble, non-judgmental manner: The wolf shall dwell with the lamb, the leopard with the kid, and so on.

So the longing for, and vision of, the unique, divine-human Character of our Lord Jesus Christ was very much alive centuries before anyone had set eyes on Him. And perhaps surprisingly, today the prophet's vision refreshes mine, when my own has faltered or become weak through forgetfulness, carelessness, or some of the spiritual baggage I've accumulated throughout my week. Today let me be open to the great and small reminders from "so great a cloud of witnesses" surrounding me, both from the past and present. Let my vision and longing for Him be refreshed in the fellowship of the Spirit, offered in His one Body, that I may be led, with others, by "a little child," Who comes forth out of the stem of Jesse.

JANUARY 4

PREPARING HIS WAY

"The beginning of the gospel of Jesus Christ, the Son of God. As it is written in the prophet Isaiah: 'Behold, I am sending my messenger ahead of you, who will prepare your way; the voice of one crying out in the wilderness: Prepare the way of the Lord, make his paths straight. John the baptizer appeared in the wilderness, proclaiming a baptism of repentance for the forgiveness of sins. And people from the whole Judean countryside and all the people of Jerusalem were going out to him, and were baptized by him in the river Jordan, confessing their sins." (Mk 1:1-5)

So, John the Baptist "prepares the way of the Lord" by proclaiming "a baptism of repentance," that is, of "metanoia" (change of mind or change of focus). The people are being prepared for the "new," for the One who, as John testifies, "is more powerful" than John himself (Mk 1:7), by unburdening themselves of the "old" through confessing their sins.

As I prepare for the appearance of the Lord in the great feast ahead, be it His birth in Bethlehem (for those of us on the Older Calendar, who are still following the star), or His coming to the River Jordan to be baptized for His earthly ministry (for those who now prepare for Theophany), let me hear "the voice of one crying in the wilderness." Let me refocus today, once again, unburdening myself of the "old" and embracing the "new" opening up before me, in the ever-new, ever-surprising Person of my Lord Jesus Christ. Let me confess my sins, handing them over to the One who comes to "take away the sin of the world," (Jn 1:29) removing the roadblocks to my relationship with Him, with myself, and others. Today let me let Him "make His paths straight" in me. Amen.

JANUARY 5

RENEWAL OF ALL CREATION

"Prepare, O Zebulon, / and adorn yourself, O Naphtali; / River Jordan, cease flowing / and receive with joy the Master coming to be baptized. / Adam, rejoice with our First Mother / and do not hide yourself as you did of old in Paradise; / for having seen you naked, / He has appeared to clothe you with the first garment. / Christ has appeared to renew all creation."
(Byzantine Troparion-hymn of the Forefeast of Theophany)

Indeed, Christ renews "all creation" in His coming. And He does this not only "spiritually," by enlightening us through the light of His word, as He did in His preaching in the land of Galilee as prophesied: *"Land of Zebulun, land of Naphtali, on the road by the sea, across the Jordan, Galilee of the Gentiles—the people who sat in darkness have seen a great light..."* (Mt 4:15-16, cf. Is 9:1-2).

Christ renews "all creation" also physically, by taking on our human body, within our historical time, and inserting Himself into our material world. The Lord's enlightening "immersion" into our material reality is most clearly thematized in our celebration of His baptism in the Jordan. He immerses Himself in water, which makes up well over half of the human body, and covers over 70% of the Earth's surface.

Thus the material world, including my body, is renewed and enlightened in communion with Christ. For Christians, the body is not something from which we seek escape; nor is it to be disparaged or discounted in our "spiritual" journeys. Clothed in Christ, in baptism, we once again receive the "first garment" of God's perfect creation. We receive His purity, His perfection, in soul and in body, and no longer "hide ourselves," as Adam and Eve did "of old in Paradise."

Today let me remember that my "spiritual" journey also includes my Christ-enlightened body, and my care of it in my daily routine. Let me make healthy choices, whether eating, drinking, washing, or sleeping, as one "clothed in Christ." Because He is "the enlightenment of our souls and bodies," as we say in the Prayer of the Gospel, and to Him I send up glory today, with the Father and the Holy Spirit. Amen!

JANUARY 6

ACCEPTING HUMAN MINISTRY

"Then Jesus came from Galilee to John at the Jordan, to be baptized by him. John would have prevented him, saying, 'I need to be baptized by you, and do you come to me?' But Jesus answered him, 'Let it be (so) now; for it is proper for us in this way to fulfill all righteousness.' Then he consented. And when Jesus had been baptized, just as he came up from the water, suddenly the heavens were opened to him and he saw the Spirit of God descending like a dove and alighting on him. And a voice from heaven said, 'This is my beloved Son, in whom I am well pleased.'" (Mt 3:13-17)

St. John the Baptist was "sent from God" (Jn 1:6) for a specific ministry to the people; to "make straight the paths of the Lord" in the people's hearts, by calling them to "the baptism of repentance" or "metanoia," a change of mind/focus (Lk 3:3), which involved the confession of "sin" or "missing the mark" (in Greek the word "sin," "amartia," means "missing the mark").

Did Christ need a "change of mind" and hence a "baptism of repentance"? No, because He never sinned. But we do need it, time and again, because we lose focus and "miss the mark." And we need the help of other human beings, the ministry of other human beings, in changing course and "repenting"; we cannot do this alone. So Jesus subjects Himself to John's divinely-instituted ministry, as one of us. He shows us the importance of accepting the ministry of another human being, in this case John, in the whole business of "repentance," which clears up or "makes straight" His paths, the paths of His baptism in the Spirit.

Today let me be open to the ministry of other people, because it is "well-pleasing" to my Lord, according to the will of His Father, in the Holy Spirit. Christ "let it be" this way even with Him, when He accepted the ministry of another human being. So let me "let it be" this way with me, in Him.

JANUARY 7

NOT KNOWING IS OK

"And all those who heard it marveled at those things which were told them by the shepherds. But Mary kept all these things and collected (συμβάλλουσα) them in her heart." (Lk 2:18-19)

Mary, the Mother of God, witnessed many events, the meaning of which She did not entirely understand at the time these events occurred. There was much uncertainty and ambivalence in Her life. For example, when She and Joseph found themselves with no place to stay, when it came time for Her to give birth. God didn't seem to be providing for them, even though the new-born Child, as She knew, was no ordinary One. But She simply accepts the ambivalence, keeping these things in Her heart.

God sends me uncertainty and ambivalence as well. I don't always understand what's going on, or what is going to happen, in relationships, in financial matters, and various other situations. But when the uncertainty begins to dampen my spirits, let me remind myself that God does, in fact, know, and understand, everything far better than I do. Let me pray today for His will for me, even if I don't know or understand it, and the grace to realize it in my life.

JANUARY 8

HE SHOWS UP

"This is the day that the Lord has made; let us rejoice and be glad in it. Save us, we beseech you, O Lord! O Lord, we beseech you, give us success! Blessed is the one who comes in the name of the Lord. We bless you from the house of the Lord. The Lord is God, and has appeared unto us..." (Ps 117/118: 24-27)

Indeed, He appears unto us. He shows up. This is the Great Fact for us, which we celebrate in the great feasts of His appearance(s): Nativity and Theophany. The very first step of Christ's self-giving, self-sacrifice, is His showing up. Just like our own self-giving, in any relationship, begins with just showing up; being there.

As I celebrate the feast, let me "rejoice and be glad in it," in quiet contemplation of His self-giving, of His showing up, despite the awkward and even perilous consequences. He shows up, despite the poverty, despite the disturbance of the status quo (for Herod & Co.), despite the lack of financial and emotional resources for a proper welcome. He shows up, to offer new fellowship, new communion, with Him and in Him.

So let me also show up today, for Him and for others, despite the vulnerability or sacrifice this may entail. And let me be there to "bless Him from the house of the Lord," sharing in the vision of His appearance among us. It is the appearance of "the One who comes" into my life, again and again, so that I, in my turn, can come and greet Him and others in His name. "The Lord is God, and has appeared unto us." Glory be to Him.

JANUARY 9

SMALL STEPS

"Not everyone who says to me, 'Lord, Lord,' will enter the kingdom of heaven, but only the one who does the will of my Father who is in heaven." (Mt 7:21)

These words are uncomfortably straightforward. They immediately remind me that I fall short of Christ's call. And yet I know that these words are loving, because they are said by Christ. These are not the unreasonable demands of a tyrant. That's the way it is with the word of God: It is both a difficult and gentle truth.

Because I know this truth is given with love, I also implement it with love, with a proper love of myself, in small steps. Not like an unreasonable tyrant. Today I can make small adjustments to my schedule, to avoid a sinful routine. I can be a little more present for other people, and listen before I speak. I can face my responsibilities as best I can (say, reply to that unpleasant email, or tend to at least one or two of those unopened envelopes piled up on my desk). I can seek to give encouragement and praise, when necessary, rather than seek it for myself. I can be grateful for the small kindnesses of others, and for God's loving grace in my life.

JANUARY 10

GROWTH THROUGH PAIN

"Early on the first day of the week, while it was still dark, Mary Magdalene came to the tomb and saw that the stone had been removed from the tomb. So she ran and went to Simon Peter and the other disciple, the one whom Jesus loved, and said to them, 'They have taken the Lord out of the tomb, and we do not know where they have laid him.'" (Jn 20:1-2)

When Mary Magdalene (together with the other women) initially delivers the news of the empty tomb to the disciples, she thinks that the news is bad. Her feelings, at this point, are sorrow and unpleasant surprise. The unnamed "they" are blamed; "They" have taken her beloved Lord.

When someone or something I love is taken from me, let me not attribute to "them," whoever they are, what God has done. Because God does not do anything with the purpose of causing me harm. Through the pain of separation He leads me to growth and new life, as it happens at birth: the mother experiences pain in labor, and the baby immediately cries upon separation from the mother's womb. We know that the initial tears of both mother and child are a good thing, because they're a sign of new life and new growth. Just like the Cross is a sign of victory.

Today I remind myself of this sign, if I am faced with the pain of separation in any form. And I ask, in prayer, for the grace to grow through it, in the light of His glorious resurrection. *"Truly, truly, I say to you, unless a grain of wheat falls into the earth and dies, it remains alone; but if it dies, it bears much fruit."* (Jn 12:24)

JANUARY 11

MOVING FROM JUDGING TO HELPING

"...how can you say to your brother, 'Let me take the speck out of your eye,' when there is the log in your own eye? You hypocrite, first take the log out of your own eye, and then you will see clearly to take the speck out of your brother's eye." (Mt 7:2-5)

I don't have perfect self-knowledge, nor do I always see "the log in my own eye." In that state I only feel annoyed, frustrated, or helplessly baffled by other people's issues. But I do have a tool to help me see my own issues, and that's self-examination. I find it helpful to sit down and make a list, noting those things I repeatedly do, and then wish I hadn't done.

I can't turn these things around overnight, nor do I have the power to turn them around on my own, without God's loving help. But I can begin this prayerful process by taking an honest look at myself, and then handing my set of shortcomings over to God, so He can build with me on the foundation of humility. From this vantage-point I can lend others a hand from time to time, not as a self-appointed judge, but as a fellow-struggler.

JANUARY 12

THE HEART OF THE MATTER

"Incline not my heart to words of evil, to make excuses for sins..." (Ps 140/141: 4, according to the Septuagint translation)

"Sins" in this sense are not the primary obstacle to me leading a God-centered life. If I go to confession and am just preoccupied with "sins," I find that they will be the same ones over and over again. I need to look more deeply, into what is literally the "heart" of the matter. After all, before I make a bad choice and "sin," my heart must be inclined to do so. What is my heart's "inclination"? It's what I first and foremost strive for today; what I see as my central purpose. That affects all my thought processes and actions. I need God's grace in my heart to keep it inclined in the right direction; toward Him. His grace can do that. As it says in the final Old Testament reading of Pentecost: *"I will give you a new heart and put a new spirit within you; ...I will put My Spirit within you and cause you to walk in My statutes, and you will keep My judgments and do them."* (Ezek 36:26-27)

So I begin my day with prayer and some beneficial reading, opening my heart to the divine energies of the Holy Spirit. This is a sort of re-charging of my heart in the morning, which helps it stay on course.

JANUARY 13

RESPONSIBILITY = ABILITY TO RESPOND

"If anyone wishes to come after Me, he must deny himself, and take up his cross and follow Me." (Mt 16:24)

I recently heard someone say something perhaps obvious, but that I hadn't thought about quite in this way—that "responsibility" means "the ability to respond." So, facing up to my daily responsibilities, which can sometimes seem a drag, is simply that: responding to a call. And the bigger picture is, it's Christ's call to me, to carry my cross and follow Him. That's also what it means to be part of Church, or "ekklesia," which comes from the Greek "ek-kaleo": It means "the called out (ones)." Implicitly this means "the responding ones" as well!

The truth is, I have to go to a dinner today that I don't feel like going to. It's not a big deal, but neither are some other little things that I want to avoid or procrastinate away,

until I remember Who it is calling me. *"For my yoke is easy,"* He says, *"and my burden is light."* (Mt 11:30) This is true, when I see things in His light.

JANUARY 14

WITNESSING vs. ARGUING

"'If you are the Christ, tell us.' But He said to them, 'If I tell you, you will by no means believe. And if I also ask you, you will by no means answer me or let me go. Hereafter the Son of Man will sit on the right hand of the power of God...'" (Luke 22:67-69)

Here Jesus doesn't bother arguing with the chief priests and teachers, because He knows it's pointless. But then He goes on to witness to the truth of the matter: *"Hereafter the Son of Man will sit on the right hand..."*

I often fail to recognize when arguments are pointless—unless someone actually wants to know, and is asking a genuine question. It's not my job to go around arguing with people who aren't open to what I have to say.

But it's always my job to bear witness to Christ, as He bore witness. Not only and not even primarily through my words, but through daily life according to His. And I can do that, if I am in daily communion with Him, carrying His agenda, not mine, in my heart. *"Be my witnesses, and I too am a witness, says the Lord God, and my servant whom I have chosen."* (Isaiah 43:10)

JANUARY 15

NOT UNDERSTANDING "GOD'S WILL"

"Thy will be done, on earth as it is in heaven." (The Lord's Prayer, Mt 6:10)

These words, addressed to the Father, Who is in heaven, are first prayed by Christ, Who was here among us, on earth, when He prayed them. Through Him and in Him the will of the Father was being done *"on earth, as it is in heaven."* And so God's will continues to be done on earth, through Christ and in Christ.

I might not understand what "God's will" is in my various situations, prospects, relationships, and so on. And that's OK, because figuring out God's will is not a commandment. Desiring it is. That is, recognizing that my own will isn't enough.

Today I do understand that my will isn't enough. My own ambitions, motivations, and intentions easily go astray by something like self-seeking; they can also be paralyzed by fear, sloth, or whatever. I know I need to leave room for the grace of God's perfect will, to keep my will on track. Daily communion with Christ opens that door, when I pray with Him, *"Thy will be done."*

JANUARY 16

KEEPING IT SIMPLE

"And, behold, a woman, who was ill with an issue of blood twelve years, came behind him, and touched the hem of his garment: For she said within herself, If I just touch his garment, I shall be whole. But Jesus turned around, and when he saw her, he said, Daughter, take heart; your faith has made you whole. And the woman was made whole from that hour." (Mt 9:20—22)

It took great faith to think as this woman did. But the action she took was so simple; almost naïve: *If I just touch His garment...* She simply came close, and touched. Despite the potential embarrassment, rejection, or whatever else she could have imagined, had she thought out her little plan more thoroughly.

I can tend to over think things, creating barriers and complications to communion with God. But He is not complicated. When I feel overwhelmed, and life gets overcomplicated in my own head, let me hand it all over to Him, because in Him things are simple. I just need to come, get in touch, and keep in touch. Even if it's just the edge of His garment, it has healing on offer. And that doesn't change.

JANUARY 17

LOVING HIS EPIPHANY

"As for you, always be sober, endure suffering, do the work of an evangelist, carry out your ministry fully. As for me, I am already being poured out as a libation, and the time of my departure has come. I have fought the good fight, I have finished the race, I have kept the faith. From now on there is reserved for me the crown of righteousness, which the Lord, the righteous judge, will give me on that day, and not only to me but also to all who have come to love (τοῖς ἠγαπηκόσι) *his appearing* (τὴν ἐπιφάνειαν αὐτοῦ)." (2 Tim 4:5-8)

In the final words of this passage, the Apostle reveals the motivation for his entire journey of "fighting the good fight" and "keeping the faith." His entire journey, for which he is about to receive "the crown of righteousness," has stemmed from love. St. Paul came to love the Lord's "epiphany" or appearance. This, he is saying to Timothy, is the foundation of "the work of an evangelist," and everything that comes with it: "always being sober" and "enduring suffering" and "carrying out ministry."

My Lord Jesus Christ "appears" or reveals Himself in different, specific ways and times to each of us, just as He revealed Himself in a unique way to Saul, when he was in the middle of zealously persecuting Christians. And the youthful Pharisee, Saul, was immediately struck, even blinded, with love for the Person of Jesus Christ, Who thus interrupted Saul's misguided zeal.

Today let me open up to Christ's "epiphanies" to me, in the midst of whatever I am doing. Let me let Him interrupt any misguided ambition or attitude, be it self-centeredness, anxiety, or misguided desire, and embrace His love. It calls me to true fulfilment, sometimes through other people, sometimes through situations, sometimes through my own emptiness. "Come and abide in us," I say to His Spirit today, opening up to the One Who has opened up to me, in His loving epiphany.

JANUARY 18

SACRAMENTS AND ME

"My son, give Me your heart, and let your eyes observe My ways." (Prov 23:26)

Every step I take to salvation, on my journey of following Christ, including participation in the sacraments, must include my wholehearted wanting to do so. The sacraments don't work "magically," nor does the Holy Spirit work forcibly, according to some automatic formula, against my will or against my heart.

So let me take extra care to embrace His work, also in the sacraments, wholeheartedly. If I am seeking communion with Him in the Eucharist, let me understand that I truly want communion; to be one with the Body of Christ. If I am seeking forgiveness for my sins at Confession, let me bring to the table true "repentance," a true "change of mind." If I want to get married, let me first discern that I truly want this union in my heart, forever, like the one that exists between Christ and His Church. And so on. (Don't worry, people, I don't want to get married. Just threw that one in.)

Let me not take the sacraments for granted, and ask God for the willingness to embrace them wholeheartedly. Because He wants my heart, and not a robot going through certain, automatic motions: *"My son, give Me your heart,"* He says, *"and let your eyes observe My ways."* (Prov 23:26)

JANUARY 19

CAN'T START A FIRE WITHOUT A SPARK

"I baptize you with water for repentance," says John the Baptist. "But after me comes one who is more powerful than I, whose sandals I am not worthy to carry. He will baptize you with the Holy Spirit and fire." (Mt 3:11)

Baptism is often thought of as a "washing away" of our sins. But it is so much more. It is Spirit and fire, specifically because He was baptized. And, sharing our human nature, He was One of us. We don't "imitate" Christ's baptism; we participate in it. And we don't just get "washed"; we are buried and re-born to new life, in His Spirit and His fire.

However, just as Jesus was baptized at the very beginning of His public mission, so is our baptism just the beginning. I did, indeed, receive the gift of life in the Holy Spirit, as well as the gift of His "fire," like a spark, in my heart, at baptism. But this "fire," which is often but a spark, needs to be constantly tended to and rekindled when necessary. A daily "re-focusing," - that is, daily "repentance," does this, when I take a bit of time for it, in prayer, contemplation, and self-examination. Let me remember this gift of Spirit, and fire, which I carry around in my heart, so that I tend to it on a daily basis.

JANUARY 20

SHINING IN DARKNESS

"In him was life, and the life was the light of all people. The light shines in the darkness, and the darkness did not overcome it. There was a man sent from God, whose name was John. He came as a witness to testify to the light, so that all might believe through him. He himself was not the light, but he came to testify to the light. He was the true light that enlightens everyone coming into the world." (Jn 1:4-9)

Today I am reminded that Jesus Christ, "the light of all people," does indeed "shine in the darkness." This is why I need not hesitate to approach Him, in prayer, despite the shortcomings and "dark spots" in my understanding of Him. I do not understand Him perfectly, and yet this lack of understanding is no obstacle to communion and enlightenment in Him. It is also no obstacle to testifying to Him, as John the Baptist did, although John did not "know" the Son of God, Whom "no one knows except the Father" (Mt 11:27). It is not entirely different in our human relationships: our dedication and love for one another "functions" despite the fact that we don't perfectly "know" one another or any human being, including ourselves.

Only God knows us as we are, and we are only given to know Him when enlightened by His true light, His Son, Who "enlightens everyone" who steps into His light. Let me not hesitate to do that today, taking some time for heartfelt prayer and a bit of reading of His word. *"In Him was life,"* says the Gospel of John, *"and the life was the light of all people,"*— of all people, yesterday and today, with no exceptions.

JANUARY 21

RE-DEFINING SUCCESS

"But Jesus called them and said to them, 'You know that those who are considered rulers over the Gentiles exercise lordship over them, and their great ones exercise authority over them. Yet it shall not be so among you; but whoever desires to become great among you shall be your servant. And whoever of you desires to be first shall be slave of all. For the Son of Man did not come to be served, but to serve, and to give His life a ransom for many." (Mk 10:42-45)

Here Jesus re-defines what many people understand as "greatness" or, in modern-day terms, "success." The measure of greatness, according to Him, is service; the extent to which one serves; gives of oneself.

So let me see any work I do today in this light; in the light of service to others, rather than self-serving. This means if I'm doing something, be it cooking a meal for loved ones, or singing in the church-choir, or giving a talk somewhere, let it be to share of myself, rather than to impress. If I give someone a call, let the other person be heard rather than just unload my own opinions or problems. I find this approach is quietly rewarding, anyway, while self-seeking is insatiable. As such, it only leads to dissatisfaction and frustration. God's approach to work, as it happens, is easier than one governed by the evasive concept of self-seeking "success."

JANUARY 22

BUILDING WITH GOD

"Everyone then who hears these words of mine and does them will be like a wise man who built his house on rock." (Mt 7:24)

It's easy to misunderstand our spiritual journey as a bunch of negatives: Don't do this, don't do that. From this point of view, my faith turns into mere "religion" in the pagan sense; that is, a burdensome obligation before a demanding divinity. But faith in the living, Triune God is actually about the big "Do," of building, step by step, and growing, from day to day, on the foundation of God's Word, in His grace.

Of course, the affirmation of my will, to bring it into harmony with God's will, means distancing and excluding that which is not His will. But let me keep my eye on the underlying, affirmative choice I am making today: to build and grow and move forward, in God. I pray today that He build with me, and do with me, as He will.

JANUARY 23

DEALING WITH DIFFERENCE

"...when you come together in the church, I hear that there are divisions among you; and I partly believe it. For there must also be differences/heresies (αἱρέσεις) among you, so that those who are reliable/tested (δόκιμοι) may be made manifest among you." (1 Cor 11:18-19)

Obviously, this passage talks about a very common occurrence among human beings: differences of opinion and divisions. (We need not understand the word "heresies" here in the later, dogmatic sense, because the Apostle is talking about disagreements within the Church, *"when you come together in the church"*). And he is saying that our reaction to disagreements, be they great or small, is a measure of our "reliability," or we could also say "genuineness," as members of a community.

This tells me that I need to take care, and watch my reaction to any polarizing and divisive issues, which can potentially wreak havoc both within me, and in my relationships with my immediate or larger community. Before I jump in and contribute to discussion, either in person or online, I need to ask myself: Is it worth it? Am I building up, or damaging? Am I leaving room for the grace of the Holy Spirit, or is my own agenda in the forefront, cutting me off from Him?

Let me be careful today, and remember that any disagreement is a test for me, to keep Him in the picture. So I'm not one of *"those,"* as it says in the Psalm, *"who say: Our tongue we will magnify; our lips are our own—who is the Lord to us?"* (Ps 11/12:4)

JANUARY 24

SERVING HIM WITHOUT FEAR

"Thus he has shown the mercy promised to our ancestors, and has remembered his holy covenant, the oath that he swore to our ancestor Abraham, to grant us that we, being rescued from the hands of our enemies, might serve him without fear, in holiness and righteousness before him all our days..." (Lk 1:72-75)

This prophecy, spoken by Zacharia after the birth of his son, St. John the Baptist, mentions us serving God "without fear, in holiness and righteousness before Him." What kind of "fear" is Zacharia talking about? The kind that is an obstacle to "holiness and righteousness before Him," before God.

The non-holy and non-righteous kind of fear usually involves: 1. Fear of people and their opinions, and/or 2. Fear of economic insecurity. If I pay attention, I find that most "sins," most misdirections of my will, are somehow connected to these fears and related ones, like fear of rejection, failure, or even of success. So my cross-carrying journey to "holiness" and "righteousness,"—that is to say, my "salvation," consists largely of letting go of these bad kinds of fear, and replacing them with faith.

Today let me renew my prayerful contact with Him, Who came and served without fear, even unto death, a death on the Cross, that we "might serve Him without fear." Let me let His grace remove any crippling, un-holy and un-righteous fears today, and move forward with Him and in Him. *"The Lord is my light and my savior,"* I say today, as so many have said before, *"whom then shall I fear?"* (Ps 26/27:1)

JANUARY 25

HAVE MERCY

"Blessed are the merciful, for they shall obtain mercy." (Mt 5:7)

The word "mercy" is so often mentioned in Byzantine church-services, particularly in the brief prayer, *"Lord, have mercy"* (*Kyrie eleison*). The Greek word for "mercy" (*eleos*) means much more than some external "withholding of punishment" (which is what we usually understand it to mean in English). It is a divine energy; that is to say, its source is God—so we constantly ask Him for it. In our terms it is an internal disposition; an overflowing of the heart with compassionate, self-giving love. So, when I ask God for "mercy," I am asking not only to receive it, but to carry it on; to be a vessel of His "mercy" in this world.

I often don't notice the small opportunities I have, on a daily basis, to "have mercy" or "show mercy." There may be a person or people dependent on me in some way, looking to me, in some small way, for compassion or at least recognition. Today I can take my demands and expectations of them a notch down; it might make their day to hear an encouraging word from me, rather than criticism.

And I myself fall into this category, of people in need of my "mercy": I can be gentler with myself today, letting go of unreasonable demands and expectations, and remembering to take care of myself, with God's nourishing word, and in the Spirit of His divine "mercy."

JANUARY 26

POWER IN WEAKNESS

"But he said to me, 'My grace is sufficient for you, for my power is made perfect in weakness.' Therefore I will boast all the more gladly about my weaknesses, so that Christ's power may rest on me." (2 Cor 12:9)

Here St. Paul honestly witnesses to God's power in his life, despite his own weaknesses. The Apostle's witness is very powerful precisely because he shares it genuinely, admitting to his weakness, his struggle.

Today I remember this honesty of the great Apostle Paul, when I try to witness to Christ in the context of my own world. My struggle is fortifying to others only when I share it honestly, without pretending or posing; being myself. Because God's grace shows forth in our weaknesses, when we witness to Him honestly, being ourselves and sharing ourselves with fellow-strugglers.

JANUARY 27

GROWING WITH THE WEEDS

"He put another parable before them, saying, 'The kingdom of heaven may be compared to a man who sowed good seed in his field, but while his men were sleeping, his enemy came and sowed weeds among the wheat and went away. So when the plants came up and bore grain, then the weeds appeared also. And the servants of the master of the house came and said to him, 'Master, did you not sow good seed in your field? How then does it have weeds?' He said to them, 'An enemy has done this.' So the servants said to him, 'Then do you want us to go and gather them?' But he said, 'No, lest in gathering the weeds you root up the wheat along with them. Let both grow together until the harvest, and at harvest time I will tell the reapers, Gather the weeds first and bind them in bundles to be burned, but gather the wheat into my barn.'" (Mt 13:24-30)

In this parable the Lord describes the coexistence of good and bad in this world, both within me, and within the broader society of believers, the Church. Through this parable He prevents unrealistic expectations of our "purity" along the journey to salvation. To be sure, I need to desire perfection and strive for it. But it is in God's power, not mine, to make perfect and to sanctify, at His pace and in His time.

So today I remember that somehow, in ways I may not understand, it is beneficial for me to live with certain "weeds" or shortcomings, both within me and in the context of my Church. As it says here, I not only coexist with these "weeds," but I "grow" with them: *"both grow together,"* says Christ, *"until the harvest."* I remember today that God can and will remove the "weeds," in His own time.

JANUARY 28

FAMILY FIRST?

"While he was still speaking to the crowds, his mother and his brothers were standing outside, wanting to speak to him. Someone told him, 'Look, your mother and your brothers are standing outside, wanting to speak to you.' But to the one who had told him this, Jesus replied, 'Who is my mother, and who are my brothers?' And pointing to his disciples, he said, 'Here are my mother and my brothers! For whoever does the will of my Father in heaven is my brother and sister and mother.'" (Mt 12:46-50)

Jesus has a loving mother and other close relatives, but He nonetheless doesn't abandon the people to whom He is ministering at this moment, while "still speaking to the crowds," to rush off and greet His immediate family. Why not?

Here, Christ is warning against familial exclusivity; that is, the type of family that is closed in on itself, preferring its own little familial circle to the exclusion of others. Such a self-serving and self-centered family life is not only egotistical, but can lead to various forms of unhealthy familial codependency. Hence a Christian family, the "little church" within the broader society, is not self-isolated, but called to be inclusive of others; to share its warmth and love with those "outsiders" who may be in need of attention and inclusion. Today I am called to share the gifts of my own family's love and warmth with those in need who may cross my path.

JANUARY 29

SEPARATED BY RELATIONSHIPS

"He entered Jericho and was passing through it. A man was there named Zacchaeus; he was a chief tax collector and was rich. He was trying to see who Jesus was, but on account of the crowd he could not, because he was short in stature. So he ran ahead and climbed a sycamore tree to see him, because he was going to pass that way. When Jesus came to the place, he looked up and said to him, 'Zacchaeus, hurry and come down; for I must stay at your house today.' So he hurried down and was happy to welcome him. All who saw it began to grumble and said, 'He has gone to be the guest of one who is a sinner.'..." (Lk 19:1-6)

Zacchaeus is not able to see Christ in the crowd, and this isn't only because he was short. Zacchaeus was despised by the crowd, and deservedly so, because he was a corrupt tax-collector. So, pushing his way to the front of this crowd would not have been an easy option for him; he may have ended up with a black eye.

Zachhaeus's relationships with other human beings force him, a wealthy, accomplished man, up a tree. It's the best he can do under these circumstances, which distance him not only from the crowd, but from seeing Christ. So the first thing Zacchaus resolves to do, after the Lord unexpectedly sheds His grace-filled light on Zachhaus's predicament, is to make amends with others: *"Lord,"* he says, *"...if I have defrauded anyone of anything, I will pay back four times as much."* (Lk 19:8)

Today let me see if any broken relationships keep me from seeing Christ, from letting Him into my "house." And let me become willing to make amends, where I can. Because my Lord is willing to enter my house, even among any mess I have made, if only I am willing to let Him in. "Lord," I say today, come "to be the guest of one who is a sinner," and shed Your light on my predicament. Amen.

JANUARY 30

LIVING IN THE NOW

"Glory be to the Father and to the Son and to the Holy Spirit, now and ever and unto the ages of ages." (A doxology of Byzantine-Rite church services)

This oft-repeated doxology reminds me of the need to focus on my present-day; on the now. Because, although it does indirectly mention the past ("and ever"), and extends into eternity ("the ages of ages"), the focus of this brief doxology is first and foremost on the "now."

In practical terms this means that today I must not be discouraged by the "what ifs" of my past, nor be distracted from my immediate responsibilities, situations, and relationships by imagining others that I would like to have in the future. I can't be grateful for, and attentive to, my present reality, if I am constantly imagining a different one. Today I am called to accept myself, other people, and situations as they are, rather than what I would like them to be. Let me be grateful for the wisdom in what God is sending me now, so that I can ascribe glory to Him, and have His glory be made manifest in my life, in the now.

JANUARY 31

BRINGING FORTH THE NEW

"Then he said to them, 'Therefore every scribe who is instructed in the kingdom of heaven is like the owner of a house, who brings forth out of his treasure things new and old." (Mt 13:52)

In this passage Christ is talking about those who are "instructed" in Christian teaching, and minister "out of this treasure" in some way. I find these words relevant to any of us more or less intellectual people, who aren't content just to believe, but make an effort to learn about faith, and study it at length. This study then compels us to share this knowledge, to "bring forth" from this treasure, in some form or other—whether we are priests or not. Even if my "ministry" is only to myself, I do "bring forth" from the storeroom of my heart and mind, in some form.

What strikes me about this passage today is that Jesus mentions bringing forth "things new,"—not just "old." And, as many commentators have noted, He does not mean the "Old" Testament and the "New." What He means is that I am called to ever-new insights about my faith, in ever-new situations, on a daily basis. I am not just called to repeat what has been said or thought in the past, but to live my faith anew every day, giving new birth, in my own context, in the context of today's Church, to the Word of God. That's why the Mother of God is classically seen as a symbol of the Church, which, in every new generation, gives new birth to the Word of God.

That's a challenging and exciting prospect. So I remind myself today to embrace it, "bringing forth" the treasures of the Word of God in the context of my own life, in ever-new ways.

FEBRUARY 1

WAITING TO MEET HIM

"Now there was a man in Jerusalem whose name was Simeon; this man was righteous and devout, looking forward to (προσδεχόμενος) the consolation (παράκλησιν) of Israel, and the Holy Spirit rested on him. It had been revealed to him by the Holy Spirit that he would not see death before he had seen the Lord's Messiah. Guided by the Spirit, Simeon came into the temple; and when the parents brought in the child Jesus..." (Lk 2:25-27)

So Simeon did all this "waiting." Not just waiting, but expecting and longing in hope, in faith, for The Expectation (προσδοκία), as the Messiah was often referred to in Tradition. Because faith, as Hebrews 11 reminds me, "is the assurance of things hoped for, the conviction of 'things not seen.'" (Heb. 11.1) And many saints before Simeon "died in faith, not having received the things promised, but having seen them and greeted them from afar." (Heb 11:13)

Today I'm reflecting on the "righteousness and devotion" of this waiting, this longing, which blesses this "cloud of witnesses," together with St. Simeon, even before the fulfilment in Christ. This "looking forward to the consolation" is apparently essential to meeting Christ, and already a blessing in and of itself. "Blessed are those who hunger and thirst for righteousness," says the Lord, "for they shall be filled." (Mt 5:6)

So today let me direct my desires and hopes toward Light, directing my vision toward Christ, in His Spirit-filled word. He has come, indeed, to meet me. So let me let Him make that meeting happen, in the temple of everything He sends into my life today.

FEBRUARY 2

CROSS-CARRYING LOVE

"Then Simeon blessed them, and said to Mary his mother, 'Behold, this child is destined for the fall and rising of many in Israel, and for a sign which will be spoken against. Yes, a sword will pierce through your own soul also, that the thoughts of many hearts may be revealed." (Lk 2:34-35)

On this occasion, when Jesus is brought into the temple on the fortieth day after His birth, St. Simeon prophetically tells Mary, the Mother of God, about a "sign," and about the "sword" that shall pierce Her soul. He is talking about the cross. More specifically, he is talking about Her cross, because Her love for Her Son made His cross Her own.

These words carry a sad message about those who will "speak against" the Cross. But they also celebrate the love for Christ exemplified by the All-Holy Virgin, and all others who, through love, become co-carriers of His cross. Today the cross continues to "reveal the thoughts of many hearts," including my own. I can take it up today, or shrink away from it, or even "speak against" it, in different ways. Let me embrace it today, in the same Spirit as She did, in the Spirit of love for Her divine Son. And today I ask for grace-filled help on this journey from Her, who as a co-carrier of the cross is "full of grace."

FEBRUARY 3

WONDER AND SURRENDER

"...and when the parents brought in the child Jesus, to do for him what was customary under the law, Simeon took him in his arms and praised God, saying, 'Master, now you are dismissing (ἀπολύεις, releasing) *your servant in peace, according to your word; for my eyes have seen your salvation, which you have prepared in the presence of all peoples, a light for revelation to the Gentiles, and for glory to your people Israel.' And the child's father and mother wondered* (θαυμάζοντες) *at all that was said about him."* (Lk 2:27-33)

Two things are happening in this passage:
    1. Wonder and
    2. Surrender.

On the one hand, St. Simeon is filled with wonder, seeing this Child and His "parents." So Simeon takes Christ in His arms and "praises God," proclaiming his famous prophecy—a prophecy not only about salvation coming to "all peoples," but about his own death, to which he now readily surrenders. On the other hand, St. Joseph and the Mother of God also "wonder" at all that is said, as their cross-carrying, self-offering journey with this Child continues to be full of surprises. Indeed they "wonder" as they do not fully understand, because "wonder" begins where comprehension ends. And yet they will continue to walk this journey, in surrender to God's will. Even when "a sword will pierce the soul" of the All-Holy Virgin, as Simeon tells Her in the next passage (Lk 2:35).

Today let me stop and wonder at what God is showing me in my life, rather than fight to attain control of the situations and people He sends me today. Because "salvation" or "recovery" is a something, and indeed a Someone, I receive. It is not a Someone I "figure out" or control. Let me be open to meeting Christ today, in openness to His light-giving will. In wonder at, and surrender to, His incomprehensible grace.

FEBRUARY 4

REDEMPTION FROM WHAT?

"Now there was one, Anna, a prophetess, the daughter of Phanuel, of the tribe of Asher. She was of a great age, and had lived with a husband seven years from her virginity; and this woman was a widow of about eighty-four years, who did not depart from the temple, but served God with fastings and prayers night and day. And coming in that instant she gave thanks to the Lord, and spoke of Him to all those who awaited the redemption of Jerusalem (λύτρωσιν Ἰερουσαλήμ)." (Lk 2:36-38)

So the prophetess Anna, a woman, came to the temple and "in that instant," with no prompting or blessing from any human being, gave thanks to the Lord, and, what is more shocking still, "spoke." She spoke "of Him" to all those willing to listen, to all those who "awaited the redemption," who awaited "deliverance," "release," or "liberation" of Jerusalem. From what?

One may have thought, from the political power of the Romans. But we know better, in hindsight, that this was not the "redemption" that our Redeemer brought. He did not, in fact, bring me any particular brand of politics. The "release" that Christ brings me is from the bondage of "self." He brings me a new focus—His light, His Person, and the power of His grace, to which I can hand over my preoccupations and burdens, taking up His "burden" instead, a burden that is "light." (Mt 11:30) No longer do I need to chase around in circles, inside of me, various issues and problems, on my own.

Let me be liberated today, in my Redeemer, letting Him into my schedule, in prayer and contemplation of His word, in the freedom of His Spirit. Let me let Him release me through His gifts of humility, meekness, love, and service, which take me out of myself and allow me both to listen and to speak "of Him" and "in Him." For His is the kingdom, the power, and the glory, today and forever.

FEBRUARY 5

ASKING FOR WISDOM

"In Gibeon the LORD appeared to Solomon in a dream at night: and God said, 'Ask what I shall give you." (And Solomon replies:) *"...Give...your servant an understanding heart to judge your people, that I may discern between good and bad...' And the speech pleased the LORD, that Solomon had asked this thing."* (1 Kings 3:5, 9-10)

Of all the things King Solomon could have asked for, he asks for "this thing" that is wisdom; that is, "discernment between good and bad." What is remarkable to me in this well-known passage is not primarily that the young Solomon (who was just a boy at the time) valued wisdom above all things, but that he recognized that it is a gift from God.

So, I need to ask God for "wisdom" or "discernment." And I must say, as I get older, I increasingly see the need for it in my own life. I often simply don't know what is truly a good thing, a good decision, and what is a bad one. I am not sure how to understand a certain situation; whether I should try and change it, or just accept it. I sometimes don't know when to say something, and when to shut up; when I need to tackle my work, and when I need to just be still and do nothing; when I'm truly being helpful, or just people-pleasing, and so on.

Today I remember to ask God for "an understanding heart," and the wisdom to "discern between the good and bad," before all things. Because this is a gift from Him, and it pleases Him when we ask "this thing."

FEBRUARY 6

HURRY AND COME DOWN

"(Zacchaeus) was trying to see who Jesus was, but on account of the crowd he could not, because he was short in stature. So he ran ahead and climbed a sycamore tree to see him, because he was going to pass that way. When Jesus came to the place, he looked up and said to him, 'Zacchaeus, hurry and come down; for I must stay at your house today.'" (Lk 19:3-5)

Zacchaeus is a rich tax-collector, which means he led a corrupt life and became rich by corrupt means. But he makes this small effort to see Christ, by—rather awkwardly—climbing up a tree. And then Jesus unexpectedly rewards Zacchaeus's awkward effort, telling him to come down, because He wants to visit the corrupt tax-collector's house.

I also make some efforts, often awkward ones, to get a glimpse of Christ. And I know, frankly, that my life isn't what it should be, and that these "efforts" aren't what they should be either. I don't pray nor read the word of God nearly enough.

Nonetheless, the little I do can make me feel like I've "climbed" a bit higher, above the heads of other people.

Today let me hear the Lord's loving and unexpected voice, telling me to "hurry and come down." Otherwise, perched as I awkwardly am, in my little tree, I can't greet Him in my house. He needs my feet planted firmly on the ground of humility, as His were, so He can break bread with me.

FEBRUARY 7

WRITTEN FOR US

"For whatever things were written before were written for our instruction, that we through the patience and comfort of the Scriptures might have hope." (Rom 15:4)

Here St. Paul states the obvious about the Scriptures: that they were written for us. That is, for us actually to read them, and to be instructed and comforted by them. And that we might have hope; the hope of His Kingdom. They are not written as some kind of legal or political system, as a plan for an earthly kingdom. So I need not bash other people over the head with my Bible, because I'm not called to impose my reading of it on anyone but myself.

Today I remind myself of the gifts I receive through a daily reading of Scripture, even if it's just a little bit: instruction, patience, comfort, and hope. And I thank God today, from the bottom of my heart, that He did not leave me without instruction, without consolation, or without hope, in this world. He accompanies me with His Word, reminding me daily that I am not alone.

FEBRUARY 8

FELLOWSHIP OF THE WEAK & THE STRONG

"...Then Peter and the other disciple (John) set out and went toward the tomb. The two were running together, but the other disciple outran Peter and reached the tomb first. He bent down to look in and saw the linen wrappings lying there, but he did not go in. Then Simon Peter came, following him, and went into the tomb. He saw the linen wrappings lying there, and the cloth that had been on Jesus' head, not lying with the linen wrappings but rolled up in a place by itself. Then the other disciple, who reached the tomb first, also went in, and he saw and believed; for as yet they did not understand the scripture, that he must rise from the dead." (Jn 20:3-9)

Peter and John run to the tomb, having heard the disturbing news from Mary Magdalene that it was empty. It is understandable that John, the youngest of the disciples, runs faster than the older Peter. What is more remarkable is that John, who faithfully remained by the Cross to the very end, still has an open heart to Peter, who just recently thrice denied Christ. So at this point, John is "stronger" than Peter, but John's heart is no less open to him.

In fact, John follows Peter's lead when they get to the tomb. John's sensitive nature doesn't allow him to enter the tomb. He stands in trepidation or perhaps confusion, just peeking in to see the abandoned linen wrappings. Here, Peter's strength of character is a help to John, because Peter doesn't think twice when he gets to the tomb. He hurries inside, and John follows. Now, inside the tomb, John is once again the "stronger" one, because John "sees and believes," while Peter remains in the dark. Peter, apparently bogged down by his denial of Christ, is not quick to recognize light and hope when they stare him in the face. Thus a denial of Christ makes us condemn ourselves, even when God is offering us light.

I remind myself today of this remarkable fellowship of the disciples, both in strength and weakness. God supports my faith, at its strong and weak points, through other faithful, whatever their strengths or weaknesses. Let me have an open heart today, and remember that God works through other people.

FEBRUARY 9

SEEING THE SIGNS

"Then the Pharisees and Sadducees came, and testing him asked that he would show them a sign from heaven. He answered and said to them, 'When it is evening you say, It will be fair weather, for the sky is red; and in the morning, It will be foul weather today, for the sky is red and threatening. Hypocrites! You know how to discern the face of the sky, but you cannot discern the signs of the times. A wicked and adulterous generation seeks after a sign, and no sign shall be given to it except the sign of the prophet, Jonah.' And he left them and departed." (Mt 16:1-4)

The Pharisees and Sadducees were usually in disagreement with one another, but they were unified in their opposition to Christ, because He did not act according to their arrogant and self-centered expectations. The Lord had already shown them plenty of "signs," because every miracle He worked, healing the sick, feeding a multitude of the hungry, and drawing crowds of the poor and neglected to hear His healing word, was a sign with which He chose to reveal Himself. But the Pharisees and Sadducees are blind to these signs in the here and now, among the people surrounding them. The arrogant are capable of being attentive to things like the weather, but not to the living and breathing human beings near them. And now they demand a sign "from heaven."

Thus I can easily be distracted from the "signs" with which God is choosing to reveal Himself in my life, through the situations and human beings in my immediate surroundings. I can become preoccupied with other issues, like far-away events I follow in the news (never satisfying), or even the weather, in a way that distracts me from my immediate responsibilities; in a way that distracts me from the presence of Christ and His signs in my own life.

So let me keep my heart and my eyes wide open today, to the signs of my Lord's presence in the people and situations He sends me in the here and now.

FEBRUARY 10

KNEELING IN PRAYER

"Then he (Jesus) *withdrew from them about a stone's throw, knelt down, and prayed, 'Father...'"* (Lk 22:41-42)

So Jesus "knelt down" and prayed. Now, I know that there are various outer and inner forms of prayer. For example, we can go about our business, doing whatever it is we do, and continuously be aware of God's presence, appealing to Him silently, from the heart, or perhaps whispering our prayer to Him throughout the day. A friend of mine, who is a very busy mother of several small children, recently told me that she does this.

But then she added that, from time to time, she must kneel down and pray, because it is "a more receptive position." I found this insight very helpful: Indeed, we receive God's grace not only in soul, but also in body. So, communion with God, in prayer, involves my whole being, in soul and in body. It involves physical actions, like kneeling.

Today I make it a point to kneel down before God, for just a little bit, in prayer. Let me be more receptive to His grace, both in body and in soul.

FEBRUARY 11

A TIME FOR REST

"Now it happened that he went through the grain fields on the Sabbath; and as they went his disciples began to pluck the heads of grain. And the Pharisees said to him, 'Look, why do they do what is not lawful on the Sabbath?' But he said to them, 'Have you never read what David did when he was in need and hungry...?' And he said to them, 'The Sabbath was made for man, and not man for the Sabbath." (Mk 2:23-27)

The word Sabbath comes from the Hebrew "shabath," meaning "to cease, desist, rest." In the passage above I learn two things about the Sabbath: 1. In the Spirit of Christ, Who is "Lord of the Sabbath" (Mt 12:8), one has a new freedom to interpret and apply the law of the Sabbath; 2. A special time for "ceasing, desisting, resting" is a God-given gift, made for "man(kind)," for all of us.

Setting aside the whole issue of Saturday vs. Sunday as the day of rest (in any event, in the West both Saturdays and Sundays are "days off"), I remind myself today of the simple truth that I need a special time "to cease, desist, rest." I need a time to re-connect, in a special way, with God and family and community, by "desisting" from other concerns. Nowadays it is more challenging to find this time, when the internet has many of us "on" or even formally at work 24/7. I need to make a conscious effort, a free choice, to accept the God-given gift of "the Sabbath made for man," in some way that I can.

Today let me accept this gift with gratitude and hear God's voice saying to me, *"Be still, and know that I am God."* (Ps 45:10)

FEBRUARY 12

WHOSE KINGDOM?

"Thy kingdom come..." (Mt 6:10)

As far as "kingdoms" go, I have a variety of choices today, as to which one I will inhabit. I can choose to play "king" myself, trying to control everyone and everything around me. Or I can make some other person or some other thing my supreme authority, and then depend on this person or thing, so it/they determine my actions, aspirations, mood, and so on. But I know, at this point in my life, that both these options lead down an unhappy road; a road of either lonely self-reliance, or burdensome dependency.

I'm grateful today for the various reminders, beginning with the Our Father, of the Kingdom I'm called (yet not compelled) to embrace, in freedom: "Thy kingdom"; God's kingdom. I affirm this choice also at the beginning of every Divine Liturgy: The priest proclaims, "Blessed is the Kingdom of the Father and of the Son and of the Holy Spirit, now and ever and unto the ages of ages," and I sing, "Amen!"

I re-affirm that "Amen" this morning, saying "Thy kingdom come," with its own laws, centering in the Cross. It has its own priorities and "logic," from the Logos. Let Him be my King today. *"For Thine is the kingdom and the power and the glory, of the Father and of the Son and of the Holy Spirit, now and ever and unto the ages of ages."* Amen!

FEBRUARY 13

OPENNESS TO CHANGE

"Now after John was arrested, Jesus came to Galilee, proclaiming the good news of God, and saying, 'The time is fulfilled, and the kingdom of God has come near; repent, and believe in the good news.'" (Mk 1:14-15)

Earlier this morning in downtown Vienna I saw a little girl walking to school in a princess costume, because Ash Wednesday is coming up and the celebration of "Fasching" (the pre-Lenten carnival) is in full swing here. The costumes signify a readiness for transformation or transition—in a general sense, from winter to spring, and in a christianized sense—from darkness to light, in "repentance" ("metanoia," meaning a change of mind or focus).

Today I'm grateful for this reminder to be open to change, the change made possible by "the good news" (even if for me Lent is still several weeks away). Let me be open to change today, where it is possible and needed, asking God for the courage, wisdom, and power to carry it out according to His will. And let me "believe in the good news" of the change He brings me, rather than fearing change, letting Him establish His kingdom in my life, as He sees fit.

FEBRUARY 14

DIVINE ABANDONMENT

"About three in the afternoon Jesus cried out in a loud voice, 'Eli, Eli, lema sabachthani?' (which means 'My God, my God, why have you forsaken me?'). (Mt 27:46)

We can't even come close to understanding the extent of Christ's suffering on the Cross, nor the enormity of the burden He carries at this moment, bearing the sins of the world.

I know that as God, our Lord always maintained His union with the Father. But in Christ's human nature, which He chose to take on in its entirety, He bears at this moment, during His salvific sufferings, also the entirety of the human tragedy of sin—and this includes one of the results of sin: the loss of the sense of God's presence. Jesus, indeed, had not only a human body, enduring the physical tortures of the Cross, but also a human soul. And His soul bears at this moment a sense of utter abandonment.

But what He does in this moment of extreme agony is cry out in the words of a Psalm: *"My God, my God, ...why have You forsaken me?"* (Ps 21/22:1) So, although no human suffering or sorrow ever comes close to what my Lord felt on the Cross, He does show me that no matter what, at any hour of darkness, I am not to cease to cry out in prayer. It is part of the journey of the Cross; a journey that leads to the coming light of the Resurrection.

FEBRUARY 15

MEETING HIM IN THE NOW

"Simeon took him (Jesus) *in his arms and praised God, saying, 'Now you are dismissing your servant, Master, in peace, according to your word; for my eyes have seen your salvation, which you have prepared in the presence of all peoples, a light for revelation to the Gentiles and for glory to your people Israel.'"* (Lk 2:28-32)

This particular moment in Salvation History, this particular "Now," is a celebration of Simoen "seeing" Christ, with his own two eyes. It is a celebration of the gift of His physical presence among us, and all its grace-filled consequences: "Now," because of the Great Fact of His incarnation, we can embrace Him and behold Him, not only "spiritually" but also physically, in wholesome communion with Him.

Indeed "salvation," in Christ, is now present and active in my physical surroundings and within me, because I am given to "see" Christ, if I have "the eyes to see." It is "a light" that has been "prepared in the presence of all peoples," including us, if we choose to be present to His presence, in us and among us. In practical terms, in my here and now, this "being present to His presence" means entering into contact with Him on a daily basis, in heartfelt prayer and openness to His presence and voice in my life.

Today let me be present to Christ's presence among us, so that I can "meet" Him in the ways He comes to me today, be it in the mundane situations and responsibilities I am confronted with, or more obviously in church-celebrations like the one we celebrate today on the Older Calendar, of the Meeting of the Lord. Let me be open to meeting Him today, wherever I am, and whatever I happen to be doing.

FEBRUARY 16

STAYING FOCUSED IN A STORM

"...And early in the morning he (Jesus) came walking toward them on the sea. But when the disciples saw him walking on the sea, they were terrified, saying, 'It is a ghost!' And they cried out in fear. But immediately Jesus spoke to them and said, 'Take heart, it is I; do not be afraid.' Peter answered him, 'Lord, if it is you, command me to come to you on the water.' He said, 'Come.' So Peter got out of the boat, started walking on the water, and came toward Jesus. But when he noticed the strong wind, he became frightened, and beginning to sink, he cried out, 'Lord, save me!' Jesus immediately reached out his hand and caught him, saying to him, 'You of little faith, why did you doubt?'" (Mt 14:25-31)

Peter is able to walk toward Christ, on the tumultuous water, while his eyes are on Christ. But when Peter's attention turns to the storm and he "notices the strong wind," he is naturally overcome by fear and begins to sink. At this point he cries out, "Lord, save me!"—and the Lord "immediately" catches him.

God does not promise to prevent "strong winds" from happening in my life. All sorts of trials and tribulations may happen, like an unexpected illness, the loss of a job or some other form of rejection, the loss of a loved one, or even calamities like a war, a hurricane, an earthquake, and so on. There can also be inner "storms" like unhealthy or conflicting desires and ambitions.

God tells me, however, not to have fear, and to focus on Him amidst a storm, because He is close and ready to offer a helping hand. So whether I'm walking or sinking in any "storm" today, let me replace fear with faith. Let me discern Christ in the midst of it, saying to me, *"It is I; do not be afraid."*

FEBRUARY 17

THE TWO BIG QUESTIONS

"But Mary (Magdalene) stood weeping outside the tomb. As she wept, she bent over to look into the tomb; and she saw two angels in white, sitting where the body of Jesus had been lying, one at the head and the other at the feet. They said to her, 'Woman, why are you weeping?' She said to them, 'They have taken away my Lord, and I do not know where they have laid him.' When she had said this, she turned around and saw Jesus standing there, but she did not know that it was Jesus. Jesus said to her, 'Woman, why are you weeping? Whom are you looking for?' Supposing him to be the gardener, she said to him, 'Sir, if you have carried him away, tell me where you have laid him, and I will take him away.' Jesus said to her, 'Mary!' She turned and said to him in Hebrew, 'Rabbouni!' (which means Teacher)." (Jn 20:11-16)

According to the Gospel of Mark, after His resurrection Christ first appeared to Mary Magdalene (Mk 16:9). The very first words uttered by the risen Lord, then, are two very consoling questions to a grieving woman:

1. *"Woman, why are you weeping?"* and
2. *"Whom are you looking for?"*

These are the two big questions He continues to pose to all men and women, to all of us, on life's journey, with its tears and its yearnings. Why are you weeping? And who is it you're looking for? It took Mary Magdalene a brief moment to recognize the ultimate, infinite consolation of these words. But for others of us it can take much longer to realize that the answer, the risen Lord, is right there in front of me. I can tend to misdirect my search and look for the answers in the wrong places.

Today let me begin my journey once again, and recognize the Lord's loving voice, amidst any of my sorrows or yearnings, asking me: *"Woman, why are you weeping?"* and *"Whom are you looking for?"*

FEBRUARY 18

SURRENDERING TO HER HELP

"Guide me in the paths of salvation, O Theotokos, for I have defiled my soul with shameful sins, and have wasted all my life in slothfulness, but by Your intercessions deliver me from all uncleanness." (Second half of Byzantine Lenten Prayer, "Open Unto Me the Doors of Repentance")

And so, just before we begin the great journey of Lent, I ask for help. Because all sorts of unwanted junk or "uncleanness" has accumulated in my spiritual "house." As we sing in this prayer, I have "defiled" my soul, which literally means "trampled on" it (from the Old French "defouler," to trample on). Today I surrender it all, letting go of what's been hoarded or tucked away. But I don't do it on my own, asking for the help of the Theotokos, and indeed of the entire Church, of which She is not "only" the symbol, but the grace-filled, willing and caring Birth-Giver.

Help is on offer today, also in the Rite of Forgiveness, as we grant and receive forgiveness from one another, empowering one another for the upcoming journey. Let me reach out today by suiting up, showing up, and entering into the communal "house-cleaning" of mutual forgiveness. I also ask forgiveness of anyone reading this, my beloved zillions. May we all be "guided in the paths of salvation," be it quickly or slowly, as we open up and let ourselves be nudged in the right direction, by an ever-caring Mother.

FEBRUARY 19

UNREASONABLE FORGIVENESS

"Then Peter came and said to him, 'Lord, if my brother sins against me, how often should I forgive? As many as seven times?' Jesus said to him, 'Not seven times, but, I tell you, seventy times seven.'" (Mt 18:20-22)

I read the above passage this morning and thought: What kind of person would sin against another certain person "seventy times seven"? It sounds like someone stuck in the same sinful routine, and falling into it over and over again—like an addict. And this person, says the Lord, is to receive forgiveness, over and over again—as "unreasonably" simple as that may sound.

But in fact this is the "unreasonable" way God approaches my sins, many of which I tend to repeat, over and over again. He forgives me, over and over again. Let me be grateful for this amazing fact today, and do likewise. Let me throw "reason" to the wind, when it comes to oft-repeated sins against me. Let me forgive myself and others, because forgiveness, very simply, sets me free.

FEBRUARY 20

THE DOORS OF REPENTANCE

"Open to me the doors of repentance, O Giver of Life..." (Lenten Prayer, sung at Byzantine Sunday matins)

"Repentance" (i.e. "metanoia," a change of mind) is a transition, so it needs to be "entered," like a door. While the "doors" of repentance are inside me, the power to open them, to open my heart, mind and body to the sometimes-scary prospect of change, is outside me, in the Giver of Life. So in the prayer quoted above, which we sing this weekend for the first time, and keep singing throughout Lent, we ask God to nudge us forward, toward the springtime of Lent.

Today let me let God open me up to the life-giving changes unfolding now, in the Lenten season. I need not be impatient or self-justifying in my "progress," as the Pharisee was (Lk 18:11-12), but rather open up to God's life-giving mercy, as did the tax-collector (Lk 18:13). Because it is God alone Who sees me as I am, and where I am, and it is His to "justify" my journey in His light, when I let Him be Who He is, the one source of Life and Justice.

FEBRUARY 21

LENT, A NEW BEGINNING

"In the beginning God created the heavens and the earth. The earth was without form, and void; and darkness was on the face of the deep. And the Spirit of God was hovering over the face of the waters. Then God said, 'Let there be light'; and there was light. And God saw the light, that it was good; and God divided the light from the darkness. God called the light Day, and the darkness He called Night. So the evening and the morning were the first day." (Gen 1:1-5)

This is read in my church today, on the very first day of Lent. We are taken way back, to the "beginning," to the great mystery of Creation; The answer to the great question, Why is there something rather than nothing? Because God loved it into being. He doesn't "need" anything or anyone, because God is perfect Being. But He brings us and all of this, our world, into being anyway, because He wants us to "be." He wants to share His Being. And now that we "are," however imperfectly, He continues to call us to "be" more fully, more perfectly, in Him. His creative energies continue to work on me, when I let Him in.

Today let me re-discover His creative call to me, to "be." Let me let Him share His Being with me, as I begin Lent, and begin to care for my spiritual "garden" and for my body in the new, creative ways Lent opens up for me.

FEBRUARY 22

A LIBERATING FEAR

"O Lord, hear my prayer, give ear unto my supplication in Your truth; hearken unto me in Your righteousness. And enter not into judgment with Your servant, for no one living is righteous before You." (Ps 142/143: 1-2)

The "fear of God," that is, the fear of His judgment, is a liberating thing. This is true for two reasons:
1. God, as the source of justice and truth, is the only perfect Judge. As distinct from human beings, He does not embrace prejudice, nor does He form trivial opinions or hold petty grudges; and
2. His justice is not "fair." He can be quite unreasonable, bestowing mercy, no strings attached, to the repentant heart.

A fear of judgment is a gift, inherent to a normal human being from a very young age. But a proper use of this gift, I think, is something we develop and discern throughout the course of our spiritual struggle. Quite early in life, children begin to care what other children think of them, and often by their teenage years become entirely dependent on the opinions of their peers.

I can similarly misdirect this gift, by focusing primarily on human opinion of me. But when I place my focus on God's judgment, rather than on the ever-changing winds of human opinion, I liberate myself from the needless fear of what everyone else thinks. This is why the "fear of God" is a gift, ultimately teaching me humble self-acceptance. It reveals to me the liberating fact that "no one living is righteous" before Him.

FEBRUARY 23

PREPARING FOR CONFESSION

"Yea, O Lord and King, grant me to see my own faults and not to judge my brother. For You are blessed unto the ages of ages. Amen." (Prayer of Saint Ephrem, Part 3)

As I prepare to go to confession this week, for a thorough "house-cleaning," I ask for a specific kind of "vision"; to "see" my own faults. Blocking my vision are various distractions, one of which is "judging my brother." But this isn't the only distraction. I may also be distracted by secondary or external matters, which turn my confession into a sort of shopping list of this and that, which never seems to change every time I go to confession. I ask for God's help to help me "see" the major issues buried deep and hoarded in my heart, which are fundamentally distorting my focus.

These "major" issues concern the first two commandments, of wholehearted love for God, and of love for my neighbor as I love myself (Mt 22:36-40). Let me ask myself:
1. How, where and why have I blocked God from playing His role in my daily life? (self-reliance, fear, ego, etc.) and
2. How, where and why have I contributed to any broken relationships, with others and myself?

Here I find it helpful to make a list of any resentments I might be carrying around, toward certain people, myself, institutions, and responsibilities. I also list the reasons for these resentments, like fear (of loss—like loss of financial security, of image, of love, and so on), or self-centeredness. I take a good look at all this and shed God's light on it, so I can hand it all over to Him, letting go of these burdens in confession. Let me let Him unburden me, because He is always ready and willing to "open to me the doors of repentance."

FEBRUARY 24

WATCHING MY WORDS

"Set a guard over my mouth, O LORD; keep watch over the door of my lips." (Ps 140/141:3) *"O Lord, open my lips, and my mouth will declare your praise."* (Ps 50/51:15)

It is interesting to contemplate these two psalm-verses alongside each other. One of them asks the Lord to "guard" my mouth, while the other asks Him to "open" it. Of course, when the Psalms were first composed, well over two thousand years ago, the spoken word was the only kind most people used. Back then, most people did not have the resources to employ the written word, nor, obviously, did they have the keyboard or the phone to type their opinions and thoughts, as we do today.

So today, when I recite these verses of the Psalms, I ask that the Lord guide my use of words, not only when I am saying them out loud, but when I am typing them on my keyboard or on my phone. Because today, strangely, I type many more words than I say aloud. The Psalm-verses remind me that I need God's help in discerning when I need to share my words, and when I need to withhold them; when I should click "Send," and when I should abstain from that. Today let me remember to ask for the wisdom to know the difference.

FEBRUARY 25

APPROPRIATE FASTING

"Then they said to him, 'John's disciples, like the disciples of the Pharisees, frequently fast and pray, but your disciples eat and drink.' Jesus said to them, 'You cannot make wedding guests fast while the bridegroom is with them, can you? The days will come when the bridegroom will be taken away from them, and then they will fast in those days.' He also told them a parable: 'No one tears a piece from a new garment and sews it on an old garment; otherwise the new will be torn, and the piece from the new will not match the old..." (Lk 5:33-36)

The Lord's disciples are new to the whole business of spiritual life. He has chosen them from all walks of life, like that of a fisherman and of a tax-collector. So at this point they are toddlers, enjoying their first steps with Him, Who is constantly "with them," like a loving parent is with a small child. It is not yet time for grown-up activities, one of which, apparently, is fasting. At this point, the disciples, like infants, are given to "eat and drink" whenever they need to do so.

This passage reminds me of the simple fact that a life in Christ does not begin, in its early phases, with strict asceticism. It can, actually, be damaging to burden oneself, or to burden other beginners, with ascetical rules and regulations, because "the new will be torn." The body, in a state of being hungry or tired, might confuse and dampen the spirit of one who still needs the tender, loving care of an infant in Christ.

Today let me ask God for His wisdom, when it comes to the physical side of "spiritual" life. Let me let God discipline me in ways appropriate to, and healthy for, my growth in Him. *"Blessed are You, O Lord, teach me Your statutes."*
(Ps 118/119: 12)

FEBRUARY 26

GO INTO THE ARK

"Then the Lord said to Noah, 'Go into the ark, you and all your household, for I have seen that you alone are righteous before me in this generation. Take with you seven pairs of all clean animals, the male and its mate; and a pair of the animals that are not clean, the male and its mate; and seven pairs of the birds of the air also, male and female, to keep their kind alive on the face of all the earth. For in seven days I will send rain on the earth for forty days and forty nights; and every living thing that I have made I will blot out from the face of the ground.' And Noah did all that the Lord had commanded him." (Gen 7:1-5)

This passage from Genesis is read today in my church, on Tuesday of the third week of Lent. I am reminded of Noah's ark, which is traditionally seen to prefigure the Church. We survive the turbulent waters of our journey to salvation by "going in," again and again, being gathered into the community, healing, and restoration that are continuously offered in grace-filled, ecclesial reality. And then we come out, again and again, to offer new life to our world.

In the context of our 40-day Lent, I am reminded of the "forty days and forty nights" of the Great Flood, during which God "blots out" that which needs to be blotted out in me, and left behind. Today let me once again embrace Lent's great "flood" of gifts, offered to me in Tradition, so I can "come out" renewed, into the light that is coming at the end of this 40-day period.

FEBRUARY 27

A NEW TREE OF LIFE

"Then the Lord God said, 'See, the man has become like one of us, knowing good and evil; and now, he might reach out his hand and take also from the tree of life, and eat, and live forever'—therefore the Lord God sent him forth from the garden of Eden, to till the ground from which he was taken. He drove out the man; and at the east of the garden of Eden he placed the cherubim, and a sword flaming and turning to guard the way to the tree of life." (Gen 3:20-24)

Both the man and the woman in this scene had wanted a good thing, "to be like God," knowing good and evil. But they had decided to give this a try without Him, against His explicit commandment. They wanted "to be" and "to become" on their own, disregarding the Source of all "being," God, Who alone "is the One Who is." (Ex 3:14) So they misused their God-given and God-like freedom to effect change.

At the center of the mystery of creation lies the simple yet unfathomable fact that He alone can make the difference between "Not Being" and "Being." It is only with Him and in Him that we can "become" in the proper direction, toward Him, while the "serpent" can only lead us to various paths of "un-being"; of retreating from our intended purpose. The path of God-less change breaks us, because we can't carry its consequences on our shoulders alone. When God notes with dismay, "See, the man has become like one of us," He is noting the "wrong" kind of "becoming"; the man has exercised Our power, the power of the Triune God, to effect change in himself.

God remedies and turns around this "wrong" kind of "becoming" in the fulfilment of Salvation History, by becoming "One of us" in the Incarnation. He takes on the "knowledge" of our good and our evil, even unto utter abandonment and death, because only His shoulders are broad enough to carry it. As Creator, He does for us what we could not do for ourselves, and that is, "become" One with us. He gives us a new path, and a new Tree of Life, in His life-giving Cross. Let me let Him effect change in me today, as I take up His cross, that I may "become" and grow in His creative energies, toward the new unity He makes possible with Him and all creation.

FEBRUARY 28

RESENTMENT

"And forgive us our trespasses, as we forgive those who trespass against us." (Mt 6:12, from the Lord's Prayer)

I have heard many people say that when they try to pray, they feel there's some invisible wall between them and God; as if the prayer doesn't "get through." This state of affairs can last for many years, or just happen sometimes, on occasion. When it happens to me, I am reminded of this verse in the Lord's Prayer, which points me to the most obvious culprit in my predicament: resentment.

That is to say, I might be (perhaps quietly) clinging onto some wrong done against me, either by my own self, or some other person or group of people, or close family, or some institution, like my workplace, my government, or even my church. Resentments often go way back, even though recent incidents trigger old feelings of frustration, neglect, hurt, etc. It is important for me to take some time and "clean my house" of any resentments, letting go of the delusion that somehow, through my resentment, I achieve the "justice" I deserve. Because I "know" I'm right, you see. This sense of "justice," bred in resentment, eats away not only at my human relationships, but prevents my communion with God. I can't even pray the Lord's Prayer honestly, while clinging to resentment.

So let me look to God's justice and His grace to help me forgive myself and others. Because when I say "Our Father," rather than "My Father," I am reminded that He forgives me as well as others, time and again. And this He does, over and over again, although He knows He was right, when we were wrong. He is free from holding grudges, and wants us to be free, like Him.

FEBRUARY 29

SPIRITUAL FAMINE

"...But when (the prodigal son) had spent all, there arose a severe famine in that land, and he began to be in want. Then he went and joined himself to a citizen of that country, and he sent him into his fields to feed swine. And he would gladly have filled his stomach with the pods that the swine ate, and no one gave him anything. But when he came to himself, he said, 'How many of my father's hired servants have bread enough and to spare, and I perish with hunger! I will arise and go to my father, and will say to him, 'Father, I have sinned against heaven and before you, and I am no longer worthy to be called your son. Make me like one of your hired servants.' And he arose and came to his father. But when he was still a great way off, his father saw him and had compassion, and ran and fell on his neck and kissed him..." (Lk 15:14-20)

What a blessing is this "famine" experienced by the son who wandered off from his Father's home! It is God's tap on the shoulder, this feeling of "running on empty." And the good news is, I can always "return," because my Father is willing to "run," not just walk, to meet me, clothe me, quench my thirst, and feed my famished heart.

Let me be grateful today for the blessing of the hole in my heart; for the emptiness and, indeed, "famine" God sends me whenever I wander off and chase yearnings or ambitions outside His house. I need not escape the yearning any longer, nor enslave myself to any "citizen" of the far-away country of my choice. Today let me embrace God's choice for me, His own home, and come back. *"Blessed are those who hunger and thirst for righteousness, for they shall be satisfied."* (Mt 5:6)

MARCH 1

IDLENESS & DESPONDENCY

"O Lord and Master of my life, a spirit of idleness, despondency, love of power, and idle talking give me not." (Lenten Prayer of St. Ephrem, Part 1)

How very "post-post-modern" of St. Ephrem that the spirit of "idleness" (inactivity, sloth, procrastination) and its outgrowth of "despondency" (various forms of depression and feelings of unfulfilment) are the very first concerns of his famous prayer. In our time, when opportunities abound for every form of distraction and entertainment, whenever and wherever th WiFi is working, these "spirits" have become our everyday companions.

St. John Climacus says that despondency makes one "look out the window" (in his context, of the monastic cell, The Ladder XIII.13). Indeed it makes me look "elsewhere," away from the here and now, which, in despondency, ceases to satisfy. Despondency makes one lukewarm toward one's own vocation; toward one's own "mission" in life. It can make a previously happily-married man wander off to seek another woman.

The good news is that the challenge of despondency, when I stand up to it in Christ, in the grace-filled tools He offers me, leads to immense spiritual growth. "Nothing brings so many crowns," writes that same author, St. John Climacus, "as a battle with despondency." (XIII.12)

So let me begin this morning with an active, conscious, gratitude for, and attentiveness to, the here and now. Let me take a bit of time to be alone with God, in heartfelt prayer on my knees, thanking Him and asking Him to discipline me in His simple ways, guiding me and nudging me forward amidst the pesky calls of idleness and despondency.

MARCH 2

RE-GENERATIVE DARKNESS

"Now it was about the sixth hour (noon), and there was darkness over all the earth until the ninth hour (ca. three o'clock PM). Then the sun was darkened, and the veil of the temple was torn in two. And when Jesus had cried out with a loud voice, he said, 'Father, into Your hands I commit my spirit.' Having said this, he breathed his last (ἐξέπνευσεν, gave up his breath)." (Lk 23:44-46)

That Friday afternoon the Son of God gives up His life, His breath, to bring us new life. This crucial—literally crucial—"breath" is both an end and a beginning. It is the end of the separation between God and human beings, signed by the veil that separated the Holy of Holies, God's earthly dwelling-place, from the rest of the Temple and the rest of the world, the dwelling-place of mankind. Through the "tearing in two" of Jesus Christ, Who endures the separation of soul and body in death, the old separation between God and us is dramatically, emphatically removed, torn asunder.

Thus a new creation begins; a renewed "Yes" of the Creator toward His creation. And it begins as the old creation began in Genesis, with "darkness" (Gen 1:2, "and darkness was upon the face of the deep"). God "dims the lights" in His salvific Theo-drama (as von Balthasar so aptly put it), to re-focus my attention on His new light, which is soon to arise from the Tomb.

Today let me open my heart, mind, and body to God's emphatic "Yes" to me and all creation. And let me not fear any darkness or fragmentation, that is, any "tearing in two," through which God may send me in His re-generative, re-creative process. *"And the light shines in the darkness, and the darkness did not overcome it."* (Jn 1:5)

MARCH 3

GOD-GIVEN SEXUALITY

"Flee fornication! Every sin that a person commits is outside the body; but the fornicator sins against the body itself. Or do you not know that your body is a temple of the Holy Spirit within you, which you have from God, and that you are not your own? For you were bought with a price; therefore glorify God in your body." (1 Cor 6:18-20)

This passage was part of the Epistle-reading in my church yesterday, on one of the Sundays of the "Lenten Triodion." So the Church is drawing our attention to an essential participant in the Lenten journey, the body, and more specifically—sexuality. The Apostle is saying—in case we were avoiding taking a prayerful look at this part of our "human" being—"Do you not know," do you not acknowledge, contemplate, and gratefully embrace the fact "that your body is a temple of the Holy Spirit within you?" And then he says, "Therefore glorify God in your body," not only in what you eat and drink, but in your sexual behaviour.

Today I am reminded of the simple, yet amazing fact, that sexuality, like hunger for food and thirst for drink, is a God-given capacity. It can lead to growth and new life when placed where it belongs, in the service of His greater glory. Conversely it can stunt growth and be destructive, if I misguide this God-given gift in self-seeking and self-reliant ways; If I hide this gift away from God, or neglect shedding a prayerful light on matters sexual, not handing over to Him that "which is not my own." It is His, because He put it there. So let His will be done in my body, as I want it to be done in my mind and soul. Let me hand over to Him all things, in a "whole-minded" fashion. *"But grant unto me, Your servant, a spirit of whole-mindedness, humility, patience and love."*

MARCH 4

COME AND LET US WALK

"For out of Zion shall go forth the law, and the word of the Lord from Jerusalem. He shall judge between the nations, and rebuke many people; They shall beat their swords into plowshares, and their spears into pruning hooks; Nation shall not lift up sword against nation, neither shall they learn war anymore. O house of Jacob, come and let us walk in the light of the Lord." (Is 2:3-5)

This is a passage from today's reading of the Prophet Isaiah, from whose book(s) we read on the weekdays of Byzantine Lent, at the service of the Sixth Hour. How awe-inspiring, to go back and "remember" God preparing us, humanity, for the Light; for His Son, Who was to come and teach us, that we not "learn war anymore." We thus step into the "shadow" of the Old Testament during Lent, so that we re-discover and revive our yearning for the "Light to the revelation of the Gentiles." (Lk 2. 32)

Let me have ears to hear and eyes to see the great lessons being taught to me in yet another day of the great tradition of Lent. Let me let God teach me to "beat my swords into plowshares, and my spears into pruning hooks," as I surrender my usual ways and let in the light of Lent. *"O house of Jacob, come and let us walk in the light of the Lord!"*

MARCH 5

A SALVIFIC SADNESS

"By the rivers of Babylon—there we sat down and there we wept when we remembered Zion. On the willows there we hung up our harps. For there our captors asked us for songs, and our tormentors asked for mirth, saying, 'Sing us one of the songs of Zion!' How could we sing the Lord's song in a foreign land? If I forget you, O Jerusalem, let my right hand wither!" (Ps 136/137: 1-5)

This Psalm, which expresses the sadness of the Jewish people in exile after the Babylonian conquest of Jerusalem in 607 B.C., is sung at Byzantine matins on the three Sundays preceding Lent. It prepares us for the voluntary "exile" of Lent, during which we focus in a special way on the sadness and yearning of humanity after Adam's "exile" from paradise, and before the coming of The Awaited One, Jesus Christ. On the weekdays of Lent, for example, we "abstain" from celebrating the joyous service of Divine Liturgy, and thus "hang up our harps" for most of the week.

Today let me not hesitate to recognize my human sadness, my yearning to "come home" to my Father's land of perfect harmony, peace, and unity. Let me not slip into self-contentment and imagined self-sufficiency, which is the kiss of death to spiritual growth and thirst. Today let me "remember" the heavenly Jerusalem, from which I distance myself, again and again, amidst my responsibilities and relationships. I need not cover this up in "songs" and "mirth," as I prepare for Lent, but rather take some time to "sit down," to "weep," and to "remember Zion."

MARCH 6

WISDOM vs. ANXIETY

"The Lord by wisdom founded the earth; By understanding He established the heavens; By His knowledge the depths were broken up, and clouds drop down the dew. My son, let them not depart from your eyes —keep sound wisdom and discretion; So they will be life to your soul and grace to your neck. Then you will walk safely in your way, and your foot will not stumble. When you lie down, you will not be afraid; Yes, you will lie down and your sleep will be sweet. Do not be afraid of sudden terror, nor of trouble from the wicked when it comes; For the Lord will be your confidence, and will keep your foot from being caught." (Prov 3:19-26)

Let it not be said that "existential angst" was discovered by the modern-day. This ancient text knows all about it. And what is the antidote to it? God's wisdom, God's discretion and "knowledge." How often do I ask Him for wisdom? Not often enough.

Today let me ask God for wisdom, understanding, discretion and knowledge. Let Him renew in me the ultimate "knowledge," that He, simply put, "is." Because at the root of anxiety is a losing sight of God's presence. Anxiety comes when I leave God out of the picture, and proceed in self-reliance, attempting to carry the world on my own shoulders. Today let me let God in, and replace fear with faith, so *"the Lord will be my confidence, and will keep my foot from being caught."*

MARCH 7

LOVING IMPROPRIETY

"...And a woman in the city, who was a sinner, having learned that he was eating in the Pharisee's house, brought an alabaster jar of ointment. She stood behind him at his feet, weeping, and began to bathe his feet with her tears and to dry them with her hair. Then she continued kissing his feet and anointing them with the ointment. Now when the Pharisee who had invited him saw it, he said to himself, 'If this man were a prophet, he would have known who and what kind of woman this is who is touching him—that she is a sinner...'" (Lk 7:37-39)

Two people, and two different approaches to Christ in this passage: Simon the Pharisee, the religious authority of his time, very properly hosting the meal to which he's invited our Lord. And a nameless woman, known to us only as "a sinner," who makes quite a scene as described above. She wasn't invited to the table, and has nothing to say for herself. Yet her actions, rather inappropriate, say everything.

The Lord famously praises this woman and admonishes Simon, saying to His host: *"Do you see this woman? I entered your house; you gave me no water for my feet, but she has bathed my feet with her tears and dried them with her hair... Therefore, I tell you, her sins, which were many, have been forgiven; hence she has shown great love. But the one to whom little is forgiven, loves little."* Then He says to her, *"Your sins are forgiven."* And *"Your faith has saved you. Go in peace."*

It's OK not to have anything to say for myself. And it's even OK not to go through the appropriate motions, according to someone else's ideas of propriety, when approaching God in our brokenness. He has little interest in external piety, when it "loves little."

So let me not hesitate and approach Him today, however I can, with a loving and contrite heart. Because He remains true to His word: *"A sacrifice unto God is a broken spirit; a heart that is broken and humbled God will not despise."* (Ps 50/51:17)

MARCH 8

SEEING AND BELIEVING

"Now faith is the assurance of things hoped for, the conviction of things not seen. Indeed, by faith the ancients received approval. By faith we understand that the ages were prepared by the word of God, so that what is seen does not originate from visible things." (Heb 11:1-3)

So in faith we "see" the visible, and "understand" its invisible Source. Thus the visible can, in faith, be a constant reminder of the invisible; In faith, the visible is a channel for divine revelation. Thus we use visible symbols and icons in our liturgical Tradition, so that they point us to the invisible. Our "vision" does not stop, so to say, at the icon, but extends beyond it, toward the One or the ones depicted on it.

Today I say thank you to God for engaging my senses as He does and and always did, in various ways. These "ways" include the simple, everyday examples of beauty, like the crocuses now sloppily in bloom here and there; These "ways" also include the very big, extraordinary way He stepped into our history, letting us see His Son incarnate, walking and talking among us. I thank You today, my Lord, for reminding me of Yourself every day, in Your beautiful images. *"By coming to save the world, O Saviour, You have filled all things with joy."* (Troparion of the Sunday of Orthodoxy)

MARCH 9

THE LEARNING NEVER STOPS

"Blessed are You, O Lord, teach me Your statutes."
(Ps 118/119: 12)

If I make at least a small effort to keep my focus on God, to listen deeply, and to see, deeply, what He is revealing to me today, then I continue to learn; I remain teachable. *"But blessed are your eyes because they see, and your ears because they hear,"* Christ says to His followers (Mt 13:16). I should note that He had harsh words not for the "unworthy," but for the unteachable.

Today might bring unexpected circumstances, unexpected or unpleasant behavior (either my own or of others). How will I respond to what comes my way today? Let me remember that Christ is calling me to keep my eyes and ears open, according to His word. I can let His grace into every situation, so that I learn more about His agenda today, rather than impose my own. The learning never stops, if I remain teachable.

MARCH 10

MAKING DECISIONS & ANXIETY

"Do not be anxious/worried about anything (μηδὲν μεριμνᾶτε), *but in everything by prayer and supplication with thanksgiving let your requests be made known to God."* (Phil 4:6)

I sometimes get quite worried, when I need to make an important decision or an important change. So I either put it off or over-think it, or both.

The Apostle reminds me today to let all this "be made known to God," and thus relieve the burden of worry and anxiety. I obviously do need to make decisions, large and small, on a daily basis, to manage my life responsibly. But worry and anxiety creeps into even simple responsibilities when I leave God out of the picture; when I fall into self-reliance, carrying the burden of my situations and decisions on my own shoulders.

Today I gratefully begin my day, by getting briefly on my knees and "letting my requests be made known to God," Who can and does give me the wisdom and courage to carry out any responsibility. He shares my burdens, when I share them with Him. Because "prayer and supplication with thanksgiving," as the Apostle assures me, relieves me daily from the burdens of worry and anxiety.

MARCH 11

AS INCENSE

"Let my prayer be set before you as incense, the lifting up of my hands as the evening sacrifice." (Ps 140/141: 2, chanted solemnly at Byzantine Vespers & Liturgy of the Pre-sanctified Gifts)

The visible burning of incense is an instructive reminder of the invisible "burning" of the heart in prayer, which rises up as an offering, as our self-giving at this evening service. The "lifting up of my hands," a physical gesture we don't practice all that much (not in my church, anyway), is also referred to here, because from ancient times the body, not only the "soul," is involved in the whole business of prayer.

Today let me "see" this intertwining of the visible and invisible; let me "see" more biblically. As Lent involves my whole being, body and soul, in its salvific traditions, let me gratefully participate in its wholesome vision, whether I'm at work or at church on this sunny, Lenten day. If I'm at work, let my fasting (in deed, word, and thought) be "set before" the Lord, as He draws me in, both in and out of church, to His way of "seeing," as I journey toward the vision of His resurrection. Glory be to Him.

MARCH 12

THE BLESSING OF CHANGE

"Then Noah built an altar to the Lord, and took of every clean animal and of every clean bird, and offered burnt offerings on the altar. And when the Lord smelled the pleasing odor, the Lord said in his heart, 'I will never again curse the ground because of humankind, for the inclination of the human heart is evil from youth; nor will I ever again destroy every living creature as I have done. As long as the earth endures, seedtime and harvest, cold and heat, summer and winter, day and night, shall not cease.'" (Gen 8:20-22)

The changeability of temporal reality, like changes in temperature, or in the times of day and night, is a blessing. One thing does not change, and that is, my obligation to tame and re-direct the "inclination of the human heart," my inclination that is "evil from youth." But amidst this constant, unchanging obligation, of spiritual struggle, I have the relief and pleasant distraction of uncontrollable changes in physical reality, like night turning to day. Why is this a relief? Because I don't have to worry about that which I don't control.

I'll note the same about changes in our liturgical "seasons." The cycles of fasts and feasts offer me changes of pace, amidst one unchanging, constant objective of working on my heart, on aligning it to God. In a word I am glad it's Lent, just like I will be glad when it's over. I thank God today for bringing His changes into my life, in ways I happily do not control.

MARCH 13

LOVE OF POWER

"Again, the devil (ὁδιάβολος) took him to a very high mountain and showed him all the kingdoms of the world and their splendor; and he said to him, 'All these I will give you, if you will fall down and worship me.' Jesus said to him, 'Away with you, Satan! for it is written, 'Worship the Lord your God, and serve only him." Then the devil (ὁ διάβολος) left him, and suddenly angels came and waited on him." (Mt 4:8-11)

The "devil" is one who slanders or misrepresents, by turning things around ("devil" comes from the Greek word διαβάλλω, to throw over). Here he misrepresents "kingdoms" as if they were his to give; as if he, Satan, were the source of "power." No, he wouldn't have any at all, as Jesus famously said to Pilate, were it not given him "from above." (Jn 19:11) The kind of "power" that Satan is allowed to offer, because of his God-given freedom, is bought at the price of "falling down"—and staying there—in slavish "worship" of creation, namely, him.

So do I strive for "power"? No, I strive for Power. It is the power of the One Source of Power, God, because outside of Him, without Him I can do nothing. When I strive to "do" without Him I am led to slavery, to one thing or another, which Satan may offer me as a God-surrogate. Let me be attentive to any dependencies like workaholism, consumerism, alcoholism, or human codependency, that may be calling me to "fall down and worship" before creation, which has no power to raise me up again. *"O Lord and Master of my life,"* I say today, this spirit, of this kind of love of power, *"give me not,"* that I may worship and serve only You.

MARCH 14

A VISION FOR EVERYONE

"Now after he rose early on the first day of the week, he appeared first to Mary Magdalene, from whom he had cast out seven demons." (Mk 16:9)

Just as the Lord always paid special attention to the outcasts and the most humbled during His earthly mission, so in His resurrection does He first and foremost honor the most humbled Mary Magdalene, a woman "from whom he had cast out seven demons." Because seven is a symbol of completeness, this means she had been completely "devil-ridden," as noted by one commentator. Similarly, the lapsed Apostle Peter, who had thrice denied Christ during His passion and bitterly wept over his denial, is singled out by the angel who announced the Lord's resurrection. He sends Peter a special message: "But go," says the angel to the women, "tell his disciples and Peter..." (Mk 16:7) Some have understood this to be a rebuke of Peter, an exclusion of Peter from "the disciples," as if the joyous news of the resurrection is sent with a rebuke. But note that only Peter is mentioned by name; by the name the Lord had given him. This is doubtlessly an honor.

On this Sunday, when we sing "Having seen the resurrection of Christ, let us worship the holy Lord Jesus...," (a hymn from the Byzantine Sunday Vigil), I am reminded that this vision, of the risen Lord, is indeed given to all of us, and first and foremost to the most humbled and repentant. I am not excluded from "seeing,"—nor is anyone, however complete their "devil-riddenness" has been, nor how deep they have fallen in the past. In humility and repentance I can receive the special message and vision of the resurrection, of triumph over sin and death in Him. For this I give thanks today to the risen Lord, "падшим подаяй воскресение" (Who grants resurrection to the fallen).

MARCH 15

HIS SPIRIT OF WISDOM

"A shoot shall come out from the stump of Jesse, and a branch shall grow out of his roots. The spirit of the Lord shall rest on him, the spirit of wisdom and understanding, the spirit of counsel and might, the spirit of knowledge and the fear of the Lord. His delight shall be in the fear of the Lord. He shall not judge by what his eyes see, or decide by what his ears hear; but with righteousness he shall judge the poor, and decide with equity for the meek of the earth..." (Is 11:1-4)

This prophecy about the Messiah is read today in my church, on yet another day of Lent. So we continue to look "forward" to the coming of this righteous Judge, Who "shall not judge" as we do, "by what his eyes see, or decide by what His ears hear." In our voluntary, Lenten exile to the times of the Old Testament, we look "forward" to the coming of a new kind of kingdom, with a King Who brings us His Spirit "of wisdom and understanding."

In any judgments or decisions I make today, let me rely not merely on what my eyes see, nor on what my ears hear. Let me rather ask for His Spirit, "of knowledge and fear of the Lord." In the Body of Christ I am not alone, with my own wisdom, judgment, or understanding. So let me ask Christ for His judgment "with righteousness," of whatever is going on today among us, "the poor and the meek of the earth."

MARCH 16

MAINTAINING BOUNDARIES

"Let your foot be seldom in your neighbor's house, lest he have his fill of you and hate you." (Proverbs 25:17)

Today I came across this ancient wisdom in the Book of Proverbs, which reminded me, simply, that I need to set and maintain boundaries with other people. On the one hand, I am certainly called to be a social being and need not self-isolate. But I also need to be careful and not overdo it with the socializing and communicating. In the context of today's world this also means abstaining from forwarding unnecessary emails or texting unnecessary pictures to my neighbor, "lest he have his fill" of me, as the scriptural warning says above, and even begin to "hate" me! Today, I think, it is much harder to set and maintain boundaries, when we are all accessible to one another online, at practically any time and any place.

So let me stop myself today, if I am tempted to overextend myself, or allow others to overextend themselves, by over-communicating, be it online, on the phone, or in person. While I need not self-isolate, finding the right time and place to ask for help, or to be of service to others, I also need some alone-time with God, as do others. Although I know this is easier said than done in today's world, I also know that God's grace helps and guides me in this respect, when I ask: *"Set a guard over my mouth, O Lord; keep watch over the door of my lips."* (Ps 140/141: 3)

MARCH 17

SPIRITUAL PROCRASTINATION

"My soul, my soul, arise! Why are you sleeping? The end is drawing near, and you will be confounded. Awake then, that Christ our God may spare you, Who is everywhere, and fills all things." (Kontakion-hymn, Canon of St. Andrew of Crete)

Every year, as the end of Lent draws near, we sing this Kontakion in the middle of the Great Canon, which calls me to retrieve a sense of urgency about my meeting and walking with Christ. He is soon to walk His final journey, taking on my sins, my death, and my hell, in order to raise me up again in His glorious resurrection. But I tend to procrastinate and even "sleep," as His disciples slept in Gethsemane, while the Lord prayed and was "deeply grieved, even unto death," that the cup He was about to drink for us pass from Him. (Mt 26:38-40)

Let me take a good look today at my spiritual procrastination, and "arise" to walk with Him again, however awkwardly and imperfectly. Let me take a quiet moment for heartfelt prayer, re-connecting with Him "Who is everywhere, and fills all things," including me, whenever I scramble to my feet and follow His call: *"See, the hour is at hand, and the Son of Man is betrayed into the hands of sinners. Get up, let us be going. See, my betrayer is at hand."* (Mt 26:45-46)

MARCH 18

GOD'S SILENT SATURDAY

"Now there was a good and righteous man named Joseph, who, though a member of the council, had not agreed to their plan and action. He came from the Jewish town of Arimathea, and he was waiting expectantly for the kingdom of God. This man went to Pilate and asked for the body of Jesus. Then he took it down, wrapped it in a linen cloth, and laid it in a rock-hewn tomb where no one had ever been laid. It was the day of Preparation, and the sabbath was dawning. The women who had come with him from Galilee followed, and they saw the tomb and how his body was laid. Then they returned, and prepared spices and ointments. On the sabbath they rested according to the commandment." (Lk 23:50-56)

On this Saturday let me reflect a bit on that Holy and Great Saturday, when our Lord lay buried. His Body rests, while His soul is anything but inactive. Already here the Lord of the Sabbath is triumphant, descending into our hell as victor, as conquerer of death and its now-crumbling empire. While His Body lies buried in the earth, the Lord is busy, working on His new creation. Just as He created Adam "from the dust of the ground" (Gen 2:7), so He is to raise the New Adam, Himself, from His burial-place in the ground, breathing new life into us in His resurrected Body.

In the meantime "they rested" up above in the visible world, "according to the commandment." They rested in the silence of that Holy and Great Saturday, quite unaware of God's silent-yet-robust activity. Today let me contemplate God's silence, which often has far more to offer than I may suspect.

MARCH 19

FAITH, LOVE, AND JUDAS

"Mary took a pound of costly perfume made of pure nard, anointed Jesus' feet, and wiped them with her hair. The house was filled with the fragrance of the perfume. But Judas Iscariot, one of his disciples (the one who was about to betray him), said, 'Why was this perfume not sold for three hundred denarii and the money given to the poor?' (He said this not because he cared about the poor, but because he was a thief; he kept the common purse and used to steal what was put into it.) Jesus said, 'Leave her alone. She bought it so that she might keep it for the day of my burial. You always have the poor with you, but you do not always have me.'" (Jn 12:3-8)

Many important things can be said about Judas's motivation for betraying Christ. I just want to note one thing, however, which strikes me today in this passage: Judas did not trust the Lord, because Judas did not love Him. While the other disciples also lack faith at times; also misunderstand His words at times; and even abandon Him and deny Him as He is led to His death—still, they love Him. This love is what keeps the door open for their healing, for the restoration of their faith, whenever their human shortcomings had diminished their faith.

But in Judas's case, his particular set of shortcomings finds no healing, because his heart is closed to the Lord. When Judas finally regrets his sin, this regret does not turn to healing, to repentance, based on love for this Person, Jesus Christ; it turns to self-loathing and suicide. "I have sinned," he says, not because I betrayed Jesus, my beloved Lord, but because I have betrayed "innocent blood." (Mt 27:4) So distanced is Judas from the Person, that He doesn't call Him by name.

Today let me open my heart to the Lord, Who calls me to come out of self-preoccupation, and accompany Him on His cross-carrying journey, in His love. Because love connects me with Him, even when faith and understanding fail.

MARCH 20

GOD'S JUSTICE

"May our mouths be filled with Your praise, O Lord, that we may sing of Your glory. For You made us worthy to partake of Your holy, divine, immortal and life-giving Mysteries. Preserve us in Your holiness that we may meditate all day upon Your justice. Alleluia, alleluia, alleluia." (Thanksgiving Hymn of the Byzantine Divine Liturgy, after Communion)

After receiving Holy Communion, I am called to "meditate upon," that is, attend to or study (μελετάω), the Lord's "justice" or "righteousness" (δικαιοσύνη) all day. It is the "righteousness" or "justice" of Christ that is our source of "righteousness" and "justice"; He is the source of our sense of right and wrong, as well as any other "worthiness" we can possess. When we partake of Him, in His grace, in His Mysteries, we partake also of His divine "justice" and carry it with us into our world.

What is Christ's kind of "righteousness"? It is a righteousness that justifies teachable sinners. That is, sinners willing to re-focus, according to His loving guidance. That is, sinners willing to let go of self-righteousness and self-justification, and accept His righteousness and justice as a gift. I inevitably cease to be self-righteous and self-justifying, when I remember this simple truth, that it is God Who is the one source of justice and holiness.

Today I gratefully meditate upon this simple truth, and thank Him for including me in His call: *"I have not come to call the righteous, but sinners to repentance."* (Lk 5:32)

MARCH 21

EXTERNAL ORTHODOXY

"Woe to you, teachers of the law and Pharisees, you hypocrites! You give a tenth of your spices--mint, dill and cumin. But you have neglected the more important matters of the law--justice, mercy and faith. You should have practiced the latter, without neglecting the former. You blind guides, who strain out a gnat and swallow a camel!..." (Mt 23:23-24)

The teachers of the law and Pharisees were very orthodox about fulfilling certain external religious obligations, while neglecting the virtues that these obligations were meant to foster: justice, mercy, and faith. The Lord is criticizing them for embracing this external Orthodoxy, which self-righteously displayed such fidelity to secondary rules and regulations, while missing their whole point.

Reading this passage today, I am reminded to beware of a purely-external Orthodoxy, which clings to secondary issues, while neglecting "the more important matters," upon which the Lord Himself insists: justice, mercy, and faith. I do, indeed, gratefully embrace certain external forms and practices of my Tradition. But these external forms and practices do not, in and of themselves, fulfill Christ's call to me. He is calling me to be filled with the Spirit of these practices, without Whom my external piety is meaningless. Christ did not come, die on the Cross, and rise again, to replace one set of external rules and regulations with another set of external rules and regulations. He came to fill us with His Spirit.

So let me seek His Spirit today, in heartfelt prayer, and ask to be filled with His gifts, of justice, mercy, and faith. *"Create in me a clean heart, O God, and renew a right Spirit within me."* (Ps 50/51:10)

MARCH 22

SELF-CENTERED FEAR

"The Lord is my light and my saviour—whom shall I fear? The Lord is the defender of my life—of whom shall I be afraid?" (Ps 26/27:1)

The opposite of faith is self-reliance, which breeds fear and anxiety. Whenever I cease to lead a God-centered life, whenever I neglect to put myself, everything, and everyone in His hands, I am left alone to play God on the stage of my concerns, challenges, situations, and relationships. Of course I inevitably find that I'm ill-suited for this role, because my own shoulders are simply too insecure a foundation for the burdens of the world. This insecurity is what brings all sorts of fear into my life, like fear of people's opinions, of failure, or of economic insecurity.

Faith turns all of this around. And by faith I don't mean just holding "firm beliefs" in my mind, or going to church once a week. By faith I mean letting God's grace into my life, by connecting with Him, in prayer, on a daily basis. I mean letting Him into the picture of any situation, relationship, or "plan" for the future.

Let me let Him in today, and ask Him, at least briefly, to do for me what I cannot do for myself. I need not fear when I walk in His kingdom, where He alone is King. *"For Thine"*—not mine—*"is the kingdom, the power, and the glory, of the Father and of the Son and of the Holy Spirit, now and ever, and unto the ages of ages."* Amen!

MARCH 23

CRIPPLING SELF-DOUBT

"And God saw every thing that he had made, and, behold, it was very good. And the evening and the morning were the sixth day." (Gen 1:31)

My spiritual journey consists mainly of developing, in God's light, in God's grace, three essential relationships, all interrelated: 1. My relationship with God; 2. My relationship with myself; 3. My relationship with other people. Today I'm thinking about the second one, my relationship to myself.

The above-cited passage in the book of Genesis reminds me that, as part of the whole picture of His creation, God sees me, as well as all other people, as "very good." This "very goodness" exists as a whole, within the interrelated whole of Creator and creation; of "every thing that He had made."

I begin to realize my dignity and my "very goodness," that is, I begin to see myself as God sees me, when I maintain my connection to Him daily, shedding His light on all my aspirations and actions. When I separate myself from God, on the other hand, I am left with a crippling self-doubt, like Adam and Eve who realize they're naked in the garden. There's suddenly a sense of shame and a loss of trust in God, in themselves, and in each other. Because it is God's grace that is the "glue," so to say, that keeps the whole, interrelated "very goodness" of creation together.

Today let me renew the God-given "very goodness" of myself, by renewing my connection to Him. His grace removes my human shame, my human self-doubt, and clothes me in His dignity. Let me move forward and grow with Him and in Him; in His wisdom, His courage, and His divine-human dignity.

MARCH 24

GRACE GIVES SPACE

"In the sixth month the angel Gabriel was sent by God to a town in Galilee called Nazareth, to a virgin engaged to a man whose name was Joseph, of the house of David. The virgin's name was Mary. And he came to her and said, 'Greetings, O full of grace! The Lord is with you.' But she was shocked (διεταράχθη) by his word and pondered (διελογίζετο) what sort of greeting this might be. The angel said to her, 'Do not be afraid, Mary, for you have found grace with God. And now, you will conceive in your womb and bear a son, and you will name him Jesus...'" (Lk 1:26-31)

The All-Holy Virgin is deeply disturbed, even shocked, by the angel's greeting. But She does not immediately say anything. She rather "ponders" what it might mean, and listens to what he has to say next. This is the reaction of one Full of Grace: She takes pause and listens, because grace places space between Her instinctive disturbance and Her words.

Today let me open up to God's grace, and ask for His power to put space between my instinctive disturbances and my words/actions. Let me take pause, when I see or hear anything disturbing, "pondering" first and speaking next, or being silent next. Let me let God's grace quiet my thoughts, if they rush to judgment, and hand over judgment to God; Let me let God's grace soften any "feelings" of discouragement or dissatisfaction, before they develop into full-blown self-pity or resentment. Like opening a window and letting in some fresh air, let me detach myself a bit today from disturbances, and let God's grace into the picture of whatever is going on. *"By the prayers of the Theotokos, Saviour, save us."*

MARCH 25

THE HOLY VIRGIN'S "FIAT"

"And Mary said, 'Behold the handmaid of the Lord; let it be unto me according to your word.' And the angel departed from her." (Lk 1:38)

One often hears about the "obedience" of the Mother of God, expressed in this famous reply to the Archangel Gabriel, at the Annunciation.

So let me reflect on the "obedience" of the All-Holy Virgin. Was it a denial of Her human "will," as we sometimes understand "obedience"? No, it wasn't. Here what we see is Her decision, made freely, and after asking for certain clarifications from the angel, to accept Her role in an extraordinary plan that was God's will. The angel came to receive Her agreement, and only departed after Her "Let it be." It is thus that the new creation begins, "the "beginning of our salvation," (as it says in the Troparion or hymn of the Annunciation)—with the creative, affirmative human word of the All-Holy Virgin. It has remarkably been compared to the Creator's "Let there be..." at the initial creation of the world.

It is important for me to understand the "obedience" to which I am called today, obedience to God's will, in this light of Her obedience. It doesn't mean switching off my will or my brain. It is rather an exercise of my will, of my willingness, and my creative energies, to embrace and follow His voice in all the situations I am met with today. *"Let it be unto me according to Your word."*

MARCH 26

COVERING MY FATHER'S NAKEDNESS

"Noah, a man of the soil, was the first to plant a vineyard. He drank some of the wine and became drunk, and he lay uncovered in his tent. And Ham, the father of Canaan, saw the nakedness of his father, and told his two brothers outside. Then Shem and Japheth took a garment, laid it on both their shoulders, and walked backward and covered the nakedness of their father; their faces were turned away, and they did not see their father's nakedness. When Noah awoke from his wine and knew what his youngest son had done to him, he said, 'Cursed be Canaan; lowest of slaves shall he be to his brothers...'" (Gen 9:20-25)

This passage, about exposing the "nakedness" of one's father, is read in church today, on Wednesday of the fourth week of Byzantine Lent. And it cuts like a knife, particularly in our day. Because today I am often tempted to rush to expose and analyze every bit of "nakedness" of the "fathers" we are given today, not only but particularly in the Church. I feel "entitled" to demand more of bishops and priests, when they fall short of our standards. Any misstep, any dysfunction in church-administration, or in the handling of modern-day issues, I am tempted to approach with unmitigated disappointment, unsympathizing discussion, and a subtle presumption of my own moral superiority.

Today let me reflect deeply on the passage above, which calls me to "cover the nakedness" of my father. Not because he is perfect, but because he is my father. And I would want my children to do that for me, if I had children and had fallen short in some way, for all to see.

MARCH 27

CHASTITY vs. "WHOLE-MINDEDNESS"

"Grant me, Your servant, the spirit of chastity (σωφροσύνη, tselomudrie, whole-mindedness), humility, patience and love." (Prayer of St. Ephraim, part 2)

The Greek word "σωφροσύνη" is often translated as "chastity," which, like the Slavonic word "chistota," tends to make us think of total abstinence, a full stop to sexuality. It thus tends to isolate or even ban all issues of sexuality from the full picture of our "spiritual" journey. But the word "σωφροσύνη" means much more, which is why its proper Slavonic translation is helpful: in Slavonic, the word is translated as "tselomudrie," which literally means "whole-mindedness." This word places issues of sexuality where they belong: within the full picture of our journey to salvation.

Issues of sexuality become problematic and "sinful" precisely when they take on a life of their own, separate from our "whole-minded" approach to God. After all, God knows about this side of our humanity, because He created it, as one of His gifts. So sexual issues, including inappropriate sexual desire, need to be placed before God, handed over to God, and discerned, like anything else, in light of other gifts of the Holy Spirit, like love, faith, patience, gratitude, and humility.

Let us pose the appropriate questions to ourselves in this area, so it's not living a life of its own: Have we let self-seeking, dishonesty, lust, power-hungriness, sheer boredom, and so on, distort our sexual conduct? Have we put ourselves first and disrespected others? Or have we disrespected ourselves in these matters?

Let me shed His light also on this area of life, in a "whole-minded" manner, and let His loving grace guide my approach to it.

MARCH 28

HUMILITY HEALS PAIN

"Take my yoke upon you and learn from me, for I am meek and humble in heart, and you will find rest for your souls." (Mt 11:29)

Self-reliance and self-centeredness lead to various forms of pain, fear, and frustration—with myself, with others, and life in general. I ultimately become self-isolated and incapable of any true relationship. Humility, on the other hand, softly moves me out of myself and opens me up to a real relationship with God, myself, and others. I can more easily ask for help when I need it; more easily let go of resentments; see my role in conflicts, and accept others and myself in God's light. I can take al step back, or just duck under the wave, so to say, when necessary.

And by humility I don't mean: wallowing in my shortcomings, pretending to be wrong when I'm not, or constantly demanding the unreasonable or even impossible from myself. That is not humility, and I know that because it does not bring "rest for my soul."

It is the meekness and humility of the God-Man that will be my mode of action today, so I keep Him close in heartfelt prayer: *Lord, Jesus Christ, Son of God, have mercy on me, the sinner.*

MARCH 29

HIS WAY OF SEEING

"Yea, O Lord and King, grant me to see my own transgressions, and not to judge (κατακρίνειν, condemn) my brother, for blessed are You, unto ages of ages. Amen." (Lenten Prayer of St. Ephrem, Part Three)

Here I am asking for God's kind of vision. He is able "to see" and yet "not to condemn" (κατακρίνειν, to judge uncharitably). I, on the other hand, can not see in His way, without His help, because we "do not see," without the light of the Lord. Our kind of vision is darkness in light of Him, Who is the Source of all justice, as Christ reminds the Pharisees: *"For judgment I came into this world, that those who do not see may see, and that those who see may become blind."* (Jn 9:39) And as the wisdom of St. Ephrem's prayer reminds me, His kind of vision opens up to me through seeing "my own transgressions," in the light of my only Lord and King.

As we enter another day of Lent, I ask Him once again to grant me to see myself and others as He sees, without condemnation. Let me recognize judgment and justice where it truly resides, in Him. For He is "blessed," and imparts blessing on all of us, in communion with Him, "unto ages of ages. Amen."

MARCH 30

SEEING HIM IN THE SACRAMENTS

"...As they (Luke and Cleopas) came near the village to which they were going (Emmaus), he walked ahead as if he were going on. But they urged him strongly, saying, 'Stay with us, because it is almost evening and the day is now nearly over.' So he went in to stay with them. When he was at the table with them, he took bread, blessed and broke it, and gave it to them. Then their eyes were opened, and they recognized him..." (Lk 24:28-31)

On the way to Emmaus, two of Christ's disciples, Luke and Cleopas, are joined by the risen Lord, Who *"expounds to them in all the Scriptures concerning Himself"* (Lk 24:27). At this point, however, they do not recognize Him, although "their hearts burned within them" while He talked (Lk 24:32).

Their eyes are finally opened, and they are given the gift of "seeing" Him only later, when "He took bread, blessed and broke it, and gave it to them." His resurrection was the beginning of a new era, the time of the Church, in which we are given the gift of "seeing" Him on a new, sacramental level. We "see" Him in the sacraments, particularly in "the breaking of bread," that is, the Eucharist.

My heart does indeed "burn," hearing the Word of God. But this Word prepares me for a deeper "vision," to "see" the risen Lord as these disciples "saw" Him, through physical participation in His "breaking of the bread." This is why our Divine Liturgy consists first of the Liturgy of the Word, when we hear the Epistle and Gospel-readings, and then of the "blessing, breaking, and giving" of His Bread, in Holy Communion.

On this Sunday let me both hear His Word and partake at His table, as the disciples did. He can, and He does, open my eyes as He did theirs, because *"Jesus Christ is the same yesterday and today and forever."* (Heb 13:8)

MARCH 31

DOING THINGS HIS WAY

"But give rather the spirit of whole-mindedness, humility, patience, and love to Your servant." (Lenten Prayer of St. Ephrem, Part 2)

Doing things in God's "Spirit" does not mean that I stop doing things. That may be obvious, but I find that it needs to be said, at least to me. On a daily basis, I must go on with responsibilities, relationships, concerns, issues, and initiatives. But I let God into the whole picture, connecting with Him in prayer, and letting Him give me what He already wants to give me, before I pray—His Spirit.

Today I go forward, in God's light, combining any interactions with people with "whole-mindedness," being careful not to approach any human being in a self-indulgent or self-seeking manner. I combine my initiatives with humility and patience, accepting and facing my responsibilities, while leaving their outcomes in God's hands. I do the next right thing, to the best of my ability, while letting God's love for me, for others, and for our sometimes-dysfunctional world, into my heart. God is willing to give me His Spirit when I ask for Him, as He invites me to: *"If you then, who are evil, know how to give good gifts to your children, how much more will the heavenly Father give the Holy Spirit to those who ask him!"* (Lk 11:13)

APRIL 1

JUST FOR TODAY

"Give us this day (σήμερον) *our daily bread."* (The Lord's Prayer, Mt 6:11)

The Lord teaches me to place my dependence on Him in a childlike manner, just for today (σήμερον). Praying the Lord's Prayer, as He taught me to pray, I make a decision to see this day, and all of today's basic necessities, both physical and spiritual, as a gift from Him. Regardless of how I translate "our daily bread" or our "super-essential bread" (τὸν ἄρτον ἡμῶν τὸν ἐπιούσιον), I know that scripturally "bread" means basic nourishment; what any human being needs to go on.

Praying the Lord's Prayer I am liberated from excessive wants, and also excessive concerns, about tomorrow or yesterday. Because excessive worry hinders my ability to go about my daily cares in His Spirit; that is, with a healthy reliance on His grace. The Lord teaches me in this prayer to simplify my spiritual journey, by renewing my reliance on Him every immediate day. I do not build my spiritual house on yesterday's prayer, nor last Sunday's, nor can I effectively be present to the cares of today by excessively worrying about tomorrow.

Let me place everything in His hands once again today, as I go about tending to my responsibilities. This is enough for today, as He reminds me: *"Therefore do not worry about tomorrow, for tomorrow will worry about itself. Each day has enough trouble of its own."* (Mt 6:34)

APRIL 2

LET US ALSO GO

"...Now Jesus loved Martha and her sister and Lazarus. So when he heard that he was ill, he stayed two days longer in the place where he was. Then after this he said to the disciples, 'Let us go into Judea again.' The disciples said to him, 'Rabbi, the Jews were but now seeking to stone you, and are you going there again?' Jesus answered, 'Are there not twelve hours in the day? If any one walks in the day, he does not stumble, because he sees the light of this world. But if any one walks in the night, he stumbles, because the light is not in him.' Thus he spoke, and then he said to them, 'Our friend Lazarus has fallen asleep, but I go to awake him out of sleep.' The disciples said to him, 'Lord, if he has fallen asleep, he will recover.' Now Jesus had spoken of his death, but they thought that he meant taking rest in sleep. Then Jesus told them plainly, 'Lazarus is dead; and for your sake I am glad that I was not there, so that you may believe. But let us go to him.' Thomas, called the Twin, said to his fellow disciples, 'Let us also go, that we may die with him.'" (Jn 11:5-16)

Four days before our soon-to-be-crucified Lord "awakens" Lazarus from the dead, He unpleasantly surprises His disciples by saying, "Let us go into Judea again." This was a bad idea, the disciples point out. But our Lord confuses them further, talking mysteriously about "walking in the day," and "the light of this world." And finally, perhaps most perplexingly, He tells them about Lazarus's death and adds, "I am glad that I was not there, so that you may believe."

So in this passage our Lord is already focused on the light He is to bring, first to Bethany, "so that we may believe," and then to the entire world, through His life-giving suffering, death, and resurrection. But the disciples don't see the "light" in this picture. They see danger and death. Nonetheless, they all resolve to follow, as Thomas says, "Let us also go, that we may die with him."

I also don't always see the "light" in the situations and paths my Lord brings into my life. But let me follow Him today, as many followed Him, and continue to follow Him, dying to self on the life-bringing path of the Cross. As Jesus heads for Bethany today, let me get up and follow, as I hear Thomas say, *"Let us also go, that we may die with Him."*

APRIL 3

CARRYING ANOTHER'S CROSS

"As the soldiers led him away, they seized Simon from Cyrene, who was on his way in from the country, and put the cross on him and made him carry it behind Jesus." (Lk 23:26)

One of the most painful and humbling sides of cross-carrying is that we might find ourselves carrying someone else's. Or somebody else might have to carry ours. This situation, as humbling or even humiliating as it can be, is graced by the precedent of our Lord's own life-giving passion. He was so weak by this point, having been beaten and tortured in various other ways, that the Roman soldiers "made" Simon from Cyrene carry His cross. The soldiers had that kind of authority.

Why? Because He willed it so. Both His "weakness," on the one hand, and the "power" of the Roman soldiers, on the other, are willed by Him. Let me accept His will on my own cross-carrying journey today, part of which might be utter weakness—my own or someone else's.

APRIL 4

A DIFFICULT DISCIPLINE

"Remember the Sabbath day, to keep it holy. Six days you shall labor and do all your work, but the seventh day is the Sabbath of the Lord your God. In it you shall do no work..." (Ex 20:8-10)

The fourth commandment, regardless of whether I dedicate Saturday or Sunday to the Lord, reminds me of an increasingly difficult discipline. And that is the discipline of finding the proper time (and place) for work and rest. It is increasingly difficult because of the 24/7 culture of the Internet, which has been called "a culture of disruption." My schedule is easily disrupted by the constant and chaotic flow of information and communication, which is always "on," as long as I am "connected" to everyone and everywhere online.

There is something in my life that particularly counteracts the disorderly time and space of the Internet. And that "something" is liturgy. At church-services, I am exposed to a linear, not chaotic, flow of information, which I am called to contemplate in prayer, together with others, "connecting" with them. And I do so within a specific, physical space of a church. I believe this is why the discipline of church-going is so increasingly difficult and even alien to many of us, immersed in Internet-culture. It is difficult even for people of faith.

Today let me ask God for His wisdom and discernment, that I might manage my time according to His will. And let me not dismiss the wisdom of church-going without thinking about it. It offers me a helping hand in the challenges of time-management, when I show up for a church-service, liberated from my phone for a while.

APRIL 5

THE FIRST LOVE

"To the angel of the church of Ephesus write: '...you have persevered and have patience, and have labored for my name's sake and have not become weary. Nevertheless I have this against you, that you have abandoned your first love. Remember therefore from where you have fallen; repent and do the first works, or else I will come to you quickly and remove your lamp stand from its place—unless you repent." (Rev 2:1, 3-5)

In the above-cited passage in the Book of Revelation, the Lord sends this message to the "angel" (in our terms, the bishop) of the church in Ephesus, and talks about a quite subtle loss of his "first love" for the Lord. This reminds me of my own "first love," that is, the love I had for Him at first, when I first consciously heard Christ's call to me. Every Christian is "called," at some point, in some way, and in this passage we are reminded to keep fresh our initial, loving response to that call; to "do the first works" we did in response to Christ, and "repent," that is, have "metanoia"—a change of mind or focus.

The way I keep "the love I had at first" fresh is through a daily "conversion," a daily re-focusing on Christ, Who calls me anew every day. I rekindle my "first love" from the moment I wake up, placing my focus squarely on Him, in heartfelt prayer and a bit of contemplation of His word. I ask that He not remove my "lamp stand from its place"; that is, the grace-filled light of His word from my heart.

APRIL 6

A NEW SELF, A NEW NAME

"Whoever has ears, let them hear what the Spirit says to the churches. To the one who is victorious, I will give...a white stone with a new name written on it, known only to the one who receives it." (Rev 2:17)

In this inspiring passage in the Book of Revelation, the Lord the Holy Spirit speaks about "the one who is victorious," the believer who co-carries the victory of Christ's life-giving Cross. By walking the journey of the cross on the cross's terms, i.e., Christ's self-giving love, humility, patience, courage and wisdom, the believer walks through life's difficulties in the quiet victory of the Spirit.

And "that person," the "victorious" one, receives a revelation, "a white stone" reminiscent of the stone tablets received by Moses, when God revealed Himself, His character, in His commandments. The "new name" written on the white stone, "known only to the one who receives it," is each and every believer's special calling or vocation, through which he or she reveals God's character in this world, by walking His cross-carrying journey. Just as we are all called *"to clothe"* ourselves *"with the new self, created according to the likeness of God in true righteousness and holiness,"* (Eph 4:24), we are all given "talents" in different ways and different measure (Mt 25:14-30). Discovering what those "talents" are, what our "new name" is, is a special gift of the Holy Spirit.

Today let me have "ears to hear"; let me hear "what the Spirit says to the churches," as elevated and strange as it may sound to me, in the Book of Revelation. And let me ask for the gift of walking my own journey, being my God-given self, "the new self" in Him and His name.

APRIL 7

WHEN GOD INTERRUPTS

"In the sixth month the angel Gabriel was sent from God to a city of Galilee named Nazareth, to a virgin betrothed to a man whose name was Joseph, of the house of David; and the virgin's name was Mary. And he came to her and said, 'Hail, O full of grace, the Lord is with you!' But she was greatly troubled at the saying, and considered in her mind what sort of greeting this might be. And the angel said to her, 'Do not be afraid, Mary, for you have found grace with God. And behold, you will conceive in your womb and bear a son, and you shall call his name Jesus. He will be great, and will be called the Son of the Most High; and the Lord God will give to him the throne of his father David, and he will reign over the house of Jacob for ever; and of his kingdom there will be no end.' And Mary said to the angel, 'How shall this be, since I have no husband?' And the angel said to her, 'The Holy Spirit will come upon you, and the power of the Most High will overshadow you; therefore the child to be born will be called holy, the Son of God. And behold, your kinswoman Elizabeth in her old age has also conceived a son; and this is the sixth month with her who was called barren. For with God nothing will be impossible.' And Mary said, 'Behold, I am the handmaid of the Lord; let it be to me according to your word.' And the angel departed from her." (Lk 1:26-38)

Thus begins God's Great Interruption of world history, and it begins with a young woman being "greatly troubled" by an unexpected greeting. Then Her visitor tells Her, "Do not be afraid." But still, She has a question: "How shall this be?" So the angel offers not only an explanation, "The Holy Spirit will come upon you…," but he points to someone Mary knows—Look, Elizabeth has also conceived… And finally the Blessed Among Women accepts God's call and says, Let it be.

Even in the case of the Most Holy Theotokos, God's call to Her first instils confusion and fear. Because She doesn't understand the "How." And yet She accepts, because She understands the "language" of the angel, the language of faith: "For with God nothing will be impossible." Today let me ask for Her help, when God gives me unexpected responsibilities, interrupting my previous concerns. *"Hail, O full of grace,"* I gratefully say to Her today. *"The Lord is with You, and through You with us."*

APRIL 8

TRUSTING OTHERS

"But Thomas (who was called the Twin), one of the twelve, was not with them when Jesus came. So the other disciples told him, 'We have seen the Lord.' But he said to them, 'Unless I see the mark of the nails in his hands, and put my finger in the mark of the nails and my hand in his side, I will not believe. A week later his disciples were again in the house, and Thomas was with them. Although the doors were shut, Jesus came and stood among them and said, 'Peace be with you. Then he said to Thomas, 'Put your finger here and see my hands. Reach out your hand and put it in my side. Do not doubt but believe. Thomas answered him, 'My Lord and my God! Jesus said to him, 'Have you believed because you have seen me? Blessed are those who have not seen and yet have come to believe.'" (Jn 20:24-29

The news of the resurrection was meant to be spread by eye-witnesses. The first to receive the news are the women, but their testimony is not believed by the disciples. And then it is the disciples who are visited by the risen Lord, when they are all gathered, except Thomas, and they pass on the news to Thomas. But he does not believe the witness of the others, demanding more evidence. So the risen Lord comes to them once again, when Thomas is present and despite the "shut doors," and gives this disciple what he had demanded. Nonetheless Christ rebukes Thomas for not having believed in the first place; for not having trusted the witness of the others. The Lord was calling the disciples to trust one another, because mutual trust was essential for their unity in faith, as Church.

Today I note that the Lord entrusted His message to human witnesses, to teach us to trust one another; to fortify one another in faith. Thus my faith is given to me, and strengthened in me, through others. Despite the "shut doors" of my fears or doubts, the Lord enters my life in the context of fellowship with other human beings.

APRIL 9

OPENING THE DOOR

"Behold, I stand at the door and knock. If anyone hears my voice and opens the door, I will come in to him and dine with him, and he with me." (Rev 3:20)

So here's another mind-blowing passage of the Book of Revelation, which I really do not read often enough. I am more aware of the passage in the Gospel of Matthew (and Luke), in which the Lord tells me: *"Ask and it will be given to you; seek and you will find; knock and the door will be opened to you"* (Mt 7:7, cf. Lk 11:9). But here in Revelation He reminds me that, whether or not I am asking, seeking, and knocking, He is always at my door, knocking and calling me to open up and let Him in. He is there, all-inclusively, for "anyone" who hears His voice. He is always willing to do that, and is doing that, even when we don't.

Let me hear His voice today, letting Him in and letting go of self-centered fear and self-reliance. Let me dine with Him, and He with me, at the table of His word, which nurtures me throughout my day.

APRIL 10

THE ARMOR OF PEACE

"Therefore take up the whole armor of God, so that you may be able to withstand on that evil day, and having done everything, to stand firm. Stand therefore, and fasten the belt of truth around your waist, and put on the breastplate of righteousness. As shoes for your feet put on whatever will make you ready to proclaim the gospel of peace. With all of these, take the shield of faith, with which you will be able to quench all the flaming arrows of the evil one. Take the helmet of salvation, and the sword of the Spirit, which is the word of God." (Eph 6:13-17)

I note today that while St. Paul uses military imagery here, he is actually making a point about peace; about "the gospel of peace." He is calling me to peace with the people in my visible surroundings, reminding me that any loss of peace/disturbance I experience on account of others is in me, in my heart. *"For our struggle is not against enemies of blood and flesh, but against... the spiritual forces of evil..."* (Eph 6:12)

Today if I feel frustrated, angry, or annoyed with any people, institutions, or situations in my life, I am reminded to look inside myself, and shed the light of the "gospel of peace" on my part in any circumstance or relationship. This doesn't mean that I have to pretend that others around me are perfect, but I am not called to control their journeys. I am called to take care of my part, with His help, with "the sword of the Spirit, which is the word of God," which clothes me in truth, righteousness, faith, and the rest of "the whole armor of God." I let Him arm me today, in His peace.

APRIL 11

KEEPING WATCH

"Therefore keep watch, because you do not know at what hour your Lord will come (ἔρχεται)." (Mt 24:42)

This passage, in which Christ tells me to "keep watch," or "pay attention," is usually translated as an admonition about the future, because we do not know when the Lord "will come" at His final "coming." However, here Christ actually uses the present tense; He says, to be precise, that we don't know when He "comes" (ἔρχεται).

The Lord "comes" to me in unexpected ways; in moments of solitude and through other people, both friends and strangers, created in His image, and through all creation, when I pay attention. Nowadays it is easy not to pay attention, when we are engrossed in our phones, oblivious to our physical surroundings so much of the time. We can be oblivious to the others riding with us in the train, or in the elevator, or even to those sitting with us at the dinner-table. Even when we're alone, walking in the park or waiting for a friend at a café, we can easily escape the moment of solitude to check the ever-present phone.

Today let me take time to be more present, to "keep watch" for how my Lord comes to me in my immediate surroundings, be it in the spring flowers, the fresh foliage of the trees, or in the various people I encounter. Let Him be present to me, and I to Him, in the places and people He reveals to me today.

APRIL 12

WORK AS PRAISE

"Praise him with the sound of trumpet; praise him with lute and harp. Praise him with tambourine and dance; praise him with strings and flute..." (Ps 150: 3-4)

This Psalm mentions various man-made instruments, calling us to "praise" God not only through words, but also through various products of our God-given creativity, through various art-forms and any work we do. It is a refreshing fact that God is praised, His name is "hallowed," not only through the beauty of His creation, but also through the work of our hands.

Today let me approach my work, whatever it may be, as "praise" to the Lord. In practical terms this means, first, asking for His guidance and help in prayer, letting go of self-reliant fears. It also means tending to my responsibilities in His Spirit; embracing those responsibilities as a service to others; letting His grace into the picture of any conflicts/difficulties, so that His gifts of gratitude, humility, courage, and patience enlighten my behavior. And finally, it means handing over the outcome of my efforts, be it success or failure, gratefully into His hands. *"Let every breath praise the Lord."* (Ps 150: 5)

APRIL 13

PROCRASTINATION

"For I do not do the good I want, but the evil I do not want is what I do. Now if I do what I do not want, it is no longer I that do it, but sin that dwells within me... Wretched man that I am! Who will rescue me from this body of death? Thanks be to God through Jesus Christ our Lord!" (Rom 7:19-20, 24-25)

Here St. Paul expresses the kind of exasperation I feel about my procrastination; when I put off the things I should be doing, and instead do things I should not be doing. But St. Paul does not just exasperatedly talk about "the problem"; he moves on to identify "the solution," exclaiming, "Thanks be to God through Jesus Christ our Lord!" In other words, he gratefully recognizes "the solution" is not in himself, but in the Power and Wisdom of God, Jesus Christ.

In practical terms, this means I need His help, and that His help is there for me. When I examine the reasons for my procrastination, at the top of the list are:
1. Self-Reliance (leaving God's help out of the picture), which leads to
2. Fear (of failure or success),
3. Perfectionism (i.e., waiting for more perfect conditions or a more perfect time for tackling the task at hand),
4. Laziness (wanting the outcome without the effort), or even
5. Resentment (like a passive resistance to an authority that gave me the task in the first place). All these spiritual "diseases" can be identified and healed, little by little, through God's grace, if I humbly accept His help and shed the light of His word on my procrastination.

Today let me open up to God's help, co-operating with Him as I face my immediate responsibilities, one by one. They are never the insurmountable mountains they seemed to be, when I approach them with a bit of faith. *"Truly I tell you, if you have faith as small as a mustard seed, you can say to this mountain, 'Move from here to there,' and it will move. Nothing will be impossible for you."* (Mt 17:20)

APRIL 14

THE PROMISE OF GROWTH

"If you sow to your own flesh, you will reap corruption from the flesh; but if you sow to the Spirit, you will reap eternal life from the Spirit. So let us not grow weary in doing what is right, for we will reap in due time, if we do not give up." (Gal 6:8-9)

Today the Apostle reminds me of the exciting reality of spiritual growth, accessible to all of us. It may be impossible to notice as it happens, like watching the grass grow, but it's an undeniable and beautiful reality nonetheless, if I "sow to the Spirit" and tend to my spiritual "garden."

Today let me do a bit of necessary "weeding," in some self-examination; Let me provide the essential nourishment, water, and light I need for growth, in some prayer and contemplation of God's word. And as I go about my work today, let me be mindful of "doing what is right," keeping His Spirit in the picture of any situation or relationship. Because we all "reap in due time, if we do not give up." And that's a promise I see fulfilled daily, when I "sow to the Spirit."

APRIL 15

SELF-ESTEEM vs. SELF-KNOWLEDGE

"Then Jesus said to them, 'All of you will be made to stumble because of me this night...' Peter answered and said to him, 'Even if all are made to stumble because of you, I will never be made to stumble.'" (Mt 26:31, 33-34)

In the final hours leading up to our Lord's arrest and passion, Peter is full of self-confidence, proclaiming that he will "never" be made to stumble. Just a few verses later Christ Himself displays a very different attitude in the face of His imminent suffering, throwing Himself on the ground in Gethsemane and praying, *"My Father, if it is possible, let this cup pass from me; yet not what I want but what you want"* (Mt 26:39). The God-Man seeks strength in prayer, while Peter seeks strength in himself.

High self-esteem is often thought to lead to high performance and success. Don't focus on your human weaknesses, I am told; focus on your "awesomeness." But such a focus actually leads to fear; to a quiet terror of making mistakes, as I defensively assert my "awesomeness" to protect it.

When I take a good look at my weaknesses, on the other hand, I actually find strength and motivation. Because self-examination leads me both to understand my deficiencies and to seek help from God and other people. This doesn't mean "letting myself off the hook" or "lowering the bar." An understanding of my particular sinful patterns helps me see them for what they are, and that is, changeable. I do change and grow as I seek and receive help, in prayer and humble openness to myself and others.

Today let me choose the path of self-compassionate change over the dead-end of self-esteem. God does not abandon me on the transformational journey of His cross, when I recognize and ask for the help that I need.

APRIL 16

A COMMON STORY

"We declare to you what was from the beginning, what we have heard, what we have seen with our eyes, what we have looked at and touched with our hands, concerning the word of life—this life was revealed, and we have seen it and testify to it, and declare to you the eternal life that was with the Father and was revealed to us—we declare to you what we have seen and heard so that you also may have fellowship (κοινωνίαν) with us; and truly our fellowship is with the Father and with his Son Jesus Christ." (1 Jn 1:1-3)

John, the beloved disciple, reminds me today of our common story. It is what the first followers of Christ "saw and heard," concerning the Word of Life, and then passed on to us, that builds our "fellowship" or "communion" (κοινωνίαν)—with all previous generations of faithful, beginning with the eye-witnesses like John; with one another today; and with God. We "commune" in His story, His revelation of Himself, and we identify with it. Because a common story means a common identity.

Nowadays we might find ourselves spending time on, and identifying with, all sorts of stories. Anything from a recent, shocking statement made by a politician, to the scandalous details of a celebrity divorce, to an animal born with two heads in Indonesia—anything that happens to pop up online or elsewhere might become our focus for considerable amounts of time, whether we consciously "care" about it or not.

Today let me be mindful about the stories I spend time on. When they draw me in, they do affect my identity, my own "story," and the "fellowship" I choose, challenging it, informing it, or building it. Let me start my day with some deep reading of the Word of Life, so that I may see all other stories, as well as my own, in His light.

APRIL 17

VICTORY OF THE WEAKEST

"A bruised reed he will not break, and a smoldering wick he will not snuff out, till he has brought justice through to victory." (Mt 12:20; cf. Isaiah 42:3)

Here, the Evangelist Matthew quotes a prophecy of Isaiah, describing Christ's healing ministry to the crowds that were following Him wherever He went. The Lord did not turn away even the weakest, the most sinful, the most disparaged, like the harlots and tax-collectors, or others considered "hopeless cases." They are likened in this passage to a "reed" or very thin branch that is "bruised," but not entirely broken, and a "wick" not aflame but still "smoldering."

Today I find great consolation and encouragement in this gentle image. It describes our Lord's humble openness to those of us who are no great pillars of spirituality; to those of us who have no great "flame" of desire and love for God's "justice."

I need not be discouraged in the weakness of my resolve today. I can take heart and bring the little I have to the table, taking small steps every day, in a bit of prayer, a bit of contemplation of His word, and doing the next right thing as best I can. I make a beginning today, and let Him do the rest. Because I have a Lord Who takes my bruised and smoldering bit of "justice" and brings it through to "victory."

APRIL 18

BLESSING HIM

"Bless the Lord, O my soul, and all that is within me, bless his holy name. Bless the Lord, O my soul, and do not forget all his benefits—who forgives all your iniquity..." (Ps 102/103: 1-3)

In this Psalm I "bless" (εὐλογέω) the Lord, which literally means "say a good word" or "praise." By "blessing" God I do not give Him something He doesn't already have, because He is the source of all good; He is the source also of all "good words" or "blessings." So when we sing this Psalm in church, we remind ourselves of this fact, adding the refrain, "Blessed are You, O Lord."

So why am I called to "bless" Him? Because it does me good. It is good for me to praise the good in this world, the source of which is God, rather than spending my time grumbling about the bad, the source of which is our bad choices. Praising the truly good, so as to "not forget all His benefits," brings me gratitude, which generates humility and peace. Grumbling about the bad in this world generates the opposite, although many seem to prefer it on social media and elsewhere. But in our church-services we spend very little time, as a liturgical community, decrying bad things, and spend almost the entire time contemplating and praising the good. The only "bad things" I am called to contemplate at any length in liturgy are my own sins. But even in this area, of my sins, I do not wallow in the "problem," but look to the Solution; to God's healing and forgiveness.

Let me "bless the Lord" today, with "all that is within me." I ask in heartfelt prayer for His gifts of gratitude and peace, that I may have eyes to see the abundance of His grace in my life and in this world. *"Blessed are You, O Lord!"*

APRIL 19

GUARDING THE MOUTH & SOUL

"He who guards his mouth and his tongue, guards his soul from troubles." (Prov 21:23)

Unfortunately this is a truth I often remember only in hindsight. I remember it after entering a useless debate, or sharing useless information, or being inconsiderate of the person with whom, or at whom, I was speaking. And yet, as discouraging as that may be, I can build on such experiences, so that today I have the foresight of this wisdom from Proverbs, rather than just remember it in hindsight.

Today let me take a small step back, and listen a bit more, in any conversation I might have. Let me think twice before sharing information, be it online or face-to-face, asking myself, Is it worth it? Let the word of God help me to help myself in *"guarding my soul from troubles."*

APRIL 20

A LIBERATING YOKE

"Put not your trust/hope in princes, in the sons of man, in whom there is no salvation." (Ps 145/146: 3)

This verse warns me about having improper expectations of human beings, including myself. And by "improper" I mean the kind of trust we have in God, in Whom we find "salvation." The word "salvation" (from the Latin "salvus," meaning "sound" or "whole," referring to people's health) means the process of our recovery or restoration to health. While God does work through other people in this process, it is His grace that brings about healing and recovery through and amidst human interaction.

Today I am mindful of letting God's grace into the picture of all my relationships, with myself and other people. No human being can fill the hole in my heart, when it wanders off and seeks fulfilment outside God, in burdensome self-reliance or human codependency.

Let me rather take His "yoke" upon me today, and carry it into all my relationships. His "yoke" liberates me from the burdens of grace-less human interaction, bringing me healing and peace. *"Take my yoke upon you and learn from me, for I am gentle and humble in heart, and you will find rest for your souls."* (Mt 11:29)

APRIL 21

DAILY RENEWAL

"Create in me a clean heart, O God, and renew a right spirit within me." (Ps 50/51:10)

Another day, another renewal. I ask today that God "renew a right spirit within me," because He does that, in ever-new ways, every day. He always has renewal and new creation on offer, "creating" in me a clean heart, when I look to Him, to His Spirit. When I look to the world, on the other hand, in a God-less manner, there is the "old" and ultimately predictable. I myself become "old" and predictable, when I turn to grace-less self-reliance, leaving God out of the picture.

I'm thinking about this wonderful, "renewable" of the spiritual journey today, because I overslept this morning. My schedule was thrown off and I felt frustrated. The world was already up and about, and I was behind.

But I have a God Who has renewal on offer, at whatever time I choose to ask for it. I am called to "walk in newness of life" (Rom. 6:4) in His Son, Who carries my burdens and nails my shortcomings to a cross. Today I hand my frustration over to Him in gratitude, and let His grace make me new, again. *"Create in me a clean heart, O God, and renew a right spirit within me."*

APRIL 22

JESUS WEPT

"When Mary (the sister of Lazarus) came where Jesus was and saw him, she knelt at his feet and said to him, 'Lord, if you had been here, my brother would not have died.' When Jesus saw her weeping (κλαίουσαν), and the Jews who came with her also weeping (κλαίοντας), he was greatly disturbed in spirit and deeply moved. He said, 'Where have you laid him?' They said to him, 'Lord, come and see.' Jesus began to weep (ἐδάκρυσεν). So the Jews said, 'See how he loved him!'" (Jn 11:32-36)

The Lord so deeply felt the grief caused by the death of Lazarus, that in His compassion He famously "wept" (ἐδάκρυσεν). Of course, Christ knew of Lazarus's coming resurrection, so it wasn't His friend's death, in and of itself, that moved the God-Man to tears. It was the very real pain of Lazarus's loved ones, the pain of the physical separation from Lazarus, for which Christ had such compassion.

I note, however, that the Lord did not "wail" ("klaio" in Greek), as the people described here did. He sincerely yet gently "wept" ("dakryo," a gentler verb in Greek). This passage tells me, if I'm grieving a loved one, it's "perfectly" human to grieve. It's even necessary to grieve—but to do so gently, with faith, in the light and hope of the resurrection.

As St. John Chrysostom says, *"He wept over Lazarus. So should you; weep, but gently, but with decency, but with the fear of God. If you weep thus, you do so not as disbelieving the resurrection, but as not enduring the separation. Since even over those who are leaving us, and departing to foreign lands, we weep, yet we do this not as despairing."* (In John 62.4)

APRIL 23

LONELINESS

"Then the Lord God said, 'It is not good that the man should be alone; I will make him a helper as his partner. ...The man gave names to all cattle, and to the birds of the air, and to every animal of the field; but for the man there was not found a helper as his partner.'" (Gen 2:18, 20)

Adam is lonely, already in his prelapsarian state (before "the fall"). Adam is not created as a self-sufficient being, but as one in need of community and companionship. This is not a "deficiency," but part of Adam's God-like nature. Adam is created in the image and likeness of God, Who also exists in community; in the Community of Three Persons, Father, Son, and Holy Spirit. And God provides us with community in different ways, throughout Salvation History.

So loneliness is a powerful emotion, particularly because it is "natural." My God-given need for community, like all my "natural" needs, is a major challenge and motivator on my spiritual journey. It motivates me to come out of myself, reaching out to God and other human beings. It motivates our creativity, inspiring great works of art and other forms of self-giving. Conversely, however, the human need for community can drive us to sin, when we search for it in the wrong places.

Today let me approach with gratitude the "hole in my heart" that is loneliness, recognizing Who it is that put it there, from the beginning. It is God, "Creator of heaven and earth, all things visible and invisible," Who calls me, through loneliness, to community and communion, with Him and other human beings.

APRIL 24

HONOR IN HUMILITY

"When he (Jesus) noticed how the guests chose the places of honor, he told them a parable. 'When you are invited by someone to a wedding banquet, do not sit down at the place of honor, in case someone more distinguished than you has been invited by your host, and the host who invited both of you may come and say to you, 'Give this person your place,' and then in disgrace you would start to take the lowest place. But when you are invited, go and sit down at the lowest place, so that when your host comes, he may say to you, 'Friend, move up higher'; then you will be honored in the presence of all who sit at the table with you. For all who exalt themselves will be humbled, and those who humble themselves will be exalted.'" (Lk 14:7-11)

So here the Lord gives me a small lesson on etiquette. What He basically says is, Don't make someone else's wedding about YOU! This may seem obvious—but still, He knows it needs to be said. It may be silly, and yet it's so human, to turn any social occasion, as well as life in general, into a self-seeking exercise in somehow gaining honor or recognition for one's self.

But the Lord is saying to me: Don't worry about that. Go and seek to honor others, putting them first, and the "host" (God) will see to the rest. It is the path of humility, which liberates me from the frustrations of self-seeking, and brings me honor at His table.

APRIL 25

HOLY, NOT PERFECT

"...A week later his disciples were again in the house, and Thomas was with them. Although the doors were shut, Jesus came and stood among them and said, 'Peace be with you.' Then he said to Thomas, 'Put your finger here and see my hands. Reach out your hand and put it in my side. Do not doubt but believe.' Thomas answered him, 'My Lord and my God!' Jesus said to him, 'Because you have seen me, you have believed. Blessed are those who have not seen and yet have come to believe.'" (Jn 20:26-29)

In this passage the risen Lord grants the "doubting" Thomas what the disciple has demanded, to physically touch His wounds, in order to believe. But Christ does not praise Thomas for his need to see and touch, of which He evidently disapproves. "Blessed are those," the Lord remarks pointedly, "who have not seen and yet have come to believe."

Thus Christ comes to His followers despite their imperfections; despite the "shut doors"—the doors we may have shut out of fear or doubt or something else. He comes to us not because we are perfect, but because we are His. All His disciples are "not of the world," and "sanctified" or "consecrated," (Jn 17:16-19), as we all are in baptism. This means that we belong to Him. "Sanctus" or "holy" means "set apart for God," or "belonging to God." It means not that we are perfect (because only God is perfect), but that we are dedicated to Him, to His purpose.

Today I am gratefully reminded that our own imperfections are no obstacle to our Lord, who comes to us despite our "shut doors," and "consecrates" us in His truth, not our own. *"As you did send Me into the world,"* He prays to the Father, *"so I have sent them into the world. And for their sake I consecrate Myself, that they also may be consecrated in truth."* (Jn 17:18-19)

APRIL 26

DO NOT BE ANXIOUS

"...And do not seek what you are to eat and what you are to drink, nor be of anxious mind (μὴ μετεωρίζεσθε). For all the nations of the world seek these things; and your Father knows that you need them. Instead, seek his kingdom, and these things shall be yours as well. Fear not, little flock, for it is your Father's good pleasure to give you the kingdom!" (Lk 12:29-32)

So the Lord reminds us to relax, in Him. He says, do not be "of anxious mind," as the RSV translation puts it. But more literally, He is saying, "μὴ μετεωρίζεσθε"—do not be tossed to and fro in the air, like a meteor. He offers us focus, or direction, which brings us peace, allowing other things to fall into place. This reminds me of a (non-theological) explanation of what "GOD" stands for: "Good Orderly Direction." I find that helpful.

Today let me "fear not," amidst my various financial, professional, or personal concerns. Let me put first things first, that is, let me start my day in a God-centered way, letting Him be my strength and focus. I take time for a bit of heartfelt prayer and grateful contemplation, so my concerns and ambitions don't toss me about in various un-godly "kingdoms," like Anxiety or Stress or Depression. Let me be part of His "little flock" today, for it is my Father's good pleasure to give me His kingdom.

APRIL 27

LIFTED UP

"So when they had come together, they asked him, 'Lord, will you at this time restore the kingdom to Israel?' He said to them, 'It is not for you to know times or seasons which the Father has fixed by his own authority. But you shall receive power when the Holy Spirit has come upon you; and you shall be my witnesses in Jerusalem and in all Judea and Samaria and to the end of the earth.' And when he had said this, as they were looking on, he was lifted up, and a cloud took him out of their sight. And while they were gazing into heaven as he went, behold, two men stood by them in white robes, and said, 'Men of Galilee, why do you stand looking into heaven? This Jesus, who was taken up from you into heaven, will come in the same way as you saw him go into heaven.'" (Acts 1:6-11)

At the time when the Lord ascends in His resurrected body, having spent forty days among us, the "men of Galilee," the disciples, still lack the grace of understanding His divine Kingship. Because they still cling to their old hopes, that Christ will "restore the kingdom to Israel." So here, just before His Ascension, He once again reminds us of the promise of the Spirit; of the "power" not political, but from above: "But you shall receive power when the Holy Spirit has come upon you."

And He further confuses them, by being lifted from their sight, so they are left standing there, bedazzled and "looking into heaven." But as the two men in white robes assure them, He has not finished His work for us, no. He "will come" again. And as St. Paul notes, Christ lifted up our renewed, human body in glory, having taken "captive" our darkness and tormentors, in order to make way for Another Comforter and His gifts. Christ is making way for the Holy Spirit, Whose time is coming, in the time of the Church, with her abundant gifts to each of us: "But grace was given to each of us according to the measure of Christ's gift. Therefore it is said, 'When he ascended on high he led a host of captives, and he gave gifts to men." (Eph 4:7-8, cf. Ps 67/68:18)

Let me be open to His gifts today, as I stare up in awe, not quite understanding the bedazzling mystery of His plan. Glory be to our Triune God, Father, Son, and Holy Spirit, Who continues to work tirelessly to lift me up, toward His kind of Kingship.

APRIL 28

I AM NOT ALONE

"I am filled with love, for the Lord will hear the voice of my supplication. Because he has inclined his ear to me, therefore I will call upon him as long as I live. The pains of death surrounded me, and the pangs of Hades laid hold of me; I found trouble and sorrow. Then I called upon the name of the Lord..." (Ps 114/116: 1-4, according to the Septuagint)

In the Psalms I find the whole spectrum of human experience on the journey of faith; From intense love and joy in the Lord, to intense sorrow and fear, like "the pangs of Hades" surrounding the soul—all these experiences are expressed here, in the Psalms, in prayer, and thus presented or handed over to the Lord.

As I chant the Psalms today, I am reminded that there is nothing, absolutely nothing, new or unique about any sorrow, fear, or trouble I encounter on my cross-carrying journey in the present day. I need not feel alienated or separated from what I imagine to be the experience of "the saints." It is a human experience, which includes love, joy, fear, sorrow, and tribulation, all handed over to the Lord in the prayers of many generations, day after day, and shared with me in the witness of the Psalms.

Today whether I stand or fall, I know I am not alone, when I refocus and join my voice to the many voices before me, who handed all this over to the Lord. *"I am filled with love, for the Lord will hear the voice of my supplication,"* as He heard theirs.

APRIL 29

ACCEPTING CHANGE

"Touch me not!" (John 20:17)

Christ says these words to Mary Magdalene, having appeared to her after His resurrection. How painfully unexpected this must have been for her. Something had changed. He is preparing her for a different, sublimer level of communion with Him: the sacramental reality of the Church.

It is often painful for me to accept change, especially in a relationship. For example, when a loved one is aging or near death. To accept parting, the parting with their physical presence, and the fact that physical touch will no longer be possible. I want to cling... But let me remind myself of the bigger picture: Through change, suffering, parting, and death I am being led to growth. More specifically, to growth in faith; to gratefully and even joyously embrace the truth of the Resurrection and all its consequences. Let me bear His cross today, not with fear or resentment, but with a focus on the Resurrection.

APRIL 30

NOT JUST ANOTHER TEACHER

"And as he walked by the Sea of Galilee, he saw Simon and Andrew his brother casting a net into the sea; for they were fishermen. Then Jesus said to them, 'Follow me, and I will make you become fishers of men.' They immediately left their nets and followed him." (Mk 1:16-17)

So, Simon and Andrew simply walk off from their job, leaving their nets, and follow Jesus. And He barely said anything to them—only the puzzling phrase I read above, which probably made little sense to them, "I will make you become fishers of men." At this point the disciples know little if anything of Christ's "teaching." They are following Him, not a teaching.

I note today that of course, Christ brings us a salvific teaching and valuable "lessons" on how to live. But this is not exclusively, not even primarily, what makes us follow Him, leaving our "nets" and other entanglements behind. There were many wise teachers before Christ, with more systematic teachings on how to live. My faith is primarily about a meeting with a living Being, the God-Man Jesus Christ, Who reveals to us the Father and sends the Holy Spirit, in the lived experience of daily life in Him. It is the strength, the power of this Being, that makes His teaching salvifically different from the teaching of others, as it says in this same chapter of the Gospel of Mark: *"And they were astonished at His teaching, for He taught them as one having authority, and not as the scribes."* (Mk 1:22)

Let me remember not to limit myself to "learning about" Christ, but also to meet Him in heartfelt prayer, letting His grace into my heart and into my entire schedule today.

MAY 1

LIBERATING CONFESSION

"Jesus said to her (the Samaritan woman), 'Every one who drinks of this water will thirst again, but whoever drinks of the water that I shall give him will never thirst; the water that I shall give him will become in him a spring of water welling up to eternal life.' The woman said to him, 'Sir, give me this water, that I may not thirst, nor come here to draw.' Jesus said to her, 'Go, call your husband, and come here.' The woman answered him, 'I have no husband.' Jesus said to her, 'You are right in saying, "I have no husband"; for you have had five husbands, and he whom you now have is not your husband; this you said truly.' The woman said to him, 'Sir, I perceive that you are a prophet...'" (Jn 4:13-19)

Our Lord is drawing the woman out of herself, letting her tell Him things He already knows—first, about her "thirst" for His kind of "water," and second, ...about that other thing. It is that thing in her life, that repeating, troublesome pattern, which needs to be said aloud and addressed, so that a real conversation with Christ can begin. And so that she can receive "living water" that will become in her "a spring of water welling up to eternal life." She can't quite say it herself, so He helps her out, and says it for her, like an experienced, skillful father-confessor: You have had five husbands... You've been trying to quench that "thirst" in the wrong place. After this, we see her eyes and heart begin to open, and she starts asking Him the right questions.

Today let me not fear a conversation like this one; a confession that liberates me from "that thing" in my life that may be blocking me from truly quenching my "thirst." My Lord can and will give me more than I can give myself, or that any human being can give me. He gives me water that becomes in me "a spring of water welling up to eternal life." So let me open up to Him today. "Give me this water," I say to Him this morning, "that I may not thirst," nor come to draw in the wrong places.

MAY 2

THIRST FOR GOD

"Let whoever who thirsts come. Whoever desires, let him take the water of life freely." (Rev 22:17)

This is a passage about desire and thirst, at the end of the Book of Revelation, at the very end of the New Testament.

I have many, varying desires and wants and needs every day. At times there is unfulfilled desire and unfulfilled ambition. Sometimes I can't even identify what it is that I desire. It's just a hole in my heart.

Let me identify that it is God, the Comforter, the Holy Spirit, Who is lacking in my heart. Let me take small steps, in brief, daily prayer, to ask Him to come and abide in me, so that I may not thirst like this, constantly. Let me hear Jesus say to me, as He says to the Samaritan woman, *"whoever drinks of the water that I shall give him will never thirst. But the water that I shall give him will become in him a fountain of water springing up into everlasting life."* (Jn 4:14) Because I can take this water "freely," as did she. Not because I am "worthy," or for any other reason. But because I desire it, and ask for it, as did she.

MAY 3

SPIRITUAL STAGNATION

"When Jesus saw him lying there and knew that he had been there a long time, he said to him, 'Do you want to be made well?'" (Jn 5:6)

This is the question Jesus poses to the paralyzed man, lying at the pool of Bethesda. It's quite a question, considering the fact that the man had been lying there, powerless to do anything about his condition, for thirty-eight years. Do you "want" healing?

But if I experience stagnation in certain areas, going around in circles with the same sinful routine, and take a closer look at this, I will find that the stagnation does have to do with this question: What do I really *"want"*? Are other "wants" taking precedence over wanting what Christ wants for me? He wants me to "arise, take up my bed and walk," as He says to this man at Bethesda; He wants me to get up and carry my cross, despite the small or big defects with which I am challenged. But apparently for some of us, like the man at Bethesda, it might take years and years to grow in this willingness, to embrace the "want" of Christ.

Let me not despair today about areas of stagnation, but ask God to help me grow in willingness, strength, and courage to do His will. Let me also ask for the patience to wait for, and receive, His gifts in His time.

MAY 4

GETTING REAL

"This is the message we have heard from him and proclaim to you, that God is light and in him there is no darkness at all. If we say that we have fellowship with him while we are walking in darkness, we lie and do not do what is true; but if we walk in the light as he himself is in the light, we have fellowship with one another, and the blood of Jesus his Son cleanses us from all sin. If we say that we have no sin, we deceive ourselves, and the truth is not in us. If we confess our sins, he who is faithful and just will forgive us our sins and cleanse us from all unrighteousness." (1 Jn 1:5-9)

Here St. John is talking about "walking in light," in God's light, which John connects with seeing the truth about ourselves and "confessing our sins." This clears the path to fellowship with God and with one another. Darkness, on the other hand, is equated here with self-deception and "saying we have no sin."

It is liberating and cleansing to see things and people, including myself, as they are, rather than how I wish them to be. It is burdensome and crippling, on the other hand, to create a land of make-believe in one's head. This may lead one constantly to be dissatisfied with the real situations and opportunities of the here and now; to neglect today's responsibilities while imagining the dream-job just around the corner; to avoid real relationships and prefer "flirtation-ships"; to put off the small things I can today, because of the heroic, great things I will do tomorrow.

Today I humbly ask God for His light to guide me in quiet self-examination. Let me prefer His loving vision of me and others to the cruel expectations I tend to create, when I walk on my own, in darkness. It is He, not me, "Who is faithful and just," as St. John says, because He forgives our sins and cleanses us from burdensome self-deception.

MAY 5

PRAYERS OF THE SAINTS

"Finally, brothers, pray for us, that the word of the Lord may speed ahead and be honored, as happened among you..." (2 Thess 3:1)

Somebody asked me recently, Why don't people in your church pray directly to God, but pray to saints? I replied that we do, indeed, pray directly to God, but we also ask for those strong in faith, the saints, to pray with us and for us; just as St. Paul asked other Christians to pray for him; just as the earliest Christians called St. Peter to come and pray when Tabitha had died, and by his prayers God granted Tabitha new life (Acts 9:36-43)—just as then, today we still ask for, and benefit from, the prayers of the strong among us, including already-deceased saints like Peter.

We still have contact, in the "communion of the saints," in the one Body of Christ, in His Spirit, with already-deceased saints, and unite with them in prayer; just as the already-deceased Moses and Elijah appeared to the disciples on the Mount of Transfiguration, speaking with Christ (Mt 17:3). *"He is not God of the dead, but God of the living,"* as Jesus Himself reminds us (Mk 12:27). While He is, indeed, a unique "mediator" between God and human beings, as St. Paul says (1 Tim 2:5), because He is the only God-Man, Christ nonetheless unites all of us in prayer, both the already-deceased and those still here, in His Body and His Spirit. God is the One Source of sanctity and grace, but there are many vessels and channels of His grace, the "saints," who are not divided, but united, in Him.

So let me not doubt the unity of Christ's Body, on earth as it is in heaven. Let me not imagine a rift where there is none, because the saints in heaven do participate in, and offer up to God, the prayers of the saints on earth, as St. John tells us in the Book of Revelation: *"...the twenty-four elders (the leaders of the people of God in heaven) fell before the Lamb, each holding a harp and golden bowls full of incense, which are the prayers of the saints."* (Rev 5:8)

MAY 6

RIGHT BEING vs. BEING RIGHT

"...and returning from the tomb, they told all this to the eleven and to all the rest. Now it was Mary Magdalene, Joanna, Mary the mother of James, and the other women with them who told this to the apostles. But these words seemed to them an idle tale, and they did not believe them." (Luke 24:9-10)

The Myrrh-Bearing women were absolutely right, when they reported to the Apostles that Christ had risen. But the Apostles didn't believe the women. It must have been frustrating for the Myrrh-Bearers, to have their testimony disregarded like that; to not be taken seriously. It wasn't until the resurrected Christ Himself appeared to the Apostles that they believed. Nonetheless, the women carried on, as members of the apostolic community, and continued to spread the message of the Resurrection. One of them, Mary Magdalene, is even called Equal-to-the-Apostles, for her missionary labors.

Let me also carry on, in peace with other people, even if they disbelieve or disregard my words—even when I know I am right, for some objective reason. Let me concentrate on "right being," before God, rather than "being right," when my message isn't heard, and leave the opinions and actions of others in God's hands.

MAY 7

HE CROSSES THE LINE

"So he came to a city of Samaria, called Sychar, near the field that Jacob gave to his son Joseph. Jacob's well was there, and so Jesus, wearied as he was with his journey, sat down beside the well. It was about the sixth hour. There came a woman of Samaria to draw water. Jesus said to her, 'Give me a drink.' For his disciples had gone away into the city to buy food. The Samaritan woman said to him, 'How is it that you, a Jew, ask a drink of me, a woman of Samaria?' For Jews have no dealings with Samaritans. Jesus answered her, 'If you knew the gift of God, and who it is that is saying to you, 'Give me a drink,' you would have asked him, and he would have given you living water.'" (Jn 4:5-10)

Indeed, at first the Samaritan woman does not see "who it is" that is speaking with her. She merely sees the externals and politics of status. She sees not Christ, but "a Jew," and herself, "a Samaritan" and "a woman," drawing an immediate, accepted line of demarcation between herself and the Stranger. But our Lord crosses this line, speaking to her not as to "a woman" or "a Samaritan," or some other category, but as to a distinct person. Differently from her, He recognizes "the gift of God" and exactly "who it is" with whom He speaks—a concrete human being—and He calls her to do the same.

Today let me recognize His voice, however and whenever He might strike up a conversation with me. And let me recognize "the gift of God" in His messengers, be they women, men, Jews, Samarians, Greeks, Russians, Americans, Georgians, Romanians, Serbs, or others. O Lord, Founder and Spirit of our unity, may You speak and be heard among us, regardless of our human lines of demarcation and politics of status, that we may have living water. Glory be to You.

MAY 8

A FREE SPIRIT

"Most assuredly, I say to you, unless one is born of water and the Spirit, one cannot enter the kingdom of God. That which is born of the flesh is flesh, and that which is born of the Spirit is spirit. Do not marvel that I said to you, 'You must be born again.' The Spirit blows where He wants, and you hear His voice, but cannot tell where He comes from and where He goes. So is everyone who is born of the Spirit." (Jn 3:5-8)

As Christ explains in this conversation with the somewhat puzzled Nicodemus, we are all called to be born, not only "of the flesh" at our natural birth, and not only "of water and Spirit" at baptism. We are called to be born again—and again, "of the Spirit." This oft-repeated process of renewal and rebirth in the Spirit, however, is not something we control. Because He comes and goes "where He wants" (ὅπου θέλει), and we cannot tell "where He comes from and where He goes."

This freedom of the governing Spirit, and our lack of control of His divine energies, which do renew and revive our own on a regular basis, is a refreshing, humbling fact. While it is my job to remain open to His grace, keeping my "house" clean to the best of my ability, I humbly ask Him to do the rest, which I cannot do for myself.

Today I gratefully recognize that we do not, and cannot, control Him, whence He comes, or where He goes. I humbly ask Him, as I start my day, *"Restore to me the joy of your salvation, and uphold me with your governing Spirit."* (Ps 50/51:12)

MAY 9

GODS AND MEN

"I said: You are gods, and all of you are sons of the Most High. Nevertheless you will die like men and fall like any one of the princes." (Ps 81/82: 6-7)

Are we all called "gods" in this Psalm? When Christ quotes this passage, "You are gods," He explains that here "He called them gods, to whom the word of God came" (Jn 10:35). So—yes. All of us, to whom the word of God "came," are called "gods," because through His "coming" we are given to participate in His divinity. He alone is divine by essence, while we are participants in divinity. We still "die like men and fall like any one of the princes."

The word of God "came" to human beings already at creation, in the creative, life-giving "fiat" of the Creator, Who willed us to be formed in His image and likeness (Gen 1:26-27). But our "God-likeness" was given to grow and deepen with God's every revelation of Himself; most particularly when the Word "came" to us in the flesh, when "the Word became flesh and dwelt among us" (Jn 1:14). And now, after the Incarnation, He shares our human nature, our humanness, and we share in His, becoming one of His, most intimately, in His Body, in which the divine energies of the Holy Spirit pour out abundantly on us: *"But as many as received Him, to them He gave the power (ἐξουσίαν) to become children of God, to those who believe in His name"* (Jn 1:12).

So today I carry with me this humbling truth, that we are "gods, and all of us sons of the Most High," in Christ. In practical terms this truth makes me take pause, and approach myself and other human beings with due honor, as those with "the power to become children of God," when we "believe in His name." Let me walk, talk, think, and act with this truth in mind, and His name in my heart.

MAY 10

ON EARTH AS IT IS IN HEAVEN

"And whenever you stand praying, if you hold anything against anyone, forgive them, so that your Father in heaven may forgive you your sins." (Mk 11:25)

What does it mean to "hold anything against anyone"? This is often more subtle than I care to acknowledge. I can "hold" a quiet, yet deep-seated resentment against someone, or a group of people, or even myself, without noticing this. For example, I might constantly perceive someone else as ungrateful for something I did or do for them; I might feel disturbed by something a close friend said about me and turn this around and around in my mind; I might feel burdened and discouraged by my own inconsiderate words or actions on the past day.

All this creates an obstacle, the Lord reminds me today, to my relationship with God. He wants me to "let it go," so that I, in my prayers to Him, am on "the same page" with Him, Who is merciful and forgiving. He wants me to seek and rely on His mercy and forgiveness, but also to learn, through seeking this contact with Him, to likewise be merciful and forgiving. Because forgiveness of others and of myself tears down the obstacles between me and God's grace. It brings me out of the dead-end of resentment and discouragement, and helps me to change and move forward, with His loving help.

Today I am gratefully reminded to "let it go," whatever I might be "holding against" anyone, and hand it over to God's mercy. Let me take note of these small or large grudges I might be carrying around, and let them be forgiven, "on earth as it is in heaven."

MAY 11

HIS CLOTHING, MY CLOTHING

"Then the soldiers, when they had crucified Jesus, took his garments and made four parts, to each soldier a part, and also the tunic. Now the tunic (χιτών) was without seam, woven from the top in one piece. They said therefore among themselves, 'Let us not tear it, but cast lots for it, whose it shall be,' that the Scripture might be fulfilled which says: 'They divided my garments among them, and for my clothing they cast lots.'" (Jn 19:23-4; Ps 21/22:18)

Today let me reflect a bit on this humiliating detail of my Lord's passion: the dividing of His "garments" (outer clothing) and casting of lots for His "tunic" (the undergarment), the removal of which left His body naked. Christ's clothing was that of an ordinary Jew of His time, but His "tunic" was seamless (a detail recorded only in the Gospel of John), like the tunics of the high-priests.

There is much to be said about Christ's clothing, but I will note just the following, to contemplate for today. My Lord humbled Himself, by wearing ordinary clothing. Ever since God lovingly clothed Adam and Eve with "tunics of skin," because they had realized they were naked after their sin (Gen 3:21), human clothing became a sign both of humility and self-knowledge.

But the God-Man transformed the meaning of our clothing, both by wearing it on His sinless, sacred body, and being stripped of it: *"...being found in fashion as a man, he humbled himself, and became obedient unto death, even the death of the cross"* (Phil 2:8), when His clothing was taken and divided amongst His executioners. He was stripped at His crucifixion, only to be "clothed with majesty" (Ps 92/93:1)—and to clothe us with His majesty—in His resurrection.

Whatever clothing I wear today, I remember the precious and simple fact that my Lord wore clothing, and was stripped of clothing, for my sake. My clothing "matters" and has new meaning, new dignity, in Him, in His one Body: *"For all of you who were baptized into Christ,"* the Apostle reminds me, *"have clothed yourselves with Christ"* (Gal 3:27).

MAY 12

ADDICTIONS

"'All things are permissible for me,' but not all things are beneficial. 'All things are permissible for me,' but I will not be dominated/ruled by anything." (1 Cor 6:12)

Addiction has to do with a loss of freedom, rather than some inherent "badness" of the "thing" to which one becomes addicted. In the case of more or less common addictions, like addiction to drugs, alcohol, sex, video-games, or the Internet, our loss of freedom happens in small steps, unnoticeably. At first, the "thing" helps us in some way, ...until it doesn't. It ceases to "help" when we are drawn to the thing against our will, because we are now "dominated/ruled" by it, which is what the Apostle is warning me against in the passage quoted above.

The good news about the suffering of addiction, however, is that it can compel me to seek God and His help in a most earnest and renewed manner. Because only God can liberate me from the powerful grip of a real addiction. *"And after you have suffered for a little while, the God of all grace, who has called you to his eternal glory in Christ, will himself restore, support, strengthen, and establish you"* (1 Pet 5:10). If I have slipped into an addiction, this can be a wake-up call from Him, to let go of self-reliance and let Him be a true part of my life.

Today I thank God, in earnest prayer, for all the things and people in my life, and ask that I be "dominated/ruled" by Him alone, seeking His liberating truth on a daily basis. *"Then you will know the truth,"* the Lord promises me, *"and the truth will set you free."* (Jn 8:32)

MAY 13

SUIT UP AND SHOW UP

"Just after daybreak, Jesus stood on the beach; but the disciples did not know that it was Jesus. Jesus said to them, 'Children, you have no fish, have you?' They answered him, 'No.' He said to them, 'Cast the net to the right side of the boat, and you will find some.' So they cast it, and now they were not able to haul it in because there were so many fish. 'That disciple whom Jesus loved said to Peter, 'It is the Lord!' When Simon Peter heard that it was the Lord, he put on some clothes, for he was naked (γυμνός), and jumped into the sea..." (Jn 21:4-7)

At this point, Peter was "naked" in several respects, because he felt shame for having thrice denied the Lord during His passion. And yet, when the risen Lord appears on the beach, and Peter hears that it is the Lord, the lapsed Apostle simply puts on some clothes and jumps into the sea to greet Him; to make things right.

So much has changed for lapsed humanity since the fallen Adam hid from the Lord God in the garden, because of his nakedness. When God called to Adam, "Where are you?", Adam replied, "I was afraid, because I was naked; and I hid myself." (Gen 3:10) The fallen Peter, on the other hand, knows better. He knows he can "suit up and show up" before a Lord Who accepts and heals the fallen. And there, on the beach, at a charcoal fire with fish and bread, the risen Lord invites Peter, along with the other disciples, to "Come and have breakfast" with Him (Jn 21:12). And shortly afterwards Christ has a conversation with Peter and allows the lapsed Apostle to reaffirm his love for His Lord.

Today I remind myself of what Peter knew well, both before and after his "fall"; that I need not hide from my Lord, whatever my shame may be. I can "suit up and show up," and find reconciliation and healing at His table. *"I have not come to call the righteous,"* He says to me, *"but sinners to repentance."* (Lk 5:32)

MAY 14

PRAYING IN PEACE

"In peace let us pray to the Lord." (Beginning of the Great Litany of Byzantine Liturgy)

This is the first petition, at the very beginning of Divine Liturgy, calling us to pray "in peace." How can I pray "in peace"? By handing everything over to God and not worrying, as St. Paul says rather emphatically: *"Do not worry about anything, but in everything by prayer and supplication with thanksgiving let your requests be made known to God. And the peace of God, which surpasses all understanding, will guard your hearts and your minds in Christ Jesus."* (Phil 4:6-7)

So I need not muster up my own "peace," but rather open myself up to the peace of God, "which surpasses all understanding," including my own understanding, and hand over to Him, with thanksgiving, all my requests and worries. "Peace" is a gift that comes from outside me, from "the God of peace" (Rom 15:33), when I hand myself over to communion with Him. His peace enables me, first, to make peace with myself, and then to carry it beyond myself, in forgiveness and acceptance of others.

Today I open myself up to God's peace, handing over my requests and worries to Him. It is this gift, His peace, that likens me to Him as a child of God, and brings happiness or "blessedness" to me and those around me: *"Blessed are the peacemakers,"* says the Lord, *"for they,"* like Him, *"shall be called sons of God."* (Mt 5:9)

MAY 15

POOR IN SPIRIT

"Blessed are the poor in spirit, for theirs is the kingdom of heaven." (Mt 5:3)

Like all of humanity, I am, by nature, "poor in (my own) spirit." That is to say, I am utterly insufficient in the spiritual sense; I am incapable of helping myself, of nurturing myself, of growing and developing in Him, without the grace of the Holy Spirit. I can't "pull myself up by my bootstraps" and save myself.

However, I don't always acknowledge this, particularly when I go about my life in self-reliance and imagined self-sufficiency. And thus it is with various teachings and religions that glorify the "Self" as the ultimate solution to human insufficiency; as if we need only look deep inside ourselves to find strength, hope, and "spirituality." This is the opposite of being "poor in spirit."

Today I begin my day in humble acknowledgement of my insufficiency in my own "spirit." Let me ask for, and rely on, the grace of the Holy Spirit, in all my duties and relationships. Because the Lord promises those who walk in reliance on Him "blessedness," and "the kingdom of heaven," already in the here and now. It is the kingdom where He is King, and not me. Glory be to Him.

MAY 16

MID-FEAST OF PENTECOST

"In the middle of the Feast, O Savior, / Fill my thirsting soul with the waters of godliness, as You did cry to all: / If anyone thirst let him come to Me and drink! / O Christ God, Fountain of our life, glory to You!" (Byzantine Troparion-hymn of the Mid-feast of Pentecost)

How appropriate that on the "Mid-feast" of Pentecost (i.e., the midpoint between the feasts of Pascha and Pentecost, according to the Older Calendar), the main hymn or "troparion" talks about spiritual thirst. When Lent is long over, the Paschal celebration has faded, and summer is upon us, I tend to drift, perhaps unnoticeably, into spiritual indifference. So, as my heart and mind begins to head for a sandy beach, the Church reminds me of a waterless desert, where I may find myself right now, barely noticing it.

The main theme of the Sundays preceding Pentecost is "water," along with spiritual "thirst." There is the kind of water that is not our ultimate answer, like the pool of Bethesda in John 5 (read in church on the Sunday of the Paralytic), and like Jacob's well in John 4 (read on the next Sunday, of the Samaritan Woman). It is only in communion with Christ, in His Holy Spirit, that my inner "thirst," the hole in my heart, is filled.

So this season, whether we're headed for a sandy beach, or a swimming pool, or perhaps a pub (shout-out to any readers in Australia ☺), let me take pause and take care, first, of "my thirsting soul." Today I come to Him and drink, as He invites me to do, on a daily basis. *"O Christ God, Fountain of our life, glory to You!"*

MAY 17

"WILLPOWER"

"Abide in me as I abide in you. Just as the branch cannot bear fruit by itself unless it abides in the vine, neither can you unless you abide in me. I am the vine, you are the branches. Those who abide in me and I in them bear much fruit, because apart from me you can do nothing." (Jn 15:4-5)

My Lord encourages me today to "abide in Him" so that I "bear much fruit," while reminding me, in no uncertain terms, that apart from Him I can do "nothing." Thus Christ clears up for me the oft-confusing and discouraging concept of "willpower": It is not a "power" at all, apart from Him. My "will" is only then a "willpower," when it is in communion with Him, and connected to other "branches," also in Him.

Modern-day psychology defines "willpower" as "the ability to resist short-term temptations in order to meet a long-term goal." And psychological studies have shown that several things can strengthen "willpower":
1. Proper motivation,
2. Having a plan in place, in case of temptation,
3. Self-monitoring, and
4. Practice. This potentially helpful information leaves several essential questions unanswered: Where does this "ability" to resist temptations come from? What is my "long-term goal"? What is "proper motivation"?

Faith provides me with answers to these questions. My Lord motivates me to seek the long-term goal of salvation, and lends me a helping hand, when I abide in His grace. I go about my daily routine, with some self-examination, a bit of reading of His word, and asking for His wisdom to "lead me not into temptation." *Thy kingdom come, Thy will be done,* I pray—whatever people, places or things I encounter today.

MAY 18

MEEKNESS

"Blessed are the meek (πραεῖς, кроткие), for they will inherit the earth." (Mt 5:5)

Now here's a word you don't hear very often: "meek." What does it mean? Meekness is a gentle attitude displayed toward other human beings and God, when confronted with specific actions toward oneself of those human beings or God. Meekness involves acceptance, withholding of judgment, patience, humility, and—especially with respect to God—teachability. Christ invites us to learn meekness from Him, promising us peace or "rest" for our souls: *"Take my yoke upon you, and learn from me, for I am meek and humble in heart, and you will find rest for your souls."* (Mt 11:29)

The intriguing promise that the meek "will inherit the earth" is also connected with the promise of peace. We see this in Psalm 36/37, which our Lord is quoting when He says that the meek shall "inherit the earth": *"Yet a little while, and the wicked will be no more,"* it says in this Psalm, *"though you look diligently for their place, they will not be there. But the meek shall inherit the earth, and delight themselves in an abundance of peace."* (Ps 36/37:10-11) In the Old Testament, one would equate "the earth" with the promised "land" of Canaan, which was the ultimate manifestation of God's favor and blessing to His people; it was the granting of the heart's desire.

In the New Testament we similarly understand "inheriting the earth" as the ultimate manifestation of God's favor and blessing, which comes with "delighting in an abundance of peace." This happens to the meek, who experience contentment in life, as well as an "abundance of peace," regardless of their outer circumstances. Because they have full acceptance of God's will for them, and have peace with precisely the things, situations, and people God has given them. This is a state of mind not guaranteed by any amount of material wealth, but by meekness. Without meekness, even the wealthiest can live in a state of unhappiness, as if they had nothing, as the Lord says elsewhere: *"For whoever has, to him more shall be given; and whoever does not have, even what he has shall be taken away from him."* (Mk 4:25)

Let me ask for His peace and His meekness, as I start my day with gratitude. *"Blessed are the meek,"* my Lord reminds me today, *"for they shall inherit the earth."*

MAY 19

PERSPECTIVE IS EVERYTHING

"The light of the body is the eye: if therefore your eye is single (whole, healthy), your whole body shall be full of light. But if your eye is evil, your whole body shall be full of darkness. If therefore the light that is in you is darkness, how great is that darkness!" (Mt 6:22-23)

My "eye" is my perspective; the way I see things, situations, relationships, and my own self.

Am I "seeing" today in God's light? Or is it a purely human agenda (my own and other people's) taking up my entire field of vision? How burdensome that can be. And what a relief it is to let light in; that is, hand it all over to God and re-focus on His presence in the whole picture. Perspective is everything!

MAY 20

HOW DO I LOOK?

"Do not worry in your soul, what you will eat or what you will drink; nor about your body, what you will put on. Is not the soul more than food and the body more than clothing? ... So why do you worry about clothing? Consider the lilies of the field, how they grow: they neither toil nor spin; and yet I say to you that even Solomon in all his glory was not arrayed like one of these." (Mt 6:25, 28-29)

Christ is not saying here that physical beauty is unimportant. After all, God "arrays" His creation with beauty, and He Himself is "clothed" with beauty (Ps 92/93:1). And we all know that we are entrusted with caring for God's creation, including our own bodies; we all need a healthy routine or discipline, regarding eating and grooming.

What He is talking about here is balance. Because the way I eat and look, including my weight and clothes, can easily become a source of excessive "worry," or even an obsession. Christ is saying to me: Don't obsess over this. I can, and I will, says God, take care of this. He is also saying: Your capacity to see it, and to emanate it, comes from Me. So there is a deeper, bigger side to "beauty." And I will constantly miss out on the bigger side if all my attention is directed at the physical one.

Today my focus will be a God-centered life, and I tend to my health, my appearance, and my well-being in His love and His light.

MAY 21

A SINLESS LIFE?

"As he walked along, he saw a man blind from birth. His disciples asked him, 'Rabbi, who sinned, this man or his parents, that he was born blind?' Jesus answered, 'Neither this man nor his parents sinned; he was born blind so that God's works might be revealed in him.'" (Jn 9:1-3)

What does the Lord mean when He says this strange thing, that neither the blind man nor his parents "sinned"? Doesn't everybody "sin," at least from time to time? Were these three people, the blind man and his parents, the only three in the history of humanity who never, ever "sinned"?

Here Jesus is using the word "sin" (*"amartia"* in Greek, which means "missing the mark"; or "missing the objective," which is salvation) in the broad sense, of what their overall objective in life was. These people, apparently, did strive for good in their lives; their focus was in the right place.

Today I want to lead a God-centered life, as my parents have. And I'll focus on Him, despite the ups and downs of whatever this day may bring, and despite the "blindness" of my human delusions and shortcomings. So that Jesus, if He looks down at me, sitting here in my blindness, can say, *"She was born blind so that God's works might be revealed in her."*

MAY 22

JESUS & PILATE

"...and he (Pontius Pilate) entered into the Praetorium again and said to Jesus, 'Where are you from?' But Jesus gave him no answer. So Pilate said to him, 'You do not speak to me? Do you not know that I have authority to release you, and I have authority to crucify you? Jesus answered, 'You would have no authority over me, unless it had been given you from above, therefore the one who handed me over to you is guilty of a greater sin.' From then on Pilate tried to release him, but the Jews cried out, 'If you release this man, you are no friend of the emperor. Everyone who claims to be a king sets himself against the emperor.'" (Jn 19:9-12)

Let me reflect a bit today on the tragic figure of Pontius Pilate. On the one hand, Pilate is no super-villain. After all, Pilate "tried to release Him." We can see that Pilate is conflicted; that his conscience is telling him that His prisoner has "no fault."

Nonetheless, he finally caves in to the demands of the Jews, against his own conscience, because ultimately, Pilate's top priority was his own position; his "office." He is concerned with asserting it, and he's concerned with keeping it. Note that the accent in Pilate's question, *"You do not speak to me?"* is on the "me." He is blinded by his own "pride of office" to the Higher Authority speaking to him through his conscience, through his wife's dream (Mt 27:19), and through the Prisoner Himself, Who reminds Pilate of the authority "from above."

Let me remind myself today, whatever position or bit of authority I may possess—either in my profession, in my community, or in my family—not to be blinded to Christ, Who may be standing before me and speaking to me through someone who does not have my position or bit of authority. Let me recognize the One Source of Authority, and hear His voice in all my actions and attitudes toward anyone I encounter today.

MAY 23

PEACE ACTIVISM

"As God's chosen ones, holy and beloved, clothe yourselves with compassion, kindness, humility, meekness, and patience. Bear with one another and, if anyone has a complaint against another, forgive each other; just as the Lord has forgiven you, so you also must forgive. Above all, clothe yourselves with love, which binds everything together in perfect harmony. And let the peace of Christ rule in your hearts, to which indeed you were called in the one body. And be thankful." (Col 3:12-15)

Yesterday as I was walking somewhere in Vienna, I saw a poster that said, "What have YOU done for world peace today?" It made me think of Mother-Theresa's well-known quote: "What can you do to promote world peace? Go home and love your family."

The Apostle Paul gives a more precise description of the same idea; of the connection between love for the people closest to us and peace. He also adds gratitude, ending this passage with the laconic "And be thankful."

I think a careful reading, and re-reading, of the passage above gives me a complete, charted-out plan for what I, personally, can contribute to peace in this world, in my little corner of it today. When I am confronted with small irritations, let me take a step back, "with compassion, kindness, humility, meekness, and patience." Let "the peace of Christ rule" in my heart, because it connects me to "the one body"; to the unity He intended, in Him. And let me be thankful today, for myself, other people, and things as they are, and not how I imagine or wish they should be.

MAY 24

PRAYERFUL READING

"Shine within our hearts, loving Master, the pure light of Your divine knowledge and open the eyes of our minds that we may comprehend the message of Your Gospel. Instill in us also reverence for Your blessed commandments, so that having conquered all sinful desires, we may pursue a spiritual life, thinking and doing all those things that are pleasing to You. For You, Christ our God, are the light of our souls and bodies, and we give glory to You, together with Your eternal Father and Your all-holy, good and life-giving Spirit, now and always and forever and ever. Amen." (Prayer Before the Gospel, Byzantine Divine Liturgy)

This is the prayer before the reading of the Gospel at Divine Liturgy, and it is meant to prepare all of us, by asking God to "open the eyes of our minds" so that we may "comprehend," "think" and "do" what we are about to hear. In practice, however, the prayer does not prepare "all of us," because in many of our churches it is read silently by the priest.

Be that as it may, this traditional prayer of the Divine Liturgy gives me an idea of what "prayerful reading" is, which I can also do privately, at home. The ancient Christian practice of "prayerful reading" (lectio divina) means combining my spiritual reading (usually, of Scripture) with prayer. Before I begin reading, I pray to God for comprehension and enlightenment (as in the prayer cited above), and then I read—not a whole lot, but deeply, in order to carry with me what I've read, for the rest of my day. It is helpful sometimes to jot down a verse that particularly moved me, to better remember it. I finish this kind of reading with a brief prayer of praise or gratitude.

Today I pray to our Lord, "The light of our souls and bodies," to "open the eyes of my mind" to His word, that it may guide and enlighten me throughout my day.

MAY 25

BLIND CERTAINTY

"So for the second time they (the Pharisees) called the man who had been blind, and they said to him, 'Give glory to God! We know that this man is a sinner.' He answered, "I do not know whether he is a sinner. One thing I do know, that though I was blind, now I see.' They said to him, 'What did he do to you? How did he open your eyes?' He answered them, 'I have told you already, and you would not listen. Why do you want to hear it again? Do you also want to become his disciples?' Then they reviled him, saying, 'You are his disciple, but we are disciples of Moses. We know that God has spoken to Moses, but as for this man, we do not know where he comes from.'" (Jn 9:24-29)

Jesus has done something entirely new; something unheard of. *"Never since the world began,"* notes the healed man, *"has it been heard that anyone opened the eyes of a person born blind."* (Jn 9:32) This is why the Pharisees refuse to recognize Christ and His healing: In Christ, God is revealing Himself to them in new ways, thus challenging what they think they "know." They think they "know" Him. And this imagined "knowledge" blinds them to God's surprises. It also effectively replaces God in their world, leading them to become judges of Him: "We know," they proclaim with certainty, "that this man is a sinner."

Today let me beware of such certainty, which can blind me to God's surprises. I am "born blind,"—with a spiritual blindness in need of His light and His vision. Left to my own devices and my own judgment, I become incapable of change; I become incapable of following the One Who calls me to ever-new change, saying: "Metanoeite!" (Repent!) Today let me be enlightened and led by Him, amidst any situations, responsibilities, and people He sends my way.

MAY 26

MARTHA, MARTHA!

"...A woman named Martha welcomed him (Jesus) into her home. She had a sister named Mary, who sat at the Lord's feet and listened to what he was saying. But Martha was distracted by her many tasks; so she came to him and asked, 'Lord, do you not care that my sister has left me to do all the work by myself? Tell her then to help me.' But the Lord answered her, 'Martha, Martha, you are worried and distracted by many things; but one thing is needful. Mary has chosen the better part, which will not be taken away from her.'" (Lk 10:38-42)

What always surprises me in this passage is not Martha's frustration with her sister (I'll admit I quite understand that part). What surprises me is Martha's unabashed frustration with Christ. "Lord, do you not care," she practically snaps at Him, "that my sister has left me to do all the work by myself?" And then she tells Him what he needs to do: "Tell her then to help me." The Lord, in His turn, lovingly replies, "Martha, Martha..."—and defends Mary. We don't hear anything about Martha's reaction to this reply, because the chapter ends here. Perhaps she dropped everything and joined Mary at the Lord's feet. Or perhaps she stomped off in a huff.

In any event, Martha, one of the women closest to our Lord, who was to be one of the Myrrh-Bearing Women, doesn't hesitate to speak to the Lord so openly, in her frustration. I note this today, reminding myself that our Lord chose and befriended, among His closest followers, not only the timid, quiet "types." And among the earliest female followers of Christ we don't see women who just tip-toe around Him, like mice. We see women who tell Him what they think, like Martha and like the Samaritan woman. They were, simply, themselves, with their gifts and flaws, as were the Apostles.

Today let me gratefully recognize that my Lord has a large variety of followers, both male and female, both shy and outgoing, contemplative and active, or something in between. Glory be to Him, Who calls me to follow Him, whatever my particular flaws and gifts may be.

MAY 27

O HEAVENLY KING

"O Heavenly King, the Comforter, the Spirit of Truth, Who art everywhere and fillest all things; Treasury of Blessings, and Giver of Life - come and abide in us, and cleanse us from every impurity, and save our souls, O Good One." (Prayer to the Holy Spirit)

On the great feast of Pentecost, we sing this ancient prayer for the first time, having "abstained" from it throughout our journey of the fifty days from Pascha to the Descent of the Holy Spirit on the Apostles. Through this liturgical "abstinence," by the time Pentecost comes around we have grown to miss, and to long for, addressing the Holy Spirit in this most direct and intimate way.

So, one journey is completed on Pentecost, as another begins, in the ever-new, ever-renewing adventure of the Spirit-filled life of the Church. Let me gratefully recognize the King, the Comforter, and the One Spirit of Truth today, letting go, once again, of other kings, other sources of comfort, and other spirits and half-truths. Let me let Him give me what He abundantly has on offer, for all of us, when we don't block Him out through man-made surrogates of His grace. *"Come and abide in us, and cleanse us from every impurity, and save our souls, O Good One."*

MAY 28

HIS UNTRADITIONAL CHOICES

"Many Samaritans from that city believed in him because of the woman's testimony, 'He told me all that I ever did.' So when the Samaritans came to him, they asked him to stay with them; and he stayed there two days. And many more believed because of his word. They said to the woman, 'It is no longer because of your words that we believe, for we have heard for ourselves, and we know that this is indeed the Savior of the world.'" (Jn 4:39-42)

Two surprising moments here: First, "many" Samaritans believe because of the testimony of a woman. And not just any woman, but one who had already had five husbands and was now with a sixth guy, who wasn't even her husband. Nonetheless, she was evidently a figure of considerable authority, whose testimony is trusted within her community. So our Lord knew what He was doing, choosing her as His messenger. Second, Jesus chooses to stay with the heretical Samaritans, with whom Jews were to have no contact at all, for two whole days. Our Lord cuts through important, yet secondary, issues of tradition and propriety, in order to bring His light to more people, that they might know "that this is indeed the Savior of the world."

How different are His choices from ours today, in matters of evangelization and church-building. We stumble over these very same, secondary issues. We hotly debate the "traditionality" of women's participation in church-matters, the status of heretics and the use of the word "church," while allowing church-unity to fall by the wayside. We are willing to hinder the unified voice of the Church, the unified testimony to Him, to be heard in this world, as we quibble about our traditions. Today I pray that my Lord help me cut through the secondary issues, and focus on the primary, as He did on those two sunny days in Samaria.

MAY 29

POWERLESSNESS

"For peace in the whole world, the well-being of the holy churches of God and the union of all, let us pray to the Lord." (Litany of Peace, Byzantine Liturgy)

Many emotions and thoughts rushed at me yesterday morning, when I heard the news of some horrible terrorist attacks. But alongside the complicated geopolitical implications, which I understand very little, it was a sobering reminder of one simple truth: human powerlessness.

In fact, there are two issues that seem to display human powerlessness more than any other, be it in the social, political, ecclesiastical, or personal spheres. And those two issues are:
1. "Peace in the whole world," and
2. "The union of all."

So these are among the very first things we pray for at the beginning of Divine Liturgy, handing them over to God's mercy. We appeal to Him for help, where we can't seem to help ourselves. And yet I must confess that I usually pay enough attention to this petition.

Today let me not take for granted the blessings of peace, for which we desperately need the Lord's help and mercy: *"For peace in the whole world, the well-being of the holy churches of God and the union of all, let us pray to the Lord."*

MAY 30

ENVY

"'...Is not this the carpenter, the son of Mary and brother of James and Joses and Judas and Simon, and are not his sisters here with us?' And they took offense (ἐσκανδαλίζοντο) at him. Then Jesus said to them, 'Prophets are not without honor, except in their hometown, and among their own kin, and in their own house.' And he could do no deed of power there, except that he laid his hands on a few sick people and cured them." (Mk 6:3-5)

Many of the people in Nazareth reacted with envy when Jesus visited His hometown with His disciples, when He was already famous for His much talked-about miracles and wisdom. They were envious, and hence they were blind to Christ.

Here's the ugly truth about envy, a pain one feels because of a desire to have the advantage(s) of another. We are most likely to feel it towards one of our own; neighbors, friends, or even relatives. "Envy" derives from the Latin "invidia," meaning "non sight." It is a blindness to "the whole picture" of myself and others as we really are, in God's sight. He sees us with all our true potential, limitations, sacrifices, gifts, and so on, which make up each person's unique vocation and journey. But envy makes me focus on some external aspect of another's life, as well as some perceived inadequacy in my own life, drawing a comparison in an imagined competition. It distracts me from the true challenges and opportunities given uniquely to me, by setting my sights on this delusion of competition. Envy blocks out gratitude and joy for my own gifts and those of others, and prevents me from growing and learning from them. It can cripple both the envious and the object of envy, because envy is "neutralized" by diminishing the object of envy. Thus Christ diminishes Himself in Nazareth, to neutralize the envy of His countrymen.

Today let me embrace gratitude, being mindful of my own gifts and challenges, as well as of the gifts and challenges of others. May the Lord help and enlighten me to see as He sees, and protect me from the delusions of envy.

MAY 31

FORGIVENESS IS THE BEGINNING

"Jesus said to them again, 'Peace be with you. As the Father has sent me, so I send you.' When he had said this, he breathed on them and said to them, 'Receive the Holy Spirit. If you forgive the sins of any, they are forgiven them; if you retain the sins of any, they are retained." (Jn 20:21-23)

The first gift of the Holy Spirit received by the Apostles, well before the outpouring of His gifts on Pentecost, was the power to forgive. Forgiveness is the beginning of spiritual life. It's the beginning of the end to self-isolation, from God and other people. It clears the way to other gifts, enabling growth.

The obstacles to forgiveness are very real, nonetheless. Not only, but especially, when I can see that the other person/people behaved badly. It's so easy for me to see that, really. But I can ask for God's grace to "see" differently, as He sees: He sees that we all struggle or behave badly, in one way or another. We're all fellow-strugglers.

I need to ask for the gift of forgiveness, because God has it on offer, if I ask: *"Is there anyone among you who, if your child asks for a fish, will give a snake instead of a fish? Or if the child asks for an egg, will give a scorpion? If you then, who are evil, know how to give good gifts to your children, how much more will the heavenly Father give the Holy Spirit to those who ask him!"* (Lk 11:11-13)

JUNE 1

SELF-GIVING IS HEALING

"That evening they brought to him many who were possessed with demons; and he cast out the spirits with a word, and cured all who were sick. This was to fulfill what had been spoken through the prophet Isaiah, "He took our infirmities and bore our diseases." (Mt 8:16-17)

Jesus takes our "infirmities" upon Himself and carries them. This self-giving of the God-Man heals.

Today I can practice self-giving in small ways, by lending an ear, taking some time to put others first in some way. I can make it a point to ask, and then actually listen, how someone is doing. Maybe I can make a phone call to an elderly or lonely relative. I can say a short prayer for someone who's done me wrong, as for a fellow struggler. I can shut up when I notice someone else's weakness, rather than put them on the spot.

A bit of self-giving, of carrying the burdens of others, is healing both for me and others around me. *"Carry one another's burdens, and in this way you will fulfill the law of Christ."* (Gal 6:2)

JUNE 2

THIRSTING AND RECEIVING

"Let anyone who thirsts come to me, and let the one who believes in me drink. As the scripture has said, 'Out of the believer's heart shall flow rivers of living water.' Now he said this about the Spirit, which believers in him were to receive..." (Jn 7:37-39)

This passage is in the Gospel-reading of Pentecost, at the Byzantine Divine Liturgy. Jesus is basically repeating what He said to the Samaritan woman, about the "living water" that He has on offer. The prerequisite for receiving this water is simple: Thirst, and come to Me.

Today let me identify this thirst, deep inside me, and focus my desires and ambitions on Him and in Him. Because it's easy to mistake that feeling, deep inside me, of insufficiency without the Spirit, for something else. I can feel something is lacking in my life, and misdirect my spiritual thirst toward some temporary "fix," be it unhealthy food, unnecessary shopping, obsessive physical fitness, workaholism, or whatever. *"Come and abide in us, and cleanse us of all impurity,"* I pray today to the Lord, the Holy Spirit, *"and save our souls, O Good One."*

JUNE 3

THE GOOD AND THE BAD

"And we know that for those who love God all things work together for good..." (Rom 8:28)

One of the best parts of having God in my life, and the revelation of His Word, is that I know I am always on a journey. No matter what setbacks or detours I experience, no matter how many times I fall, I see the light on the mountaintop. It reaches and illuminates the winding path I am on. There is eternal meaning, in light of God's Word, to every little good or bad thing in my life, even if I tend to lose sight of this fact from time to time. God's love encompasses all these things, because His love remains unchanged, regardless of my own changes of focus, my misdirection or "sin." After all, *"God demonstrates his own love for us in this: While we were still sinners, Christ died for us."* (Rom 5:8)

So if I'm discouraged today, about some sinful routine I can't seem to break, or some situation or relationship I can't seem to set straight, let me renew my love for God and faith in Him—in light of His love for, and faith in, me. Let me get on my knees and pray, at least briefly, that I may have communion with His kind of love and faith—the unchanging kind. Because He remains unchanged, and does not become discouraged, as He observes my imperfect struggles up the mountain.

JUNE 4

SCATTERED IN THE HOLY SPIRIT

"When the most High came down and confused the tongues, / He divided the nations; / But when He distributed the tongues of fire / He called all to unity. / Therefore, with one voice, we glorify the All-holy Spirit!" (Byzantine Kontakion-hymn of Pentecost)

This Kontakion-hymn refers to the division of nations in Genesis 11:1-9, when the Lord confused the languages of the people, who had attempted to build a city and the so-called "tower of Babel," the top of which was to "touch the heavens." It was the people's goal thus to ensure, as they said, "a name for ourselves, lest we be scattered abroad over the face of the whole earth." (Gen 11:3) But the Lord denied them such a unity, and "scattered them abroad from there over the face of all the earth." Why? Because the people had intended a unity based on themselves. They were not ready for the unity God intended; a unity rooted in Him.

The coming of Christ and His sending down of the Holy Spirit does not change our division into nations. He rather takes this reality and overcomes it, as only He can, using it to our benefit. He sends us out, scattered as we are, among the nations, saying, "Go and teach...," calling all to unity in Him and through Him. Today let His All-Holy Spirit overcome in me all self-isolation, that I may open up to His call, reaching out to others and letting them reach me, in His humbling grace. *"Therefore, with one voice, we glorify the All-Holy Spirit!"*

JUNE 5

DIFFERENT STYLES, SAME MESSAGE

"But to what will I compare this generation? It is like children sitting in the marketplaces and calling to one another, 'We played the flute for you, and you did not dance; we wailed, and you did not mourn.' For John came neither eating nor drinking, and they say, 'He has a demon'; the Son of Man came eating and drinking, and they say, 'Look, a glutton and a drunkard, a friend of tax collectors and sinners!' Yet wisdom is proved right by her deeds." (Mt 11:16-20)

This passage tells me that there are different forms and styles of Christian life and Christian ministry. Jesus mainly lived and walked among the people "eating and drinking," as it says here, and being "a friend of tax collectors and sinners." St. John the Baptist, on the other hand, was a desert-dweller, practicing severe asceticism. And yet, both carried the same "wisdom" or message, as the Lord indicates here by saying, "we" (*"We played the flute for you..."*). And both were judged harshly, specifically for their lifestyle, and not for their message, by the "generation" Christ is talking about here.

So various people can lead a life of faith in various ways, according to their own character and gifts. I shouldn't be quick to judge someone else's character or approach, just because it disagrees with my preconceived notion of what a life of faith looks like. God's voice and His wisdom can be spoken to us through various people and also various art forms, like music in different styles, or humor, or tragedy, or something else. Let me listen for His message today, rather than judge the messengers.

JUNE 6

AN ORDERLY EXIT

"Then Simon Peter came, following him (John), and went into the tomb. He saw the linen wrappings lying there, and the cloth (σουδάριον) that had been on his (Jesus') head, not lying with the linen wrappings but rolled up in a place by itself. Then the other disciple, who reached the tomb first, also went in, and he saw and believed..." (Jn 20:6-8)

What is it that John "saw" in the tomb that made him "believe" in Christ's resurrection? It was the linen wrappings, lying in one place, and the cloth (σουδάριον), not only lying separately, but neatly "rolled up." What had transpired here had involved no haste or chaos. Nor was it done either by irreverent thieves or ardent followers. Because thieves, having stripped Christ's Body, would not have carefully set aside the cloth, while devout followers would not have carried His Body away naked. What John "saw and believed" was evidence of the Lord's majestic exit from the tomb; He had left the darkness of the tomb in full control, "clothed in majesty" and leaving order behind, as Lord over chaos and death.

Today I ask that He bring His order into my often disorderly thoughts, actions, and words. Let His grace be in full control today, bringing light and order where previously there was darkness and chaos. *"And the light shines in the darkness, and the darkness did not overcome it."* (Jn 1:5)

JUNE 7

DEMAND vs. REQUEST

"Then one of the criminals who were hanged blasphemed him, saying, 'If you are the Christ, save yourself and us.' But the other, answering, rebuked him, saying, 'Do you not even fear God, seeing you are under the same condemnation? And we indeed justly, for we receive the due reward of our deeds; but this man has done nothing wrong.' he said to Jesus, 'Lord, remember me when you come into your kingdom.' And Jesus said to him, 'Assuredly, I say to you, today you will be with me in paradise.'" (Lk 23:39-43)

Two thieves. Both are suffering "justly," and both famously have very different reactions to the crucified Lord in their midst. But I'd like to note something else here: Both thieves actually ask the Lord for salvation, albeit in very different ways.

The non-repentant thief arrogantly demands that the Lord "prove" Himself: "If you are the Christ," he says, very much like Satan, when he tested our Lord in the wilderness, saying, *"If you are the Son of God..."* (Mt 4). So the non-repentant thief demands salvation in the form of an arrogant, quite diabolical challenge, full of a sense of entitlement. There is no sense of his own wrongs, of his own debt; also no sense of compassion for the Co-Sufferer. The Lord owes him, somehow.

The repentant thief, on the other hand, makes a humble request, and a much smaller one: "Remember me," is all he is asking. This thief is aware of his own wrongs, and humility opens his eyes to Who it is next to him, crucified. Humility also makes the repentant thief's heart capable of compassion, despite his own suffering, on his own cross.

Today I ask for the grace of humility, both in my approach to God, in prayer, and in my approach to fellow-strugglers in my surroundings. It is humility that opens our eyes to the crucified Lord in our midst, and makes us capable of compassion.

JUNE 8

CONSUMERISM

"Better a little with the fear of the Lord than great wealth with turmoil." (Proverbs 15:16)

The word "consumerism" has various definitions. What I'd like to reflect on today is "consumerism" in the sense of "a frivolous and selfish preoccupation with the buying of consumer goods in excess of our basic needs." I become afflicted with "consumerism" when I cease to lead a God-centered life and when I focus, instead, on extrinsic motivations, like the way I look, and how my appearance compares with the appearance of others. This kind of "consumerism" has to do with a lack of humble self-acceptance, as well as the anxiety, frustration, and envy that comes with this lack of self-acceptance.

It is difficult today to abstain from buying needlessly, when advertisements are practically everywhere I look. So I need God's help and grace to maintain sane spending habits. Today let me slow down a bit, and dedicate some time to heartfelt contact with Him, that I might see myself, and accept myself, as He does; as His child, with one primary purpose of growing in Him. Let me let God liberate me from the fears of human opinion, which might drive me to acquire "wealth with turmoil." Today I will be gratefully content with "a little," with the liberating "fear of the Lord."

JUNE 9

A HISTORICAL FAITH

"While he was saying this, a woman in the crowd raised her voice and said to him, 'Blessed is the womb that bore you and the breasts that nursed you!' But he said, 'Blessed rather are those who hear the word of God and obey it!'" (Lk 11:27-28)

The unnamed woman in the crowd is, I dare say, quite "graphic" in her praise of the Lord's Mother. One might think she could've simply said, "Your Mother must be so proud of You!" rather to the same effect. But instead she mentions "the womb that bore" Him and "the breasts that nursed" Him, drawing my attention to the physical side of the motherhood of the Theotokos.

While Christ in His reply turns our attention to the "blessedness" to which we are all called, together with the All-Blessed Theotokos, of hearing and obeying His word, I am struck today by the reminder of the physical, historical fact of the motherhood of the Blessed Among Women. It is an important truth, which, more than anything else in Salvation History, underlines the "realness" of the Incarnation. He was, indeed, born and nursed, and His clothing washed, not mythologically, not somehow "symbolically," but by a concrete human being—a young Jewish woman from Nazareth with no washing machine.

Today let me gratefully remember this refreshing, historical nature of our faith, which is not based on some instructive myth, nor on some abstract philosophy or collection of ethical teachings. It is based primarily on personal relationships with concrete, living persons; in communion with the divine-human Person of Jesus Christ, His Father, His Holy and life-giving Spirit, and in the "communion of the saints." It is in the lived experience of my relationships with these Persons and people that I make my journey to salvation, as I am reminded in this petition of the Divine Liturgy: *"Remembering our most holy, pure, blessed, and glorious Lady, the Theotokos and ever virgin Mary, with all the saints, let us commit ourselves and one another and our whole life to Christ our God."*

JUNE 10

GIVING SIMPLY

"Then the king will say to those at his right hand, 'Come, you that are blessed by my Father, inherit the kingdom prepared for you from the foundation of the world; for I was hungry and you gave me food, I was thirsty and you gave me something to drink, I was a stranger and you welcomed me, I was naked and you gave me clothing, I was sick and you took care of me, I was in prison and you visited me...'" (Mt 25:34-36)

A colleague of mine recently told me how difficult it was for him to visit his friend, whose leg had just been amputated. My colleague did finally visit his friend, but was reluctant to do so, because he "didn't know what to say."

I can relate to this reluctance to show up and show compassion, simply because I know I will do it imperfectly. It is a selfish kind of fear, focusing very much on me and my "performance." However, the Lord reminds me today in the above passage to go ahead and do these simple things: To feed someone hungry, to give "something" to drink to the thirsty, to welcome the stranger, to clothe, to take care, to visit. He doesn't specify how or when, but He does call me to do so, in the way I see possible, and when I am made aware of someone hungry, thirsty, lonely, sick, trapped, and so on. Some people, like parents, are constantly called to do these things for their own children, while others, like public officials, are called to do so on a larger scale. In my own position I might at least offer a word of encouragement to a struggling colleague at the office, or smile at the grumpy cashier at the supermarket, or give to a beggar on the street, or make a phone call to an elderly relative.

Today I humbly ask God to relieve me of preoccupation with the self, and give freely of what I have to give, in His grace and His light and lightness.

JUNE 11

JESUS AT HEROD'S COURT

"When Herod saw Jesus, he was very glad, for he had been wanting to see him for a long time, because he had heard about him and was hoping to see him perform some sign. He questioned him at some length, but Jesus gave him no answer. The chief priests and the scribes stood by, vehemently accusing him. But Herod with his soldiers treated him with contempt and mocked him; then he put an elegant robe on him, and sent him back to Pilate." (Lk 23:8-11)

Herod wanted to see Jesus because he "was hoping to see him perform some sign (miracle)"; that is to say, Herod wanted to be entertained by the Lord, as if He were some kind of court jester. Herod was not interested in the Person of Jesus Christ, but in His "entertainment value." Herod's human need for entertainment, which is a healthy thing in its proper place and time, had developed to the extent that he was entirely a seeker of stimulation, with no interest in spiritual growth. This put Herod on the wrong side of the cross.

Entertainment in the form of watching a show, as we do online, on TV, or on stage, provides us with relaxation and passivity; a "switching off" of certain brainwork. In small doses this kind of entertainment can be healthy and restful. But if I overdo it, for example, by binge-watching TV-series on a regular basis, I can cripple my capacity to focus, and to engage real people and real situations as God sends them to me. I can ultimately cripple my capacity and thirst for spiritual growth; my capacity and willingness for grace-filled cross-carrying.

Today let me be mindful, and ask the Lord to help me walk with Him, and in Him, on my cross-carrying journey. Let me keep my focus on Him, Who was crucified for me, that I may have truth and life; the grace-filled life He offers me, when I have the eyes to see and ears to hear what truth He has to teach me today.

JUNE 12

PRAYING FROM THE HEART

"And when you are praying, do not babble meaninglessly (μὴ βατταλογήσητε) as the Gentiles do, for they suppose that they will be heard for their many words. So do not be like them; for your Father knows what you need before you ask Him." (Mt 6:7-8)

The Lord reminds me today that when it comes to prayer, I should focus on quality rather than quantity. Christ gently warns me not to overwhelm myself, in prayer, with many words, the meaning of which I do not understand. Because I do not "magically" connect with God, through some "magical" formulas that I repeat without understanding. I must seek, in prayer, to speak with Him from my heart.

Does this mean that I ignore the many, traditional prayers, of rich theological content, available to me within my Tradition, and just pray in my own words? No. I do, of course, pray in my own words, as need be. But when it comes to traditional prayers, it is important that I seek to learn the meaning of these prayers, so that I say them from my heart, rather than "babble meaninglessly."

Today let me remember that prayer, as Christ sees it, is a loving discipline. I need not be overwhelmed by prayer, because my God is not a God Who demands words, and more words, for His "satisfaction." Through prayerful communion with Him, He teaches me to explore and know my heart, which He knows already. So let me open my heart to Him today, as best I can, that I may grow in Him, in prayer.

JUNE 13

PRAYING FOR OTHERS

"When they came to the place called The Skull, there they crucified him and the criminals, one on the right and the other on the left. But Jesus was saying, 'Father, forgive them; for they do not know what they are doing.'" (Lk 23:33-34)

Here, from His cross, the Lord demonstrates to me the ultimate form of self-giving: Despite His own, extreme suffering, He expresses concern for others, praying for them. For Christ, this historical moment, when He hangs on the cross for the life of the world, is not "all about Him." In prayer, He remains in the Spirit of human-divine fellowship, appealing to the Father in loving concern for His fellow-human beings.

When it comes to my own little cross-carrying journey today, I am reminded not to make it all "about me." Whatever difficulties or challenges I face today, be it grief, illness, conflict, disappointment, financial insecurity, misunderstanding, or whatever, let me take time to see beyond my own concerns and pray for others. It is a quiet form of self-giving that helps me move out of self-centeredness, teaching me to place God and His will in the center of my relationship with others.

So today let me contribute a bit of my prayer-time to prayer for others, placing them and myself in God's hands.

JUNE 14

UNIQUELY USEFUL

"Take care that you do not despise (μὴ καταφρονήσητε) one of these little ones; for, I tell you, in heaven their angels continually see the face of my Father in heaven. What do you think? If a shepherd has a hundred sheep, and one of them has gone astray, does he not leave the ninety-nine on the mountains and go in search of the one that went astray? And if he finds it, truly I tell you, he rejoices over it more than over the ninety-nine that never went astray." (Mt 18:10-13)

Who are "these little ones" Christ is warning us not to "despise" (καταφρονέω, literally *to think down upon*, i.e. *to look down upon*)? On the basis of the preceding verses of this chapter, we might think He means children, as well as those who are humble "like children" (Mt 18:4). But as cited above, by "little ones" He also means sheep that have "gone astray" somehow, and therefore need the special attention of the shepherd.

So He means me. And anyone else who, on a daily basis, tends to "go astray" like a wandering little sheep and needs Christ's help to get back on track. The Lord is willing to go to the trouble, for each and every one of us. And no matter how, or how often, we "go astray," He still has His angels caring for us; our angels, who "continually see the face of His Father in heaven." Are we, the often-lost sheep, really worth that kind of attention and trouble? Yes. Because we are His. And because through the learning-process of our own, particular shortcomings; of falling or straying, and then getting up or coming back, with God's help, each of us becomes uniquely useful to Him and other "little ones," who might need a helping hand in their journey.

So let me continue my journey today, with His help and in His grace. Because my God is a God Who identifies me as His, through the ups and downs. "The Lord is my shepherd," I am gratefully reminded today; "I shall not want." (Ps 22/23:1)

JUNE 15

FAITH AT EVERY HOUR

"I will bless the LORD at all times: His praise shall continually be in my mouth." (Psalm 33/34:1)

In all my activities and interactions with people, I rely on the presence, guidance, and power of God. I need to let Him in, to put every situation and relationship into His hands, on an hourly basis. *"Thy will be done."* Not mine. Not only during my brief prayer, on my knees in the morning, when I explicitly offer my life and concerns to God and His will. But around the clock: with my family, with colleagues at work, waiting in line at the supermarket, conversing with others in a blog online, replying to an email, and so on.

Let me ask myself today: Do I let God into the picture, throughout my day? Do I sense His grace and image in other people? Do I hear God's voice speaking to me through other people? Today I am grateful to Him for the beauty and wisdom He opens up to me, through other people and various things going on in my life.

JUNE 16

A LORD FULL OF SURPRISES

"When the sabbath was over, Mary Magdalene, and Mary the mother of James, and Salome bought spices, so that they might go and anoint him. And very early on the first day of the week, when the sun had risen, they went to the tomb. They had been saying to one another, 'Who will roll away the stone for us from the entrance to the tomb?' When they looked up, they saw that the stone, which was very large, had already been rolled back. As they entered the tomb, they saw a young man, dressed in a white robe, sitting on the right side; and they were alarmed. But he said to them, 'Do not be alarmed; you are looking for Jesus of Nazareth, who was crucified. He has been raised; he is not here. Look, there is the place they laid him.'" (Mk 16:1-6)

The Sabbath was over, and a new day had begun, in more ways than one. The women have a well-intended plan for this day—not a perfect one, I might add, because the stone is way too big for them to roll away... In any event, things do not go according to plan, because of the most unexpected news. He is not there, where they expected to find Him.

Let the most unexpected news of the Lord's resurrection; of enormous suffering, injustice, abandonment, physical and spiritual torture and death, unexpectedly overcome, defeated, trampled, and turned to light, joy, and eternal meaning—let this news be ever-new to me, and ever present in my heart and mind.

I do have a Lord Who overcomes the darkest of hours, and death itself, in me. I have a Lord, as someone once said, "Who knows His way out of a tomb." I also have a Lord Who often surprises me with unexpected events and circumstances, despite my well-intended plans. Let me be open to His will and His surprises today, and be willing to re-discover Him in some place other than where I had expected.

JUNE 17

CONFESSION AND BELONGING

"Confess your sins to one another, and pray for one another, that you may be healed." (James 5:16)

At times, all sorts of things can make "confession" an unpleasant prospect: fear, denial, shame, self-isolation, or simply indifference.

But when I do bring myself to reveal, first to myself and then to God and another, the burden I've been carrying around, hiding, denying, insisting upon and yet resenting—the burden of the misdirection of my will, called "sin,"—when I bring this out and "con-fess," I literally "say together with" God, and the fellowship of my Church, the truth about myself. This truth sets me free from self-isolation and brings back my sense of belonging. That is, belonging to God and the rest of humanity. My burden is shared, when I share it in confession. It is no longer carried on my shoulders alone. I come home to humility and light and peace.

JUNE 18

BE ENLIGHTENED

"Come to him, and be enlightened, and your faces shall not be ashamed." (Ps 33/34:5)

So the Psalm reminds me that I can approach the Lord, and He will enlighten me, rather than make me "ashamed." Does this really need to be said? Well, yes. I think that at times I tend to avoid approaching Him, for fear He will somehow give me this big "thumbs down" or bite my head off. This is not a grace-filled "fear of God," but a delusional self-loathing projected onto God. He doesn't seek to shame me. Nor is He "disappointed," like a self-seeking parent. God seeks to share Himself with me, to share His light, and always has it on offer, wherever or however I am—and that last part is not "news" to Him.

Today let me "come to Him, and be enlightened," in heartfelt prayer. His light enables me to see myself as He sees me, without fear or favor. Just unchanging, humble and loving acceptance. So I come to Him today and let Him give me what I can't give myself, vision. As it says in the Prayer of the First Hour: *"O Christ, the True Light, Who enlightens and sanctifies every man that comes into the world: Let the Light of Your countenance be signed upon us, that in it we may see the Unapproachable Light, and guide our steps in the doing of Your commandments, through the intercessions of Your most pure Mother, and of all Your saints. Amen."*

JUNE 19

SELF-RELIANCE = A BARREN FAITH

"Remembering our most holy, pure, blessed, and glorious Lady, the Theotokos and Ever-Virgin Mary, with all the saints, let us commit ourselves and one another and our whole life to Christ our God." (Great Litany of the Byzantine Rite)

The Mother of God and the saints are models of humility; of total reliance on God. It's impossible to "commit my whole life" to God if I try and play God myself. Even if I seem to embrace very firm religious beliefs, my faith remains barren if I approach my day with self-reliance; if I lack the humility to seek God in daily prayer. Christ is a living and active presence in my life today, when I let Him in, through humility.

JUNE 20

HIS BODY, OUR BODY

"The Lord is king. He is clothed with majesty/beauty (εὐπρέπεια)." (Ps 92/93: 1)

This verse is proclaimed at Vespers (the evening-service), on the eve of every Sunday, commemorating Christ's resurrection. So, every week this verse reminds me of two truths revealed in His rising from the Life-Giving Tomb:
    1. Christ reigns, as divine-human King over death and darkness; and
    2. His resurrected human Body, in which He is clothed as He majestically exits the Tomb, is beautiful.

In Christ, my human body is endowed with new beauty and new light. This is already evident in Bethlehem, when He first appears to us in our "clothing," sharing with us our vulnerability to cold, heat, hunger, fatigue, and even death. What is "new" and uniquely "beautiful" about this Child's Body, however, is that it is the Body of a King. But His unique "majesty," which He will also share with us, will only be revealed in His ultimate victory; in His resurrection from a tomb outside the walls of Jerusalem.

So, my Lord Jesus Christ walked in my physical vulnerability, facing cold, heat, hunger, fatigue, and even death, to bring my humanity, including my human body, new light and new beauty. Let me share in His light-giving journey today, and join Him "outside the walls"; outside the confines I construct, of self-centered fear, expectations, or discouragement. "For You are the enlightenment of our souls and bodies, O Christ God," as we say in the Prayer of the Gospel, "and to You we send up glory," with Your Father Who has no beginning, and Your Life-Giving Spirit. Amen.

JUNE 21

THE RIGHT LAND

"O God, my God, early in the morning I seek you (πρὸς σὲ ὀρθρίζω), *my soul thirsts for you, and moreover my flesh, in a dry and weary land where there is no water."* (Ps 62:1, according to the Septuagint)

This is what it's like, waking up early in the morning with all sorts of thoughts scurrying about in my head. That chattery "place" in my head, raising concerns about this and that, is "a dry and weary land where there is no water." It's also a tap on the shoulder from God, calling me to seek Him; to get up and re-connect with Him, Who alone restores me to true life and true peace, giving me to "drink" of His "living water," His humbling grace.

"Your Good Spirit shall guide me into the right land" (Ps 142:10) today; a land in which I not only do not thirst, in neediness and insufficiency, but can share with others. In His land, His water becomes in me "a spring of water welling up to eternal life." (Jn 4:14)

JUNE 22

OUR FATHER

"But when the fullness of time had come, God sent his Son, born of a woman, born under the law, in order to redeem those who were under the law, so that we might receive adoption as sons. And because you are sons, God has sent the Spirit of his Son into your hearts, crying, 'Abba! Father!' So you are no longer a slave but a son, and if a son then also an heir of God through Christ." (Gal 4:4-7)

Christ is "born of a woman" and becomes one of us, sharing our humanity, opening the door for us to share in His divinity; in His heretofore-unique dignity of being God's Son and sole Heir to God's kingdom. Is this an extravagant or empty promise? No, I don't think so. I find that God restores my lost sense of belonging, of connection, often on a daily basis, whenever I choose to enter the wide-open door of His fellowship and communion.

Today, whenever I cry out, "Our Father...," I remember gratefully that I do so with His Son, Who first prayed in this way, as one of us. No longer is any one of us truly separate, nor floating about like an island—no matter how "disconnected" or broken one may feel in the area of human relationships. God has His kingdom on offer for every one of us, including me; His entire inheritance is there, as well as a place for me at His family table—as cheesy as that may sound. He indeed has a "place," the proper place, and a proper home, in Him and with Him, for everyone. "Our Father," I say today, letting Him restore my proper place with Him and in Him. "Thy kingdom come, Thy will be done" with me today, for Yours is the kingdom, the power, and the glory. Here and now, and forever.

JUNE 23

ASKING FOR HELP

"O God, be attentive unto helping me; O Lord, make haste to help me." (Ps 69/70:1)

Sometimes I forget to ask God for help. I get overwhelmed in the midst of the day's stress, and turn my focus entirely to the chaos at hand. I can get caught up, not only in work and other responsibilities, but also in my thoughts and feelings, as well as other people's opinions, feelings, reactions, and so on. That's a lot to carry around, on my own.

It is (perhaps ironically) a daily admission of defeat, that I can't do it on my own, which gives me renewed strength, when I let God back in the picture and ask for help. His grace takes the edge off.

I find this psalm-verse very helpful when I've lost touch with the fact that God is right there, and always willing to help: *"O God, be attentive unto helping me; O Lord, make haste to help me."*

JUNE 24

DESTROYING DEATH BY DEATH

"Having beheld the Resurrection of Christ, let us worship, the holy Lord Jesus, the only Sinless One! We venerate Your Cross, O Christ, and Your Holy Resurrection we praise and glorify; for You are our God, and we know no other than You; we call on Your name. Come, all you faithful, let us venerate Christ's Holy Resurrection! For, behold, through the Cross joy has come into all the world. Let us ever bless the Lord, praising His Resurrection. By enduring the Cross for us, He destroyed death by death!" (Byzantine Paschal Hymn, sung weekly at Sunday matins)

In our church-services we often hear this phrase, that Christ "trampled" or destroyed "death by death." What does this mean? It means that He took the most unpleasant, the most difficult part of our existence, which is death, and walked right through it. He didn't avoid it. Just like He didn't avoid the other parts of being human, like feeling hunger, enduring poverty, grief, fatigue, and so on. Death is "destroyed" by Him walking through it, because it can't "hold" Him, Who is not only human, but also divine. And He takes away the "sting" of death for all of us, who share in His victory, through communion with Him. The difficult parts of our existence, including death, are now life-giving, in Him. The previously dark and difficult now leads to growth and new life. This is not a merely abstract dogmatic concept; it is something I see at work every day, when I walk through difficulties in Him and with Him, rather than avoiding them.

So my Lord shows me the path of the cross, which leads to victory, in Him. It is not through avoidance or escape from my human existence, which includes hardship, difficulty, and ultimately death. The light-filled path of the cross is about walking through it all; walking through life on life's terms, in Christ and with Christ. He brings new light to the whole picture of our human journey, on which we no longer walk in darkness. *"Through the Cross joy has come into all the world. Let us ever bless the Lord, praising His Resurrection."* Amen!

JUNE 25

WELCOMING STRANGERS

"Now after they had left, an angel of the Lord appeared to Joseph in a dream and said, 'Get up, take the child and his mother, and flee to Egypt, and remain there until I tell you; for Herod is about to search for the child, to destroy him.' Then Joseph got up, took the child and his mother by night, and went to Egypt, and remained there until the death of Herod. This was to fulfill what had been spoken by the Lord through the prophet, 'Out of Egypt I have called my son.'" (Mt 2:13-15)

I heard this passage read yesterday in church, so I've been thinking about the obvious fact that in Egypt Christ, His Mother, and Joseph were refugees. In Egypt, of all places, where this Family's ancestors had been enslaved. When they arrived with the Child in Egypt, they must have been taken in and helped by local people, just like any of us need help in a foreign country, particularly if we happen to be poor as this Family was.

So, when later in life our Lord talks about the Final Judgment, and describes what He will say to the "righteous," specifically—"I was a stranger, and you took me in" (Mt 25:35)—there were already people who had done just that—who weren't even Christians. In fact, He goes on to describe, in that same passage about the Final Judgment, how the "righteous" will reply, "Lord, when did we see you a stranger and take you in…?" (Mt 25:37-38) They had no idea that it was the Lord they were helping.

Today let me take pause, when or if any "stranger" crosses my path, and needs my help or my welcome. This may be just someone at the subway station, asking for directions, or someone who wanders into my church for the first time, or someone else. *"Do not forget to show hospitality to strangers, for by so doing some people have shown hospitality to angels without knowing it."* (Heb 13:2)

JUNE 26

THE MANY MASKS OF ENVY

"And the chief priests accused him of many things. And Pilate again asked him, 'Have you no answer to make? See how many charges they bring against you.' But Jesus made no further answer, so that Pilate was amazed. Now at the feast he used to release for them one prisoner for whom they asked. And among the rebels in prison, who had committed murder in the insurrection, there was a man called Barabbas. And the crowd came up and began to ask Pilate to do as he usually did for them. And he answered them, saying, 'Do you want me to release for you the King of the Jews?' For he perceived that it was out of envy (διὰ φθόνον) that the chief priests had delivered him up. But the chief priests stirred up the crowd to have him release for them Barabbas instead." (Mk 15:3-11)

A while ago I reflected on "envy" (from the Latin "invidia," i.e. "non sight"), a blindness that occurs from the desire to have what someone else has. But now here it is, once again. The chief priests masked their envy, accusing Christ "of many things." Christ gives no answer to these charges, because they are masks.

Envy tends to mask its ugly face, which is why it is sometimes hard to detect, both for the envied and the envious. It can be masked in a political ideology, or in righteous indignation, as it is here, in the case of the chief priests, who pretend to be protecting ancient traditions and structures. It can conversely be masked in flattery and even infatuation, attempting to get close to the envied and thus acquire what he/she has "by association." This can be the basis of stalking celebrities, and then quietly rejoicing over their "fall" in some scandal.

Today let me get in touch with God in grateful prayer, at least a bit, and also take time for some self-examination, in His light. Because His grace, His divine energies, bring me the ability to see myself and others as He sees us; not in competition with one another, but as unique persons with unique journeys, each with his/her own challenges and blessings. "Thy will be done," I say today, with me and with others, "on earth as it is in heaven."

JUNE 27

GOD WITH US

"Let Your mercy, O Lord, be upon us, even as we have hoped in You." (Ps 32/33:22)

This Psalm-verse is frequently repeated in Byzantine church-services (e.g., every day as part of the "Great Doxology," or occasionally on its own, as a "Prokeimenon"). But really, I don't repeat it enough. The verse expresses, in a nutshell, the basic attitude I must always have toward God: An openness to His mercy, on the one hand, and true hope in Him, or true God-dependency, on the other. Note also that the verse is expressed in the "we" form, reminding me that I make my journey of faith in fellowship with others.

There are three basic, inevitable "relationships" that constantly need to be worked on, or made right, to foster my openness to God's mercy and my hope in Him: My relationships with
1. myself,
2. other human beings, and
3. money.

While the multifarious challenges of these three, inescapable relationships can seem to obstruct my God-dependency, they actually help me grow in Him, if I choose to do so. I grow in Him on a daily basis, when I "cope" with the insecurities of self, others, and financial matters by opening them all up to His mercy, and letting Him guide and enlighten me through them.

Today let me step out of self-reliance and fear, and let God's mercy into the picture, because He is, indeed, "with us," when we let Him in. *"Let Your mercy, O Lord, be upon us, even as we have hoped in You."*

JUNE 28

REALITY CHECK

"Jesus said, 'I came into this world for judgment (εἰς κρίμα) so that those who do not see may see, and those who do see may become blind.' Some of the Pharisees near him heard this and said to him, 'Surely we are not blind, are we?' Jesus said to them, 'If you were blind, you would not have sin. But now that you say, "We see," your sin remains.'" (Jn 9:39-41)

Christ comes into this world "for judgment," that is, to give us His assessment, His vision, if you will, of our state of affairs. Without His vision, on my own, I am blind. This is the point He is making to the Pharisees—and to me, whenever I am inclined to "see" things my way, without shedding His light on them. His light is the "reality check" I need on a daily basis, lest I slip into certain, common delusions about myself, others, and events/circumstances around me. In communion with Him, I am liberated from the insecurities, frustrations, and resulting fears of "wishful thinking," and am given humble acceptance of myself, other people, and things as He sees them; as they are.

Today let me open up to the light of God's "judgment," by taking a bit of time for heartfelt prayer and reading of His word. His judgment, in His Spirit, brings me neither apathy nor despair. It brings me the humble acceptance of cross-carrying, step by step. He can, and He does, give me the strength to do the next right thing, when I walk in His light.

JUNE 29

WALKING THROUGH FEAR

"When he had stopped speaking, he said to Simon (St. Peter), 'Launch out into the deep and let down your nets for a catch.' But Simon answered and said to him, 'Master, we have toiled all night and caught nothing; nevertheless at your word I will let down the net.' And when they had done this, they caught a great number of fish, and their net was breaking. So they signaled to their partners in the other boat to come and help them. And they came and filled both the boats, so that they began to sink. When Simon Peter saw it, he fell down at Jesus' knees, saying, 'Depart from me, for I am a sinful man, O Lord!" (Lk 5:4-8)

When Simon-Peter is initially confronted with the person of Jesus Christ, his reaction is fear. "Depart from me," he says, "for I am a sinful man." This is not "the fear of God," which is a gift of the Holy Spirit. Peter fears his own "unworthiness," and this fear makes him want distance from the God-Man. It won't be the last time that St. Peter "denies" Christ on the basis of fear. When he thrice denies Christ during His final trial, it is on the basis of a different fear—the fear of other people's opinion.

And yet Christ calls this fallible human being to become a "fisher of men"; to become the one-and-only, the great Apostle Peter. And Peter keeps answering that call, despite the setbacks of his own, very human, fears.

I'm encouraged today by this "humanness" of the Apostle Peter. Fear is an underlying obstacle, even when I don't notice it, to entering into a true relationship with God, or anyone else, for that matter. I am called to walk through my fear, however, and keep following His call, despite my own "unworthiness," or other people's opinion.

JUNE 30

THE AMBITION TO "HAVE"

"As he was setting out on a journey, a man ran up and knelt before him, and asked him, 'Good Teacher, what must I do to inherit eternal life?' Jesus said to him, 'Why do you call me good? No one is good but God alone. You know the commandments: 'You shall not murder; You shall not commit adultery; You shall not steal; You shall not bear false witness; You shall not defraud; Honor your father and mother.''" He said to him, 'Teacher, I have kept all these since my youth.' Jesus, looking at him, loved him and said, 'You lack one thing; go, sell what you own, and give the money to the poor, and you will have treasure in heaven; then come, follow me.' When he heard this, he was shocked (στυγνάσας,) by this word and went away grieving, for he had many possessions." (Mk 10:17-22)

To give away "what he owned" and to "come, follow" Christ was too much for this man, because he still had the sense of "having" temporal possessions. It's not his material wealth, per se, which keeps this still-young man (he is called "young" in Mt. 19:20) from following the God-Man. It is his false sense of "having" anything at all, which prevents him from recognizing the Everything staring him in the face, and "loving" him. This young man's vision is only "darkened" (στυγνάσας, made gloomy) by the potentially-liberating Word of God, because his vision is attached to "having" outside Him.

The ambition to "have" what we can only "have" for the time being, temporal possessions, can keep spiritual thirst at bay, while we are still chasing them—because they still fulfill, still seem to be the ultimate "good." Until they aren't. Until we begin noticing the "hole in the heart," which won't go away, no matter what we seem to "have," calling us to recognize that nothing and "no one is good, but God alone."

Today I gratefully recognize this hole in my heart, which called to me "looked at me and loved me," as Christ did this young man, when he was still chasing shadows. Let me recognize Him today and follow Him, that I may have everything in Him and with Him. Amen!

JULY 1

LEAD US NOT INTO TEMPTATION

"...And lead us not into temptation; but deliver us from the evil one." (Lk 11:4)

This part of the Lord's Prayer usually gives rise to questions. But today I'd like to reflect on the answer; the answer to which it points. It points me to the ultimate answer, the ultimate solution to the challenges of "temptation": God's power. The Lord tells me in His prayer something I have been learning from experience: that my own "power," be it of will, of self-knowledge, of scientific or psychological analysis or whatever, is not the ultimate answer to the challenges of "temptation" or "the evil one." While I have found that I can quite ably, at times even scientifically, take apart the workings of the will and mind, I am nonetheless not able to put them back together again. The power to "restore" wholeness to my humanity in its thinking, wanting, and acting, belongs to God. That is to say, "salvation" is a job only He can accomplish, in us and with us.

Today let me focus on the Solution, because the "problem" is well-known to me. Let me seek the power of God throughout my daily routine, in communion with Him. Because I have tried my own power, and failed. Let me let God be the God of my life today, letting His will be done. *"For Thine is the kingdom, and the power, and the glory, forever. Amen."*

JULY 2

COMPASSION

"When he saw the crowds, he was moved to compassion for them, because they were worn out (ἐσκυλμένοι) and neglected (ἐρριμένοι), like sheep without a shepherd." (Mt. 9:36)

The crowds described here are "worn out," or, as we would say today, stressed out. And they are "neglected" or abandoned, scattered, left to their own devices. Both these conditions, of being stressed or neglected in some way, or perhaps rejected in some way, are something most of us experience from time to time, maybe even on a daily basis. Let me note that Jesus is moved to *compassion* when He sees this.

Let me also note that these two feelings:
1. stress and
2. some form of neglect or rejection, small or large are the primary reasons for a "bad mood," not only for me, but for other people as well.

Before I react to my own issues or other people's today, let me remember that when Jesus sees us, He is moved to compassion.

JULY 3

DON'T GET IN THE WAY

"He must become greater; I must become less." (Jn 3:30)

St. John the Baptist says these words about Christ. Although St. John was a great teacher and had a large following, benefiting many with his teaching and example, he did not distract his disciples from Christ through his own agenda or person. He paved the way for people to come to Christ.

I keep this in mind as a model for any kind of ministry to other people. And also for the way I "minister" to myself. Don't let self-centered fears, self-seeking, or self-reliance, that is, the voices in my head, block out Christ and His voice. He must become greater, and I less.

JULY 4

THREE WINDOWS OF DAILY LIGHT

"Let your light so shine before men, that they may see your good works and glorify your Father in heaven." (Mt 5:16)

Three things help me, on a daily basis, to maintain sanity in my spiritual house: prayer, contemplation, and self-examination. I know that I need at least a little bit of each of these, usually in the morning, to walk before God and stay open to His will and His grace in my life.

When sometimes I don't feel like getting up in the morning to have that conversation with God, and to prayerfully read a bit, and to review my recent actions, words, and thoughts, where they may have been wrong, I find it very motivating to remember Christ saying to me: *Let your light so shine before men...* It does make a difference, not only for me, but for others, if I carry light, rather than darkness, to those with whom I come into contact today. This thought gets me out of bed.

JULY 5

ALREADY AND NOT YET

"For the grace of God has appeared, bringing salvation to all people, training us to renounce impiety and worldly passions, and in the present age to live lives that are whole-minded, upright, and godly, while we wait for the blessed hope and the appearing (ἐπιφάνειαν) of the glory of our great God and Savior, Jesus Christ. He it is who gave himself for us that he might redeem us from all iniquity and purify for himself an extraordinary people (λαὸν περιούσιον), zealous for good deeds." (Tit 2:11-14)

So the saving grace of God "has appeared" (ἐπεφάνη) already, in the coming of "our great God and Savior" in the flesh. And yet we still "wait for the appearing" of His glory in full, in the final fulfilment, when time shall end. This "waiting for" more to come; this forward-looking to the resurrection of all, along with the grace of God that already "has appeared," is the basis of our "zeal," of our being "zealous for good deeds."

Today let me keep in my heart this little motivational talk that St. Paul gives to Titus, and through Titus to me. Let me pay attention, in heartfelt gratitude, to the grace of God that already "has appeared" most abundantly in my life, in so many situations, relationships, events, in ups and in downs, both yesterday and now, this very morning. And let me look toward the future, our common future, as "an extraordinary people" in Christ, Who "gave Himself for us" that we may have eternal Meaning, eternal hope, and eternal growth. Whatever has happened, whatever is happening now, and whatever is yet to happen today, in Him it all moves me forward, gently and meaningfully. Both now, and ever, and unto the ages of ages. Amen!

JULY 6

UNNOTICEABLE GROWTH

"He put before them another parable: 'The kingdom of heaven is like a mustard seed that someone took and sowed in his field; it is the smallest of all the seeds, but when it has grown it is the greatest of shrubs and becomes a tree, so that the birds of the air come and make nests in its branches.'" (Mt 13:31-32)

Sometimes I tend to think of prayer-life as something enormous; as a huge, almost unsurpassable mountain before me. This is a delusional and damaging thought, because what it does is make me put off any attempt at communion with God. I avoid stepping up to the plate, imagining obstacles like my "unworthiness," unresolved issues, sinful routines, or whatever.

But the Lord gently reminds me in this parable that my faith is a little inconspicuous thing, like a small mustard seed in my heart. If I just nurture it, bit by bit, with some sunlight and water on a daily basis, it gradually grows. I might not even notice it, because other things in life are somehow louder and more prominent. And yet, however unnoticeably, God's grace in my life grows and can make a difference for others around me, if I patiently continue to nurture this little seed in my heart.

The grace of the Gospel is also like this in the broader scheme of things: it does transform the world, and offer even outsiders shelter in its branches, whether they notice that hospitality or not.

JULY 7

AMONG TRANSGRESSORS

"And with him they crucified two bandits, one on his right and one on his left. And the scripture was fulfilled that says, 'and he was numbered among transgressors.' (Is 53:12) Those who passed by derided him, shaking their heads and saying, 'Aha! You who would destroy the temple and build it in three days, save yourself, and come down from the cross!'" (Mk 15:27-30)

So Jesus died as He lived, "among transgressors." That is to say, among us. But the line between those truly "with Him" and those "not with Him" is not drawn in terms of "righteousness" and "sinfulness." No. The difference between those truly with Him and those not with Him lies in self-perception. There are "transgressors" in this picture who feel entitled and self-righteous, like the passers-by who "derided Him," together with one of the bandits crucified with Him, while another, the repentant one, acknowledges that, "we are getting what we deserve for our deeds" (Lk 23:41).

On this Friday, the day of the Lord's crucifixion, I'm thinking about this "place" in which our Lord chose to be, "among transgressors." He went to this "place" not because He had to, not because He "was getting what He deserved for His deeds"; He placed Himself there, among us, to bring us out of that place, together with Him. And He shows me this "way out," this way toward His light, which involves two essential steps:
1. Acknowledgment of my "place," my place as a true transgressor; and
2. Acknowledgment of His "way out," with a willingness to take His outstretched hand and follow.

Today let me acknowledge, in humble self-acceptance, my place "among transgressors," so I can both receive help, and help others, if need be, from a place of humility and weakness. Because this is the place from which our Lord offered Himself to us. *"Remember me, Lord,"* I say today, *"when You come into Your kingdom."*

JULY 8

CHOOSING MY FRIENDS

"That day Herod and Pilate became friends—before this they had been enemies." (Lk 23:12)

This passage, which relates how Herod and Pilate formed a friendship when they collaborated in leading Christ to His cross, holds a simple message for me: Not all friendships are good. Both these men were on the wrong side of the story of the Cross, and it is precisely this that brought them together, as friends. They "enabled" each other, as participants in the trials that led to His crucifixion.

So let me say I should be careful about the friendships I form and foster, at the risk of making this reflection too morose. Some friendships can put me on the wrong side of the Cross, that is to say, "enable" me or someone else to cast it off, while I am attempting to be, in my own small way, a co-carrier of His cross. I don't need to "judge" anyone else's journey, but I do need to see situations and relationships honestly, with God's help. I need not see myself as a victim of other people's choices, expectations, or vision, but of my own.

So I don't go around judging everyone today, but I also don't need to embrace everyone's friendship. I am obliged to "love" everyone. I don't need to "like" everyone, however, nor be friends with them.

JULY 9

HE GIVES TO EACH OF US

"But each of us was given grace according to the measure of Christ's gift. Therefore it is said, 'When he ascended on high he made captivity itself a captive; he gave gifts to his people.' (When it says, 'He ascended,' what does it mean but that he had also descended into the lower parts of the earth? He who descended is the same one who ascended far above all the heavens, so that he might fill all things.) The gifts he gave were that some would be apostles, some prophets, some evangelists, some pastors and teachers, to equip the saints for the work of ministry, for building up the body of Christ, until all of us come to the unity of the faith and of the knowledge of the Son of God, to maturity, to the measure of the full stature of Christ." (Eph 4:7-13)

Indeed, Christ entered into "all things," not only "ascending" and elevating our humanity in His divine dignity. He also "descended" into the lowermost parts of our "hell," of the human experience, even unto death. His light thus touches the best in us, and the worst in us. Because there is nothing, absolutely nothing in my experience, in my daily falling or rising, which He isn't willing to take on, heal, and transfigure in Him, in His body.

Whatever "place" I am in today, whatever level of "maturity," let me let Christ in, and begin anew in Him, in the building up of His body, wherever or however I am. The gifts of "the unity of the faith" and of "the knowledge of the Son of God" are already given, in Him. I have only to embrace them, in whatever "measure" I can today, if only by showing up, by being there, among others gathered in His name. Let me not close off today nor self-isolate, but enter into communion with my resurrected Lord, Who "made captivity itself a captive." Let me let Him liberate me today, in His grace of unity and knowledge, which "each of us was given according to the measure of Christ's gift." Amen.

JULY 10

THE WAY OF PEACE

"...And you, child, shall be called the prophet of the Highest: for you shall go before the face of the Lord to prepare his ways; To give knowledge of salvation unto his people by the remission of their sins, through the tender mercy of our God; whereby the Sunrise from on high shall visit us, to give light to them that sit in darkness and in the shadow of death, to guide our feet onto the way of peace." (Zacharia's Prophecy, Lk 1:76-79)

In the past few days I've been thinking a lot about "the way of peace" mentioned here by Zacharia, the father of St. John the Baptist, in his prophecy about his own son, and about "the Sunrise" or "Orient" from on high, the Messiah. We know that this "way of peace," which gives "light to them that sit in darkness," is the way of the Cross. Because the Messiah, Jesus Christ, walked the way of the Cross, which is called in Byzantine hymnography "the weapon of peace."

I've been thinking about this because of a close friend of mine, a single mom whose 10-year-old daughter is being bullied in school. My friend's efforts to help her child seem to have been futile, including her repeatedly going to the school, talking to teachers and parents, and asking the parishioners at our church here for prayers. The teachers and parents seem to be increasingly indifferent or hostile, and her daughter continues to come home in tears, occasionally to get into fights, and so on. I'll also note that my friend doesn't have the options either of home-schooling or changing schools.

So at this point it seems we are witnessing the harsh reality of a young child being taught the way of the Cross; the way of taking up "the weapon of peace." I don't see any other "light" in this picture. Because alternatively she could be taught the way of bitterness, resentment, self-pity and self-isolation. May His light shine in our darkness and our powerlessness today, for the young and the old, that our feet may be guided by "the tender mercy of our God," onto "the way of peace."

JULY 11

A SHARED EXPERIENCE

"O magnify the Lord with me, and let us exalt his name together. I sought the Lord, and he heard me, and delivered me from all my tribulations." (Ps 33/34:3-4)

How powerful, how encouraging, that the Psalmist witnesses to his personal experience. He doesn't just say, "O magnify the Lord with me," because this is what upstanding, proper citizens do, or this what "our tribe" does, or this is the cleverest philosophy on the market. No, he says, "I sought the Lord, and He heard me," and He "delivered me." I tried this way, His way, and it works.

Indeed, faith has been salvifically "infectious," precisely because it has been passed on by eyewitnesses to the Word at work, to the Lord at work in people's lives. I'm thinking about this because of something I happened to read, just last night, in the writings of the psychologist C. Jung—and I'm sorry but I can't resist quoting this: "It is not ethical principles, however lofty, or creeds, however orthodox, that lay the foundations for the freedom and autonomy of the individual," Jung writes, "but simply and solely the empirical awareness, the incontrovertible experience of an intensely personal, reciprocal relationship between man and an extramundane authority which acts as a counterpoise to the 'world' and its 'reason.'"

Today I am gratefully reminded of the power of human witness, of fellow human beings, whose experience, strength and hope strengthens my own, when I am weak or faltering. Today I seek the Lord, and He hears me, because others sought Him before me, and I know He heard them. *"O magnify the Lord with me, and let us exalt his name together."* Amen!

JULY 12

SEEING "THE OTHERS"

"Then Paul stood in front of the Areopagus and said, 'Athenians, I see how extremely religious you are in every way. For as I went through the city and looked carefully at the objects of your worship, I found among them an altar with the inscription, 'To the unknown god.' What therefore you worship as unknown, this I proclaim to you..." (Acts 17:22-23)

St. Paul begins his famous Areopagus Sermon with the vital words, "I see..." And he goes on to make several observations, to the 'agan Athenians, about their religiosity. So the great Apostle to the Gentiles first took the time to "see" and appreciate the mindset of his (mostly hostile) audience, noting also its good sides, before sharing quite a different sort of Good News with them. St. Paul's effort really to see "the others," the Athenians, rather than simply dismissing their world-view from the outset, opens his heart to these people.

Today this wisdom of St. Paul reminds me first and foremost to note the good in those who disagree with me (in matters great or small), before engaging in dialogue with them. Because if my heart is closed to those with whom I'm speaking, then their hearts will—naturally—be closed to mine.

JULY 13

SEEKING GLORY

"How can you believe, when you receive glory from one another and do not seek the glory that comes from the only God?" (Jn 5:44)

Thus the Lord asks those who are rejecting Him, those who not believe in Him, how they could possibly believe, when they "do not seek the glory that comes from the only God," but are focused rather on human "glory." Christ's question, "How can you believe, when…," points to a blindness, a blindness caused by a focus on what is essentially and unavoidably delusional—merely-human opinion. He is not saying that human opinion is always "bad." He is saying that a focus on it, to the exclusion of "seeking" God's glory, makes faith impossible.

This passage reminds me today to re-focus, if I happen to slip into people-pleasing, into seeking the approval, justification, or praise of other people. I do this practically by default, if I cease consciously and actively to "seek the glory that comes from the only God." Why is this whole business of "glory" so important, and so potentially-damaging? Because if I focus on a God-less kind of glory, which is unavoidably not-omniscient, and hence not "true," then I strive to become someone or something "not true." Only God can know me as I am, as His creation. Only His "approval," His vision of what or who "is very good" (Gen 1:31), can grant me the grace of being the "very good" He created me to be, in humble self-acceptance, in His humility, in His loving grace.

Today let me let God liberate me from the brutal insecurities of seeking human "glory," which blind me to true vision of God, myself, and others. "For Thine is the kingdom, the power, and the glory," I say to Him today. Let me be today the "very good" He sees in me, in Him.

JULY 14

HALLOWING HIS NAME

"Our Father who art in heaven, hallowed be Thy name..." (Mt 6:9)

God's "name" can be said to be His "reputation" among us. Whenever I "name" Him or hear His name(s), according to the various names He has revealed to us, I immediately relate to Who God "is," as far as I have heard, learned, and experienced. I know from received Tradition, and through living Tradition, that God, first of all, "is"; and that He is all-loving, all-powerful, all-knowing, all-glorious, and indeed, all-holy. He is, in fact, the one Source of love, power, knowledge, glory, and holiness. And He imparts these energies to me when I "recognize" Him, and look to Him, as their Source.

So, God Himself doesn't need to be "hallowed" to be "holy." But His "name," according to which we relate to Him, can be more or less "recognized as holy," or "hallowed," by us (be hallowed, that is to say, glorified, as St. John Chrysostom writes, ἁγιασθήτω, τοῦτ' ἔστι, δοξασθήτω). Or not. It is in the realm of my free will to "give God a bad name," by mistrusting Him, by underestimating or otherwise distorting His perfect being, His perfect love, His perfect beauty, His perfect will, and so on. I can slip into these distortions of God's "name," time and again, by distancing myself from enlightening contact with Him, by replacing Him with something or someone else, or by projecting my fears, ambitions, and limitations on Him.

Today let His name be hallowed in my life, lest I look in the wrong places for love, power, knowledge, glory, or holiness. *"Our Father, hallowed by Thy name."* Today, and forever. Amen.

JULY 15

LOVING THE LIGHT

"...And this is the judgment, that the light has come into the world, and people loved darkness rather than light because their deeds were evil. For all who do evil hate the light and do not come to the light, so that their deeds may not be exposed. But those who do what is true come to the light, so that their deeds may be clearly seen, for they have been done in God." (Jn 3:19-21)

Yes, indeed. It is by doing what is "true" that I come to the Light, and so come to love the Light rather than darkness. The Light is God Himself, the Creator, so I receive creative energy by moving toward Him, however small and however slow my steps may be.

It is not an immense effort on my part, to do the next right thing, rather than avoiding it. But such daily, small steps are ever-regenerating, ever-new, because they are done "in God," Who, unlike "darkness" is not a "nothing." I mean "darkness" or "evil" is the absence of Light, so its deeds are not creative, and thus never new. If I choose to "do evil," I find that in essence I just do the same thing over and over again, in circles, in self-centered circles, the result of which is having nothing of value to share; having nothing to give. That's why "evil" is full of neediness and isolation, in the self, which desires to be served and yet not to serve, and by all means to "not be exposed." It is averse to vulnerability.

Today let me open up to the Light, in a bit of heartfelt prayer, as well as honesty toward myself and others. Let me recognize the Great Fact that, "the light has come into the world" and is willing to walk with me, and share my vulnerability, on the light-giving and love-giving path of His cross.

JULY 16

TO SHARE OR NOT TO SHARE

"Death and life are in the power of the tongue, and those who love it will eat its fruits." (Proverbs 18:21)

Ouch! Yes, my words can spread "life," or my words can spread "death." Not only by way "of the tongue," as it was when Proverbs were written. Today my sharing of words happens increasingly online, in what I choose to "forward" or "share" via text-message, tweet, email, or otherwise. I'm thinking about this today, because yesterday I received a nasty email, and then forwarded it to a close friend, saying something to the effect of, Look, she's at it again, this one. I shouldn't have done that. I could have "stopped the madness," so to say, by just keeping it to myself. Simple abstinence in forwarding, and wise use of "DELETE" would have been a beneficial exercise in compassion and withholding of judgment.

So today let me be a bit more abstinent with "the power of the tongue," which nowadays is magnified through the abundance of words I can choose to share, or not to share, online. If I happen to come across damaging or death-bringing information, let it stop with me, rather than be spread by me, so that others are not subjected to "eating its fruits." And let me be grateful today for lessons learned yesterday, in light of God's always life-giving Word.

JULY 17

THE FELLOWSHIP OF THE SPIRIT

"O Lord, You sent down Your All-Holy Spirit at the third hour to Your Apostles. Do not take Him away from us, O Good One, but renew us, who pray to You." (Byzantine Troparion of the Third Hour)

It is almost nine o'clock (i.e. "the third hour"), and I am running late. I received some disturbing news earlier this morning from a dear friend, who has been diagnosed with a huge tumor, and must soon undergo very serious and unexpected surgery. She is my age, and stronger than I am in faith, I must say, because in this case, quite amazingly, I found her words to me, full of humble practicality, very strengthening and consoling, while I had nothing to offer but dumbfounded grief and pain for my beloved friend.

Today, at this Third Hour, let me be strengthened and renewed by the grace of the Holy Spirit, sent down so abundantly and continuously upon us, in dear friends, in our fellowship of the Spirit, in the one Body of Christ. May He be our continued Source of strength, humility, courage, and mutual love, in one another and through one another, on our cross-carrying journeys, toward the Light of His and our resurrection. *"O Good One, renew us, who pray to You."*

JULY 18

SIN IN GOD'S SIGHT

"Against you, you only, have I sinned, and done this evil in your sight: so you are right in your verdict, and justified when you judge." (Ps 50/51:4)

King David composed this famous Psalm (*"Have mercy on me, O God, according to your great mercy..."*) after committing adultery and murder—the two sins, one would think, that most directly violate another human being. And yet he says to God, "Against you, you only, have I sinned..."

This is because ultimately, only God's righteous judgment can properly assess "sin" and its gravity. It is ultimately only God, as lawgiver, Who can "see" where and how I transgress His law, and only His grace allows me to "see" as He does. Human opinion, on the other hand, my own and that of others, is capable of looking upon sin with pleasure, or distorting its gravity, or labeling something a "sin," which God doesn't see as "sin" at all. And I can easily be distracted from my actual "sin," by focusing on something external, which isn't an issue for God.

Today let me be open to "seeing" as God does, "according to His great mercy," by humbly asking for this gift in prayer.

JULY 19

SPEAKING FROM THE HEART

"A good man brings good things out of the good stored up in his heart, and an evil man brings evil things out of the evil stored up in his heart. For the mouth speaks what the heart is full of." (Lk 6:45)

I don't always have something good to say. Sometimes I feel bogged down by various self-centered concerns, so the words that come out of my mouth tend to be useless. Occasionally they become even damaging or hurtful to other people.

In the passage quoted above the Lord reminds me of a simple truth: that the problem lies not in my words, but in my heart. I need to look into my heart, and see what it's been embracing and focusing on. Has my focus floated over to self, and all its fearful preoccupations?

Let me take a little time to re-focus on God, and humbly ask for His grace to fill my heart, clearing away the debris it's been collecting. *"Treasury of good and Giver of Life, come and abide in us, and cleanse us of all impurity. And save our souls, O Good One!"*

JULY 20

SOLITUDE

"And after he had dismissed the crowds, he went up the mountain by himself to pray. When evening came, he was there alone..." (Mt 14:23)

Did Jesus really "need" solitude, at the top of a mountain, to pray? As Son of God, One of the Holy Trinity, I presume He was in constant communion with the Father and the Holy Spirit. But He did take on my humanity, in all its entirety, and here He demonstrates a very human need: to take time out for solitary prayer, at some appropriate place (in this case, an unspecified mountaintop).

I need to remember this need, among my other needs: I need occasional solitude, and an appropriate place or places, specifically "to pray," to have a conversation with God. In the present-day it is especially easy for me to forget this human need, because I can take my mobile device anywhere, and be "connected" to everyone else.

Today I shut off my connection to everyone else, for just a bit of time after I wake up, to connect with Him in prayer, and in some quiet reading of His word. Because He showed me that to do so, in solitude, is human.

JULY 21

GROWTH IN CRISIS

"Jesus, full of the Holy Spirit, returned from the Jordan and was led by the Spirit in the wilderness, where for forty days he was tempted by the devil. He ate nothing at all during those days, and when they were over, he was famished. The devil said to him, 'If you are the Son of God, command this stone to become a loaf of bread.' Jesus answered him, 'It is written, "One does not live by bread alone."' (Lk 4:1-4)

Here Jesus is feeling "famished," that is, He has come to the point in His fasting where He needs food...or else. So this is a "crisis," which is defined by Merriam-Webster as "a turning point for better or worse," and "a time when a difficult or important decision must be made." I'll note that a "crisis" is connected to an intense need of some sort; when I perceive that something is lacking, and I need to do something about it.

Note also that this perception of something "lacking" can be false. We can perceive an intense "need" for people, places, things, or conditions that we may not need at all; or not in the way we think we need them. We are particularly vulnerable to such "temptation" when we are hungry, lonely, or tired. These states of mind or body can force us into a decision that is wrong; a decision to misuse our God-given gifts, our powers of argumentation, or beauty, or authority, or money, to acquire that which we think we need to fill our void. While this is no easy "temptation," the decision we make at this point can lead to immense growth. If we resolve the crisis in God, in His nurturing presence, handing it over to Him and earnestly relying on His help, we make an empowering step toward Him and grow. And we acquire experience, which we can then share with others, empowering others around us. That's how our Lord comes out of this situation, as it says at the end of this passage: *"Then Jesus, filled with the power of the Spirit, returned to Galilee."* (Lk 4:14)

Today let me let Him in, and fill my void. Let me reach out in humility and service to other people, in light-filled fellowship, in His Spirit, when I have the need for help. And let me let God discipline me in His simple ways, taking care of my physical and spiritual needs according to His rules of love, compassion, and humble self-acceptance. Amen.

JULY 22

SURRENDER

"One of the criminals who were hanged there kept deriding him and saying, 'Are you not the Messiah? Save yourself and us!' But the other rebuked him, saying, 'Do you not fear God, since you are under the same sentence of condemnation? And we indeed have been condemned justly, for we are getting what we deserve for our deeds, but this man has done nothing wrong.' Then he said to Jesus, 'Remember me, Lord, when you come into your kingdom.' He replied, 'Truly I tell you, today you will be with me in Paradise.'" (Lk 23:39-43)

So one of the criminals is still fighting, still arguing, still feeling entitled and wronged, even at this point. But the other one surrenders on his cross and to his cross, saying, "we indeed have been condemned justly." This surrender, this full stop to arguing with and demanding from God, opens the repentant criminal's eyes, bringing him to recognize his Lord and to make—not a demand—but a feeble request: *"Remember me, Lord, when you come into your kingdom."* And this brief, humble prayer, made in full surrender and with no sense of entitlement, was heard beyond the criminal's wildest dreams.

For some of us, the path to surrender, which enables us truly to see and truly to pray, is not an easy one. It sometimes takes extreme circumstances, extreme loss, to stop fighting and blaming, to recognize God for Who He is, as One who "has done nothing wrong," and let Him take over.

Today let me surrender again, handing everything and everyone in my life over to His kingdom, letting Him be King instead of me. I have tried my own way, and failed. So let me be willing today, albeit imperfectly, to try His way, recognizing His perfect willingness to be there with me, on the cross right next to mine. *"Remember me Lord,"* I say today, *"when You come into Your kingdom."*

JULY 23

SPIRITUAL INTOXICATION

"Six days later, Jesus took with him Peter and James and his brother John and led them up a high mountain, by themselves. And he was transfigured before them, and his face shone like the sun, and his clothes became dazzling white. Suddenly there appeared to them Moses and Elijah, talking with him. Then Peter said to Jesus, 'Lord, it is good for us to be here; if you wish, I will make three tents here, one for you, one for Moses, and one for Elijah..."' (Mt 17:1-4)

On this occasion, Peter "does not know what to say" (Mk 9:6), because the revelation is overwhelming. But this doesn't stop him from saying something. It is a suggestion. It's something to the effect of, Lord, this is so good, let's all just stay here and live happily ever after. Forget about all those people down there.

This is a case of spiritual intoxication; of a novice in the early stages of encountering grace, a bit like someone in love for the first time. In this phase we may say and do things that look quite silly in hindsight. We might forget about our responsibilities, tend to forget about the rest of the people in our lives, and sillier yet, offer suggestions or even advice to those far more experienced than we are; to those who have been leading a spiritual life all along, before we decided to take it up.

Today let me ask God to plant my feet firmly on the ground, when my head is in the clouds. And let me receive my enthusiasm for spiritual life both with gratitude and, when need be, a sense of humor, not taking myself too seriously. Let me let Him keep things His way—light.

JULY 24

PRAYING AGAIN AND AGAIN

"Again and again, in peace let us pray to the Lord." (Litany of Byzantine Liturgy)

There are two basic things to be said about prayer:
1. Start doing it, and
2. Keep doing it. Preferably "in peace."

And that's easier said than done, particularly in the context of church community, where human tensions and shortcomings, beginning with my own, can make praying in peace a challenge. I'm thinking about this before I go off to church this morning, because certain bits of "church news" have disturbed me since last evening.

Today let me look to the King of Peace, the Source of my peace, to calm any disturbance I may feel. Let me be reminded that any loss of peace I feel is not a sign of any lack in God, but of a lack in me; a loss of focus in me. Because He remains the same, in perfect and omniscient peace, and in His perfect willingness to impart His peace on me.

So let me "duck," so to say, under the "wave" of His peace, in humility and acceptance, letting God take care of things and people as they are in my immediate community and in the world in general. *"For You are the King of Peace and the Saviour of our souls,"* not me, *"and unto You to we ascribe glory, to the Father, and to the Son, and to the Holy Spirit,"* here and now, and forever. Amen.

JULY 25

LETTING HIM INTERRUPT

"Once while Jesus was standing beside the lake of Gennesaret, and the crowd was pressing in on him to hear the word of God, he saw two boats there at the shore of the lake; the fishermen had gone out of them and were washing their nets. He got into one of the boats, the one belonging to Simon, and asked him to put out a little way from the shore. Then he sat down and taught the crowds from the boat. When he had finished speaking, he said to Simon, 'Put out into the deep water and let down your nets for a catch.'..." (Lk 5:1-4)

So this is how Christ walked into Simon Peter's life: He borrowed his boat for a while. And then, when He had finished speaking, He returned the favor to the fisherman, helping him catch some fish. And the whole transaction ends with Simon leaving everything and following Him (Lk 5:11).

How subtly, how naturally, the Lord inserts Himself into my life and helps me out in unexpected ways, when I'm open to lending Him my "boat." And by "boat" I mean my particular set of possessions or gifts, by which I make a living.

Today let me be open to sharing whatever I may have, with the simple attitude Simon Peter displayed in the passage above. The fisherman was in the middle of his workday, a frustrating workday after a long and unproductive night, during which he "caught nothing," as he says a bit later (Lk 5:5). But Simon let the Lord interrupt this day, when Jesus got into Simon's boat and "asked him to put out a little way from the shore." And the interruption led Simon to becoming far more than just a fisherman.

Today let me be useful to Him in the small ways I can, doing small favors for others when need be, so that He can make me useful in the grace-filled way that only He can. *"Come and abide in us,"* in our little boats, I say to Him today, as I open myself up to His unexpected interruptions.

JULY 26

THE GIFT OF HUMOR

"When the days drew near for him to be taken up, he set his face to go to Jerusalem. And he sent messengers ahead of him. On their way they entered a village of the Samaritans to make ready for him; but they did not receive him, because his face was set toward Jerusalem. When his disciples James and John saw it, they said, 'Lord, do you want us to command fire to come down from heaven and consume them?' But he turned and rebuked them. Then they went on to another village." (Lk 9:51-56)

So James and John helpfully suggest destroying an entire village by "fire from heaven," just because it denied them lodging. To these two brothers Christ wittily gives the nickname "Boanerges," which is understood to mean "Sons of Thunder" (Mk 3:17). It is quite a satirical nickname at the time it is given, when the two sons of Zebedee still had some serious hiccups to iron out of their approach to their mission. Calling them "Boanerges" was like nicknaming a know-it-all kid "Einstein."

Christ, like any effective teacher, is not devoid of wit and humor. And the Bible is not a book devoid of these elements, even mentioning that God laughs (Ps 58/59:8). I can easily forget this when I read Scripture, because of course the points being made, using humor, are very serious.

But I am reminded today that a certain dose of playfulness in my nature is a God-given gift. That's why children instinctively play; they in fact learn and grow through play, although they don't yet sense when it's time to stop. As adults we might have the opposite problem: not sensing when it's time to lighten up.

So if I'm taking myself or certain situations too seriously, let me embrace the gift of approaching myself and the world with a sense of humor. I continue both to learn and grow by remembering when it's time to lighten up.

JULY 27

ANGER

"But everyone must be quick to hear, slow to speak and slow to anger; because human anger does not accomplish the righteousness of God. Therefore, putting aside all filthiness and all that remains of wickedness, in humility receive the word implanted, which is able to save your souls..." (James 1:19-21)

Indeed, my anger does not "accomplish" the good I supposedly want from the situations and people in my life; the "righteousness of God." And by "anger" I don't mean feelings of irritation, hurt, and vulnerability. These need to be recognized, walked through, and healed in the light and humility "of the word implanted," rather than escaped through anger or "substituted."

Anger is called a "substitute emotion" because it lets me cover up my pain and vulnerability with the delusion of control and superiority; it lets me be distracted from the "real" issues of fear and/or resentment, which need to be, and indeed can be, healed within me—but not by me, and certainly not by my human anger, however I express it or hide it (either in angry action or apathy, or turning it inward, in depression or self-sabotage). This healing takes time, it takes slowing down—being "slow to speak and slow to anger," as I take a look at my fears and resentments, and hand them over to God and His grace of forgiveness.

Today let me "be quick to hear" what the Lord's voice has to say to me through my irritations and hurt. And let me put aside my own interpretations of these things, fed by resentment or fear, and "in humility receive the word implanted, which is able to save," to move me forward toward wholeness and unity, within myself and with others. Lord, let me see in Your light today, embracing Your grace and Your power, rather than escape into the seductive and divisive delusions of anger.

JULY 28

THE PRISON OF RESENTMENT

"Bring my soul out of prison that I may confess Your name." (Ps 141:10/Ps 142:7)

The "prison" that can keep me from "confessing the name" of the Lord, of recognizing Him for Who He is and letting Him be God in my life, is resentment. In the dark prison of resentment my growth becomes impossible. There is only blame and excuses for my every failure and inadequacy, so I become incapable both of the grace of humble acceptance and of God-willed change.

Today I am reminded to ask for help, to "bring my soul out of prison," if traces of old resentments begin to resurface, blocking out light and distorting my vision. Let me be quick to let go of these, sharing them with God and others, in rigorous honesty, so I can be free as He wants me to be; free to grow.

JULY 29

TWO KINGDOMS

"...From then on Pilate tried to release him, but the Jews cried out, 'If you release this man, you are no friend of the emperor. Everyone who claims to be a king sets himself against the emperor.' When Pilate heard these words, he brought Jesus outside and sat on the judge's bench at a place called The Stone Pavement, or in Hebrew Gabbatha. Now it was the day of Preparation for the Passover; and it was about noon. He said to the Jews, 'Here is your King!' They cried out, Away with him! Away with him! Crucify him!' Pilate asked them, 'Shall I crucify your King?' The chief priests answered, 'We have no king but the emperor.' Then he handed him over to them to be crucified." (Jn 19:12-16)

Two "kingdoms" are being set against one another here, the Kingdom of God and the kingdom of Caesar. These kingdoms are clashing not because they must, because the ultimate authority in both kingdoms, in reality, is God. Jesus reminds Pilate of this reality in the verse preceding the above passage: *"You would have no power over me,"* He says to Pilate, *"unless it had been given you from above; therefore the one who handed me over to you is guilty of a greater sin."* (Jn 19:11)

The two kingdoms are clashing here because the people involved are setting the two kingdoms against each other within their own hearts. In the case of the chief priests, they are doing so knowingly, manipulating Pilate to meet their own earthly goals. In the case of Pilate, he does so in confusion; because his entire upbringing and position in the Roman world have operated on a distorted, confused vision of Caesar as "the" ultimate authority.

Today let me keep God in the picture, whatever politics I choose to embrace. I am less likely to shout "Away with Him!" in my heart and in my politics, when I maintain my conscious contact with Him, as the one, ultimate authority in my life. *"For Thine is the kingdom, the power, and the glory,"* I say today, *"now and forever."* Amen!

JULY 30

SERVING OTHERS IS HEALING

"So when they had eaten breakfast, Jesus said to Simon Peter, 'Simon, son of Jonah, do you love me more than these?' He said to him, 'Yes, Lord; you know that I love you.' He said to him, 'Feed my lambs.' He said to him again a second time, 'Simon, (son) of Jonah, do you love me?' He said to him, 'Yes, Lord; you know that I love you.' He said to him, "Tend my sheep.' He said to him the third time, 'Simon, (son) of Jonah, do you love me?' Peter was grieved because he said to him the third time, 'Do you love me?' And he said to him, 'Lord, you know all things; you know that I love you...'" (Jn 21:15-17)

In this well-known passage, Christ restores Peter, who had recently thrice denied His Lord during His salvific passion. Christ offers Peter healing by thrice allowing the lapsed Apostle to affirm that he "loves" Him, and by thrice calling Peter to do the work that was his vocation, to minister to the Lord's sheep and lambs, that is, to serve others.

There is much that can be said about this passage, but I'd like to reflect just on the following: Christ points to Peter's calling, to minister to others in the Church, as part of his healing process. It is easy to read this passage slightly differently, by thinking that the Lord demands that Peter "prove" his love to Him through ministry. As if the Lord is saying, *"Oh yeah? You love Me? Well, prove it to Me."* But the Lord does not need proof, knowing Peter's heart, because, as Peter rightly notes, He "knows all things." It isn't the Lord Who needs "proof" of Peter's love. It is Peter who needs restoration and healing, and a vital part of this, Christ says to the Apostle, will be Peter's ministry to others, which is Peter's calling. And the refreshing fact is, this vocation hasn't changed nor erased itself because of Peter's sin.

Today I remember that service to others is healing, first and foremost for me. When I help others, I help myself. This is why it is pointless to ponder whether or not I am "worthy" to do what I am called to do. And for me, just like for every other follower of Christ, that calling is—to be of service to others, in the way that I, personally, can.

JULY 31

SANCTIFICATION BY TRUTH, NOT ESCAPE

Jesus prays for His followers to the Father: *"I am not asking you to take them out of the world, but I ask you to protect them from the evil one. They do not belong to the world, just as I do not belong to the world. Sanctify them in the truth; your word is truth. As you have sent me into the world, so I have sent them into the world. And for their sakes I sanctify myself, so that they also may be sanctified in truth."* (Jn 17:15-19)

These words in the Gospel of John, spoken in prayer by Christ for those who will follow Him, remind me that it is not His will that we be taken "out of the world." It is rather His will that we be "sanctified in truth," which is His word, in the world.

So, I remind myself, it is not in escape from my "world" that my path to sanctification lies. I have various matters, responsibilities, and relationships I must tend to in "the world." I need not fear all that, because I am not in "the world" by mistake, nor am I on my own. According to the words of the Lord, I am "sent" into it, as are all those who believe in Him. And I am given His word to accompany, guide, protect, and sanctify me.

Let me keep Scripture close, on a daily basis, so that I'm not alone with my own "truth," but sanctified and protected by His.

AUGUST 1

GROWING IN VULNERABILITY

"For the word of the cross is folly to those who are perishing, but to us who are being saved it is the power of God." (1 Cor 1:18)

When does "the word of the cross" become "folly" to me? When I slip into resentment, self-pity, and egocentrism. In these states of mind my growth is stunted, and I place myself among "those who are perishing." These states of mind are closed in on the self, asking the wrong questions, like: How have I been wronged? What haven't others done for me? And it goes around in circles, because I can't control "others"; I can't change "others."

The "word of the cross," on the other hand, is one of self-giving and hence of growth, because self-giving brings me out of myself. It brings me out, into the vulnerability and sunlight of the "power of God," where I grow through the ups and downs of humble openness.

Today let me hear, and let me do, "the word of the cross," asking the right questions: How have I wronged others? What can I do for fellow-strugglers today? Let me be open to "being saved" today, in the great outdoors of Christ's Self-giving. *"So, let us go out to Him outside the camp, bearing His reproach."* (Heb 13:13)

AUGUST 2

THE PROMISE OF LAUGHTER

"Blessed are you who weep now, for you will laugh (ὅτι γελάσετε)." (Lk 6:21)

Here is an oft-forgotten, oft-neglected promise made by my Lord to those who take up their cross: laughter! I have seen this promise come true in the lives of people who lead lives of conscious, spiritual growth and struggle: Despite their unmistakeable, focused earnestness—they often laugh wholeheartedly. They have the capacity to laugh good-naturedly at themselves, and at the absurdity of some of our human predicaments.

So laughter is a gift of the Holy Spirit, promised to those of us who open up to weeping—to weeping in His light, according to His truth. These are not tears of self-pity, resentment, or bitterness. In His grace we open up to tears of compassion, surrender, acknowledgment of our fragmentation and yearning for "salvation," that is, restoration of our lost wholeness.

Today let me open up to God's gifts, both of God's kind of weeping and God's kind of laughter. Because both of these are God-given channels of release, unlike the traps of anger or resentment. God's kind of weeping and laughter allow me to release things, to let them go in His way. *"Blessed are you who weep now,"* He says to me today, *"for you will laugh."*

AUGUST 3

MUNDANE TRIVIALITIES

"Diligent hands will rule, but laziness ends in forced labor." (Prov 12:24)

A large part of my "spiritual" journey, of my journey to freedom, in God's light, consists of facing the challenges of my everyday responsibilities "diligently." I can easily slip into excluding these responsibilities, like opening the mail and filling out necessary forms, from my "spiritual" obligations, as if my work-responsibilities were mundane trivialities. But a life in Christ is not one of "forced labor," whatever it is I happen to be doing.

I remind myself today that my Lord calls me, and indeed empowers me, to the freedom to do what I should be doing, because I want to do it. His "will" for me is most clearly expressed in my immediate responsibilities, however unpleasant they may seem. So let me embrace His will and continue my cross-carrying journey today, doing the next right thing in Him and with Him, Who liberates me from the "forced labor" that comes from laziness. *"Whatever you do, work at it with all your heart, as working for the Lord, not for human masters."* (Col 3:23)

AUGUST 4

TAKING ACTION

"Direct my footsteps according to your word; let no iniquity rule over me." (Ps 118/119: 133)

Indeed, it's all about taking actual "footsteps," even if they're small and awkward. It's not just about knowing the "word."

I'm reminded of this simple truth today, and ask God to help me take action, albeit slowly and insecurely. I ask Him to liberate me from the bondage of inactivity, and all the anxiety that comes from it. Because, as I read somewhere, true freedom is "doing what one ought to do, because one wants to do it." Today let me be open to asking for help, from God and others who can help me in my responsibilities, so that, "no iniquity rule over me." God is willing to help me, like He helps the early flowers come out from under the snow, when I can't help myself to come out and do the next right thing.

AUGUST 5

ARROGANCE BLINDS

"He also told them a parable: 'Can a blind man lead a blind man? Will they not both fall into a pit? A disciple is not above his teacher, but everyone when he is fully trained will be like his teacher. Why do you see the speck that is in your brother's eye, but do not notice the log that is in your own eye?..." (Lk 6:39-41)

If I attempt to help a newcomer to the faith, but am myself infected with arrogance, that is, self-seeking ("arrogance" comes from the Latin "arrogare," which literally means "to claim for oneself"), we both "fall into a pit." And that's not a pleasant place to be, particularly for two self-seeking people. We both end up pointing out each other's "specks," rather than doing anything constructive.

Today I am reminded that ministry to others on the path of salvation is ineffective or even damaging, if the "minister" has neglected to minister to his or her own self. Because service to others on this path is about sharing a lived experience, rather than teaching a set of abstract principles. Today let me take up my cross, once again, and tend to "the log" that is in my own eye, so that, if necessary, I can share the experience with someone else in the same predicament.

AUGUST 6

ONE SOURCE OF LIGHT, MANY CHANNELS

"You were transfigured on the mountain, O Christ God, / revealing Your glory to Your disciples as far as they could bear it. / Let Your everlasting Light also shine upon us sinners, / through the prayers of the Theotokos. / O Giver of Light, glory to You!" (Troparion or main hymn of the Feast of Transfiguration)

In this hymn of the great feast of Transfiguration, celebrated today by those of us on the Old(er) Calendar, Christ is mentioned as the Giver of Light. As One of the Holy Trinity, He is the one Source of Light, and of all that is good.

Others are also mentioned in this hymn, who are channels, though not sources, of His light:
1. The disciples (Peter, James, and John), who were with Him on the mountain, and received the grace of God's uncreated energies, "as far as they could bear it," when they were manifested in His unexpected and glorious Transfiguration;
2. "We sinners" are mentioned, as we also become recipients of God's grace, with the help of those who were vessels of His Light before us, most notably,
3. The Theotokos, upon Whom the Holy Spirit descended in a unique way, well before He shared His energies with anyone else.

So the feast of Transfiguration celebrates our mystical unity in the Body of Christ, which is realized in the sharing and passing on of grace, of which He is the One Source. His light is received in different ways by each of the members of the Body of Christ, "as far as they can bear it." Today I humbly ask that I not be left out, by the incessant prayers of the Theotokos. And I send up glory to the One who makes us all channels of His light, through one another. *"O Giver of Light, glory to You!"*

AUGUST 7

HUMILITY GETS A SEAT AT HIS TABLE

"Simon Peter said to them, 'I am going fishing.' They said to him, 'We will go with you.' They went out and got into the boat, but that night they caught nothing. Just after daybreak, Jesus stood on the beach; but the disciples did not know that it was Jesus. Jesus said to them, 'Children, you have no fish, have you?' They answered him, 'No.' He said to them, 'Cast the net to the right side of the boat, and you will find some.' So they cast it, and now they were not able to haul it in because there were so many fish. That disciple whom Jesus loved said to Peter, 'It is the Lord!' When Simon Peter heard that it was the Lord, he put on some clothes, for he was naked, and jumped into the sea. But the other disciples came in the boat, dragging the net full of fish, for they were not far from the land, only about a hundred yards off. When they had gone ashore, they saw a charcoal fire there, with fish on it, and bread..." (Jn 21:3-9)

Peter has come a long way since his very first encounter with Christ, roughly three years before the incident described above. At that first encounter three years earlier, when the Lord similarly revealed Himself through a miraculous catch of fish, Peter's reaction was fear: "Go away from me, Lord," he said to Jesus, "for I am a sinful man!" (Lk 5:8) To Peter's way of thinking, back then, his own sinfulness meant he needed to distance himself from the Lord.

But now, three years later, Peter's reaction to the presence of Christ is very different: he literally jumps to greet Him. And this is not because Peter is any less aware of his own sinfulness. On the contrary, he had just recently thrice denied Christ and was, at this point, a lapsed Apostle. Having "wept bitterly" over his lapse, Peter is broken; he is more aware than ever that he is "a sinful man." And yet he no longer seeks to distance himself from the Lord because of this, because after three years at Christ's side, Peter knows that the Lord is particularly open to the repentant sinner: "I have not come to call the righteous," He says, "but sinners to repentance" (Lk 5:32). So Peter now brings humble self-knowledge to the table, rather than isolating himself in self-centered fear.

Today, when Christ calls me to "Come and eat," let me not hesitate nor self-isolate in fear. Let me hasten, in humble self-knowledge, to His table, because He did and does, indeed, "eat with tax-collectors and sinners." (Mt 9:11)

AUGUST 8

BUILDING ON ROCK

"I will show you what someone is like who comes to me, hears my words, and acts on them. That one is like a man building a house, who dug deeply and laid the foundation on rock; when a flood arose, the river burst against that house but could not shake it, because it had been well built. But the one who hears and does not act is like a man who built a house on the ground without a foundation. When the river burst against it, immediately it fell, and great was the ruin of that house." (Lk 6:47-49)

Do I just "hear" His words, as I did yesterday morning in church, and then go about my business from Monday to Saturday, as if everything in my life depended on my own words, my own will, and my own "lights"? Yes, sometimes I do slip into self-reliance, and dependency on human word and opinion. And this God-less attitude, sometimes very subtle, can bring horrible disappointment. "Great is the ruin of that house."

But building in God, with God, and in the light of His word, letting it be "dug deeply" into my heart, gives my "house" stability. A conscious, daily contact with God, when I open up to Him in prayer and attentiveness to His word, removes the "sting" both from the ups and the downs of ever-changing life-situations. Today let me hand over any financial difficulties, professional frustrations, personal relationships, and inner challenges into God's hands, shedding His gentle light on them. *"For I am convinced that neither death, nor life, nor angels, nor rulers, nor things present, nor things to come, nor powers, nor height, nor depth, nor anything else in all creation, will be able to separate us from the love of God in Christ Jesus our Lord."* (Rom 8:38-39)

AUGUST 9

LETTING IN THE NEW

"He entered again into a synagogue; and a man was there whose hand was withered. They were watching him to see if he would heal him on the Sabbath, so that they might accuse him. He said to the man with the withered hand, 'Get up and come forward!' And he said to them, 'Is it lawful to do good or to do harm on the Sabbath, to save a life or to kill?' But they kept silent. After looking around at them with anger, grieved at their hardness of heart, he said to the man, 'Stretch out your hand.' And he stretched it out, and his hand was restored. The Pharisees went out and immediately began conspiring with the Herodians against him, as to how they might destroy him." (Mk 3:1-6)

Hell hath no fury, I would say, like the rage of a Pharisee against the new. Because a self-righteous person treasures his/her old self, and hell is incapable of offering anything new. But the Good News of my Lord brings unexpected paradoxes, like the liberating fact that a loss of the old self is a condition for finding a new one, in Him.

Today let me not fear Christ entering into my "synagogue" and stirring things up a bit. Let me let Him detach me from my old patterns, which may have me going around in circles, in self-reliance. Christ sheds new light on my darkness, offering change where I might prefer self-affirmation. Paradoxically, He makes strength arise out of my weakness, when I am willing to admit it.

AUGUST 10

THE WORD OF THE CROSS

"For Christ did not send me to baptize but to proclaim the gospel, and not with eloquent wisdom, so that the cross of Christ might not be emptied of its power. For the word of the cross is foolishness to those who are perishing, but to us who are being saved it is the power of God." (1 Cor 1:17-18)

St. Paul had received an excellent education, and possessed much "eloquent wisdom." But when he encountered Christ on the road to Damascus, Paul was first made entirely blind. In the process of "being saved," he had to first lose the capacity to see as he previously had, merely on the basis of man-made wisdom, in order to embrace Christ, the strength and Wisdom of God. This new Wisdom centered on "the word of the cross," which turns many world-wisely assumptions upside-down. St. Paul was able to embrace this word, and to "see" in a new way, precisely because he stepped onto the path of "being saved," having left the path on which he was "perishing."

Today I note to myself that both these roads, of "salvation" or "perishing" are a life-long process, and a choice I make on a daily basis. The process called "salvation" has a two-fold meaning:
1. Being healed or made whole (through communion with God and acceptance of His gifts); and
2. Being made safe, being "recovered" (from a danger, which is sin, i.e. the misdirection of my will).

And "perishing" means the opposite of all that; it's the rejection of and separation from God's healing communion, and ultimately means being "lost" to God, to self, and others.

Which road will it be today? That depends, as the Apostle reminds me, on my attitude toward "the word of the cross." Let me take it up today, and carry it with His power; with the meekness of the Lamb who was led.

AUGUST 11

PRINCIPLES vs. PERSONALITIES

"Then Jesus said to the crowds and to his disciples, 'The scribes and the Pharisees sit on Moses' seat; therefore, do whatever they teach you and follow it; but do not do as they do, for they do not practice what they teach. They tie up heavy burdens, hard to bear, and lay them on the shoulders of others; but they themselves are unwilling to lift a finger to move them. They do all their deeds to be seen by others; for they make their phylacteries broad and their fringes long. They love to have the place of honor at banquets..." (Mt 23:1-6)

The Lord reminds me here to regard the teaching, the principles, taught by legitimate teachers of the Law of God, regardless of their behavior or personalities. Jesus is not silent about the defects of the scribes and Pharisees, but He points out their legitimate authority, because they "sit," as He says, "on Moses' seat," and He commands that the people "do whatever they teach."

It is a common phenomenon, I think, of any institution that involves human beings, including the Church, that its leaders and teachers sometimes inspire criticism rather than admiration. But Christ puts my mind to rest on this account, because He lets me know He is well aware of it. In other words, God allows for this humbling reality, of His teaching being passed on—not by angels—but by those who, like me, are often far from perfect. Just as, time and again, He allows imperfect human beings to become parents.

So we are raised and taught by other human beings, imperfect as we are, throughout life, learning from one another nonetheless. Today I am grateful to Him for this humbling reality, that He has such faith in us, despite our imperfections.

AUGUST 12

HIS ENDURING PRESENCE

"Then the eleven disciples (μαθηταὶ) went away into Galilee, to the mountain which Jesus had appointed for them. When they saw him, they worshiped him; but some doubted. And Jesus came and spoke to them, saying, 'All authority has been given to me in heaven and on earth. Go and make disciples (μαθητεύσατε) of all the nations, baptizing them in the name of the Father and of the Son and of the Holy Spirit, teaching them to observe all things that I have commanded you; and lo, I am with you always, even to the end of the age.' Amen." (Mt 28:16-20)

So the risen Lord commands His "disciples" (μαθηταὶ) to go and "make disciples" (μαθητεύσατε) of "all the nations." And this is to be accomplished, He says, through two things:
1. Baptism, and, equally importantly,
2. Teaching.

The disciples weren't only to baptize, to increase the "number" or "percentage" of church-members, no. They were to "make disciples," new "learners" and followers and spreaders of His word, similar to themselves. Christ is describing the remarkable and difficult enterprise that was to become His Church.

And in this specific context, of the difficult mission of the Church, the Lord speaks of His own exclusive authority and presence as nowhere else. I find this extremely comforting. "All authority," He says here, "has been given to Me in heaven and on earth." And on earth! So—it is with My authority, not your own, that I send you to baptize and teach.

And finally, in perhaps the most comforting passage of the whole Gospel, our Lord assures us of His presence among us, on earth as it is in heaven, until the end of time: *"And lo, I am with you always, even to the end of the age."* Today, no matter what the ups and downs of our church-life are, I hear this promise, spoken by the Lord to each of us. And I carry it, like joy-creating sorrow, in my heart.

AUGUST 13

ECCLESIAL CONSUMERISM

"Do nothing from selfishness or empty conceit, but with humility of mind regard one another as more important than yourselves; do not merely look out for your own personal interests, but also for the interests of others." (Php 2:3-4)

I looked at these words this morning, and immediately thought, "Ouch!" Because the Apostle is speaking to a Church-community, within which there was, apparently, a tendency "merely to look out for one's own personal interests." This admonishment stares out at me today, as part of Holy Scripture, speaking to me most specifically about my behaviour within the context of Church.

So let me review my general attitude toward "others" in church. Do I ask myself what "I" can "get out of" church-participation? Or do I ask myself, What can I give? And let me remind myself of the "sacrificial" aspect of the Eucharist (from *sacer* and *facio*, "to make holy") that involves not only the Self-Giving of God, but the self-giving of us, to one another and to Him, that He may in His turn "give us back" to ourselves, transfigured and holy.

Today let me not be an ecclesial "consumer," but a self-giver within the harmony of the Body of Christ. *"Let us love one another that with one mind we may confess: Father, Son, and Holy Spirit, Trinity one in essence and inseparable."* (Byzantine Divine Liturgy)

AUGUST 14

CRYING OUT TOGETHER

"Now as they went out of Jericho, a great multitude followed him. And behold, two blind men sitting by the road, when they heard that Jesus was passing by, cried out, saying, 'Have mercy on us, O Lord, Son of David!' Then the multitude warned them that they should be quiet; but they cried out all the more, saying, 'Have mercy on us, O Lord, Son of David!' So Jesus stood still and called them, and said, 'What do you want me to do for you?' They said to him, 'Lord, that our eyes may be opened.' So Jesus had compassion and touched their eyes. And immediately their eyes received sight, and they followed him." (Mt 20:29-34)

In the Gospel of Matthew there is not one, but two blind men sitting by the road; two people with the same problem, sticking together and also crying out to the Lord together, seeking help. While the crowd tries to quiet the two men, treating them as something of an embarrassment, they catch the Lord's attention. He has compassion and heals them, and they follow Him.

The blind men show both humility and courage, together earnestly seeking help from the Lord. They remind me of the well-known fact that, in any trial or ailment, be it physical or spiritual, it is helpful and wise to seek the fellowship of others in a similar situation, rather than to self-isolate; and to unite with these others in prayer.

More generally, however, this reading reminds me of what any earnest prayer looks like, whether it's communal or private. In prayer, we always recognize our human "blindness," because we are all blind without the Lord's healing touch. So I ask for His mercy today, that my eyes may be opened, and I may follow Him. Because we don't follow Him in blindness.

AUGUST 15

A MYSTIFYING BEAUTY

"In giving birth you preserved your virginity, / In falling asleep you did not forsake the world, O Theotokos. / You were translated to life, O Mother of Life, / And by your prayers, you deliver our souls from death." (Troparion or main hymn of the Feast of the Dormition or repose of the Most-Holy Theotokos)

Beauty is always something of a mystery; it defies understanding. And so it is with the inimitable beauty of Mary, the Most Holy Mother of God: She presents me with a bundle of contradictions. In motherhood She maintains virginity; in Her departure She remains present; in Her death She reveals life. And in Her humility She attains glory in all generations—an antinomy She Herself pointed out, exclaiming, *"For He has regarded the humility of His servant; For behold, henceforth all generations will call me blessed."* (Lk 1:48) Also, based on the lives of many saints, She, the Most Pure of all creation, readily offers Her intercession for the least pure, for the greatest of sinners.

Quite frankly I am at a loss for words, contemplating these beautiful antinomies, brought together in the Blessed among Women. All I can say today is Thank you, to the Mother of God. I thank Her for Her quiet, grace-filled, unconditionally-loving, and beautiful presence in my chaotic life. I don't know what it is, with Her and great sinners, because it defies my understanding. But today I thank Her for it. I thank Her, the Heavenly Door, for always keeping Her door open to me, when all other doors seem closed. *"Hail, Mary, Full of Grace! The Lord is with You."*

AUGUST 16

DOES DOGMA MATTER?

"Glory to the Holy, Consubstantial, Life-giving and Undivided Trinity, now and ever, and unto the ages of ages." (Beginning Doxology, Byzantine Great Vespers)

Does it "matter" whether we embrace specific truths about God, revealed, experienced, and witnessed to in Tradition? Well, not necessarily. If I have no contact with God, His Three-Personal life doesn't "matter" in my life. But if I do step into conscious contact with Him, it matters more than anything else in the world. As C. S. Lewis writes, "The whole dance, or drama, or pattern of this three-Personal life is to be played out in each one of us: or (putting it the other way round) each one of us has got to enter that pattern, take his place in that dance."

Indeed, the "life-giving" qualities of the "undivided" and "consubstantial" Trinity do, so to say, "rub off" on us, most profoundly in the coming of the Son into our history, and walking among us, through our journey, even unto our death, and down into our hell. He joins us in all of that, in order to bring us out, with Him and in Him, into new life. He can do that, and does do that, specifically because He is "consubstantial" and "undivided" with the Father and the Holy Spirit. I can step into this exciting "drama" today, and join Him in a bit of heartfelt prayer, letting His "life-giving" grace into my life. Or I can remain apart, going around in meaningless circles of "whatever," where nothing really "matters." Let me choose God today, as He chose me. Because He is where it's all happening, amidst my work, my immediate responsibilities, and my relationships, in His life-giving "now."

AUGUST 17

MEETING CHRIST

"And it had been revealed to (Simeon) by the Holy Spirit that he would not see death before he had seen the Lord's Christ. So he came by the Spirit into the temple..." (Lk 2:26-27)

St. Simeon, who meets Christ at the temple and rejoices at seeing Him, when the Lord was brought there on the fortieth day after His birth, comes into the temple "by the Spirit."

There is a simple message for me here. And that is, any "meeting of Christ" and "seeing Christ" occurs "by the Spirit." This includes my daily life in Christ, as well as liturgical life—going to church. I remind myself today that my actions alone, devoid of the divine energies of the Holy Spirit, cannot bring me to truly "meet" and "see" Christ. This is why church-services and other forms of piety can easily become burdensome and boring, when I lose the humble awareness of my need to act, pray, seek and come, "by the Spirit." Today I humbly ask Him, the Giver of Life, to breathe life into my prayer, and to help me "see," by His grace.

AUGUST 18

EMPTY PRIDE

"He has scattered the proud in the thoughts of their hearts. He has brought down the powerful from their thrones, and lifted up the humble; he has filled the hungry with good things, and sent the rich away empty." (Words spoken by the Mother of God, Lk 1:51-53)

These words, spoken with great joy by Mary, the Mother of God, remind me today of the effects that pride and, conversely, humility, have on my heart and my life. When my heart ventures over to prideful self-reliance, (sometimes very subtly) disregarding God's presence, I remain alone with the chaos of my own thoughts and ambitions, which, without the guidance of His grace, equal emptiness. My thoughts become "scattered," because they have lost their focus.

Humility, on the other hand, gently reminds me of my insufficiency without God, and brings me to ask for help. I recognize my hunger for the "good things," and that they come not from inside me, but from God.

Today I ask Her who is Full of Grace, the Mother of God, for guidance in humility, that I not be left alone and empty.

AUGUST 19

WALKING IN HIS LIGHT

"For we did not follow cleverly devised myths when we made known to you the power and coming of our Lord Jesus Christ, but we had been eyewitnesses of his majesty. For he received honor and glory from God the Father when that voice was conveyed to him by the Majestic Glory, saying, 'This is my Son, my Beloved, with whom I am well pleased.' We ourselves heard this voice come from heaven, while we were with him on the holy mountain." (2 Pet 1:16-18)

Our faith is not based on some abstract "system" of moral values, nor on some abstract ideology, devised by the Apostles. It is rather based on the historical, eye-witness experience of God's revelation of Himself to these Apostles, like the experience of the Transfiguration, witnessed by the Apostles Peter, James, and John, on the mountain. It is the experience of the "majestic glory," of the glory of the divine, uncreated energies of the Holy Spirit—of grace, simply put, in the life of the believer. This experience is passed on and lived on, from generation to generation of believers, walking in His light.

I should not be quick to dismiss this elevated teaching on the "majestic glory" of grace, as if it is closed to me, a sinner. Because in his second Epistle the Apostle Peter makes it "known" to all of us, this "power and coming of our Lord Jesus Christ"; I know that all of the Scriptures, including this second Epistle of Peter, are written for all of us. And I know that, inexplicably, the "majestic glory" of grace somehow carries me through life, despite my "unworthiness."

So today I will carry with me the grace-filled words of the Apostle Peter, written for me. And let me hear with him the voice of God, calling to me to dispel my fears and hesitations, and rely on the energies sent to me through His Son. Because God calls me to walk in His light, when He proclaims, *"This is My Son, My beloved, with Whom I am well pleased."*

AUGUST 20

BACK TO BASICS

"Now I remind you, brothers and sisters, of the good news that I proclaimed to you, which you in turn received, in which also you stand, through which also you are being saved, if you hold firmly to the message that I proclaimed to you—unless you have come to believe in vain. For I handed on to you as of first importance what I in turn had received: that Christ died for our sins in accordance with the scriptures, and that he was buried, and that he was raised on the third day in accordance with the scriptures, and that he appeared to Cephas, then to the twelve. Then he appeared to more than five hundred brothers and sisters at one time, most of whom are still alive, though some have died..." (1 Cor 15:1-6)

In this passage the Apostle reminds the Corinthians of the basics of our faith, because some in the community had become distracted by other issues and philosophies, which distorted the basic vision initially passed on to them. This vision was not based on argument, skillfully crafted at the desk of some philosopher, nor of course at the keyboard of some blogger, but on the lived experience of human witnesses: *That Christ died for our sins in accordance with the scriptures, and that He was buried, and that He was raised on the third day in accordance with the scriptures*, and was then seen by many witnesses.

Today I am reminded of this simple fact, that my faith is about lived experience; of Christ's life-giving Cross and Resurrection, with all its consequences. My faith is not about arguments that begin and end in my mind, but about my daily partaking of the grace-filled journey of the Cross, lovingly guided by the light of the Resurrection.

Let me continue this experience today, remembering with gratitude that it is passed on to me by many others, who lived it before. They lived it and shared it in Christ, Who is, indeed, risen!

AUGUST 21

SELF-CENTEREDNESS BLINDS

"And the crowd came together again, so that they could not even eat. When his family (ο ἱ παρ ' αὐτοῦ) heard it, they went out to restrain him, for people were saying, 'He has gone out of his mind.' And the scribes who came down from Jerusalem said, 'He has Beelzebul, and by the ruler of the demons he casts out demons.' And he called them to him, and spoke to them in parables, 'How can Satan cast out Satan?...'" (Mk 3:20-23)

So when Jesus was preaching, healing, and attracting crowds of people wherever He went, both His family and the religious leaders of the time, the scribes and Pharisees, wanted Him to stop. His relatives were worried about what people were saying that "He has gone out of His mind,"—so they were concerned about their family's reputation. In the case of the religious leaders, the concern was their own authority, which was being overshadowed by this new Teacher. They were envious and fearful of a disruption of the status quo, so they try to discredit Him by casting doubt on His spirituality: *"By the ruler of the demons He casts out demons,"* they say, and of course the Lord easily disproves this illogical accusation.

Both the family and the religious leaders, then, were motivated by self-centered concerns. Their self-centeredness made them blind to the Person before them, Jesus Christ, and to His gifts. To them He was merely an obstacle to their own wants and perceived needs.

Today I am reminded to be attentive to other people's gifts, and to celebrate them, with gratitude. Let me be helpful and encouraging, when I can, rather than pull others down. Because Christ works in our midst through other people, sometimes in ways that are unexpected or even disagreeable to me. Let me take a step back today, if I find myself annoyed or envious or disturbed by someone else's journey, and praise God for unfolding the gifts of His Spirit in every unique person in my surroundings.

AUGUST 22

JESUS BULLIED

"Then the soldiers of the governor took Jesus into the governor's headquarters, and they gathered the whole cohort around him. They stripped him and put a scarlet robe on him, and after twisting some thorns into a crown, they put it on his head. They put a reed in his right hand and knelt before him and mocked him, saying, 'Hail, King of the Jews!' They spat on him, and took the reed and struck him on the head. After mocking him, they stripped him of the robe and put his own clothes on him. Then they led him away to crucify him." (Mt 27:27-31)

Right after Pilate makes his final decision, "handing over" Jesus to be crucified (Mt 27:26), the Roman soldiers do not immediately proceed to the task at hand. No, they take "time out" for this horrible, sadistic, and even ritualized scene of… bullying. Tragically, this scene plays out every day in our school courtyards. This "need" to take time out and hurt another, to mock another, is also on display in the internet, in the pointless yet very hurtful comments certain people take the time to make.

So this, too, was absorbed and carried by my Lord, in His life-giving journey of the Cross. He let Himself be undressed, "stripped," then dressed and undressed again, by bullies. And He walks through it all; He descends into our darkness, even unto our death and our hell, in order to bring it out, in His resurrected Body. He says, Look, you have shamed Me, you have stripped Me, you have bullied Me, and yet I have come back to you in light and peace. Now stop doing it to yourselves. I have nailed your frustrations, your anger, your self-loathing, and your bullying to the cross. Let all of us, the bullies and the bullied, take pause, and hear Him today, saying, *"Come to me, all you that are weary and are burdened, and I will give you rest. Take my yoke upon you, and learn from me; for I am gentle and humble in heart, and you will find rest for your souls."* (Mt 11:28-29)

AUGUST 23

COURAGE

"Near the cross of Jesus stood his mother, his mother's sister, Mary the wife of Clopas, and Mary Magdalene." (Jn 19:25)

These women, along with John, the beloved disciple of Christ, famously remained near Christ as He suffered and died on the cross. In doing so, these women and this disciple demonstrated not only the virtues of love and loyalty, but also courage. It took courage not to fall to pieces when the death of their beloved Teacher was imminent. And this courage was demonstrated not by blaming anyone or fighting back, as Peter did when he cut off the ear of the high priest's servant at Christ's arrest (Jn 18:10); Courage was rather demonstrated by simply being there, next to Him, until He died.

I am reminded today that when I face some trial or loss, like the loss of a loved one, I ask God for courage. And that means, simply, being there; being present to the circumstances and people involved. Let me be present, as I ask God for the courage to accept the things I cannot, and need not, change. Through these things He brings about change in me and others; He leads us, through the courage of the cross, to embrace the transforming light of the Resurrection.

AUGUST 24

YOU GIVE THEM TO EAT

"The day was drawing to a close, and the twelve came to him and said, 'Send the crowd away, so that they may go into the surrounding villages and countryside, to lodge and get provisions; for we are here in a deserted place.' But he said to them, 'You give them to eat.'" (Lk 9:12-13)

In this well-known incident, the Lord does not say to the disciples, "I will give them to eat." No, He says—you do it. "You give them to eat." And of course the disciples are puzzled, because they have among them "no more than five loaves and two fish," and the crowd was huge, "about five thousand men." (Lk 9:13-14)

This continues to be puzzling today, that indeed our Lord chooses to nurture us, to offer us His "food," through one another. This is true both in the case of sacramental Communion, which I receive from the hand of a priest, and in other cases on a daily basis, when I learn and grow from the actions, service, and words of other people. It is also true that I, too, can be nurturing to others, when I do not resist His call, "You give them to eat," despite the dearth of provisions in my here and now, "in a deserted place."

Today let me go and partake of the Lord's Bread, which He gives me by the hands of others. And let me be open to sharing His gifts. Because He calls all of us to be transfigured, from self-seekers and consumers, to self-givers and nurturers in Him, in our "deserted place."

AUGUST 25

A DAILY DECISION

"Then he said to them all, 'If any want to become my followers, let them deny themselves and take up their cross daily (καθ'ἡμέραν) and follow me. For those who want to save their life will lose it, and those who lose their life for my sake will save it.'" (Lk 9:23-24)

The word(s) "daily" (καθ'ἡμέραν) in Christ's commandment to "all," to take up their cross, did not enter the "textus receptus" of the Gospel, but they are abundantly attested in the most ancient manuscripts of Scripture. So my decision to take up my cross, to follow Him, and to "lose" myself, to give myself away, for His sake, is to be renewed on a daily basis.

I find this "daily" approach to cross-carrying very refreshing, very encouraging. Because God knows it would not suffice, under the ever-changing circumstances of human existence, to make this decision to take up the cross just once, or to make it only on Sundays. No, He invites me to take it up again today, on Monday, and start anew.

So let me "lose" myself again today, letting go of any neediness or self-seeking that may have crept into my heart and behaviour. Let me follow Him again, in His Self-giving, which "saves" my life, bringing me growth. The path of the cross takes me out of the stagnation and vicious circles of self-centeredness, bringing the quiet rewards of new life in Him.

AUGUST 26

BURDENS HARD TO BEAR

"But he (Jesus) said, "And woe unto you, experts in the law! For you weigh people down with burdens hard to bear, while you yourselves will not even touch the burdens with one of your fingers." (Lk 11. 46)

So, alongside the "cross" every Christian has to bear, there are also the "burdens hard to bear," with which we can and do weigh one another down. I am thinking about this because just this morning I received a very eloquent message from an Orthodox man, describing to me the proper place of women in the Church, according to his, no doubt about it, expert command of "the norms of the Church."

May the Lord give me His strength, His willingness, and His wisdom today, to carry also the burdens placed readily upon us by "experts in the law."

AUGUST 27

GOOD GRIEF

"For godly grief produces a repentance that leads to salvation and brings no regret, but worldly grief produces death. For see what earnestness this godly grief has produced in you, what eagerness to clear yourselves, what indignation, what alarm, what longing..." (2 Cor 7:10-11)

Christianity is neither optimistic nor pessimistic, nor is it neutral. And that is so because it is true; it is life, based on the true story of God's free choice to die for His creation, and our free choice either to rise or fall. Hence a life in Christ is not some predictable pattern, like a philosophy. "It is not a philosophy," as G. K. Chesterton writes, "because, being a vision, it is not a pattern but a picture." And this picture is one of a hopeful, yet no less earnest struggle, of the Church Militant, with its joys and its sorrows.

The Apostle reminds me today of "godly grief" that produces repentance. It is quite different from the crushing despair of "worldly grief" that produces death. I need not banish "godly grief," because it is a gift. It is a feeling of discomfort that moves me to action, to change my focus and return home. This dynamic is one that gives me life; it is one that instills in me a longing, a desire to move forward. Let me be attentive to this gift today, and embrace my desire to grow in Him.

AUGUST 28

HER LIFE-GIVING CROSS

"I will take the cup of salvation, and call on the name of the Lord." (Ps 115:4 / Ps 116:13)

This Psalm-verse functions as the "Communion Verse" for all Byzantine feasts in honor of the Mother of God, including the feast of the Dormition (or repose) of Mary, the Most-Holy Virgin and Mother of God, celebrated today by those of us on the Old(er) Calendar. Why? And I don't mean "why" the Old(er) Calendar, although that is a good question, ☺ but why this verse for all Marian feasts?

The Mother of God is being praised for the "cup" of the cross, of which He prayed on that night in Gethsemane, that it be taken from Him, if possible (Mt 26:39). She co-carried the cross, with Her Divine Son, to an extent greater than any other Christian, than any other co-carrier of His cross, ever. This is why, on the Byzantine feast of Her Dormition, we also have the Epistle-reading from Philippians 2:5-9, which calls us to remember His cross and have the "mind" of the Cross: *"Let this mind be in you which was also in Christ Jesus... He humbled Himself and became obedient to the point of death, even the death of the cross"* (Phil 2:8). The Mother of God had this cross-carrying "mind," in Her Christ-loving and hence Christ-like journey.

Thus Her death, like Her life, is Christ-like, in that She conquers death. The tomb could not hold Her, just as it could not hold Her Son. *"For being the Mother of Life,"* it says in the Kontakion-Hymn of this feast, *"She was translated to life."*

Today, as we celebrate the mystery of the Mother of Life, accompanying Her in Her repose-but-not-departure, let me ask for Her help and guidance on my cross-carrying journey, to which all of us are called: *"Let this mind be in you,"* the Apostle says to me, *"which was also in Christ Jesus."* As it was also in Her, Full of Grace, I ask for Her help, whenever *"my lamp is going out."* (Mt 25:8)

AUGUST 29

THE "RIGHT" THING ISN'T ALWAYS RIGHT

"When (King Herod's) daughter Herodias came in and danced, she pleased Herod and his guests; and the king said to the girl, 'Ask me for whatever you wish, and I will give it.' And he solemnly swore to her, 'Whatever you ask me, I will give you, even half of my kingdom.' She went out and said to her mother, 'What should I ask for?' She replied, 'The head of John the Baptist.' Immediately she rushed back to the king and requested, 'I want you to give me at once the head of John the Baptist on a platter.' The king was deeply grieved; yet out of regard for his oaths and for the guests, he did not want to refuse her. Immediately the king sent a soldier of the guard with orders to bring John's head. He went and beheaded him in the prison, brought his head on a platter, and gave it to the girl. Then the girl gave it to her mother." (Mk 6:22-28)

This is a story of two people, Herod and his daughter Herodias, doing the "right" thing, according to the moral and political correctness of their circumstances. Herod, on the one hand, has sworn very publicly to his daughter to grant whatever she wishes. So then, although the king is "deeply grieved" by her request, he feels obliged to grant it "out of regard for his oaths and for the guests." He would lose face both in front of his political subjects and his family, were he to go back on his word. His daughter, on the other hand, acts out of her unhealthy dependency on her insane mother: She runs to ask her mother what to ask for, and then eagerly "rushes back" to ask for the head of John the Baptist. In her eagerness to please her mother, Herodias even throws in the chilling detail, "on a platter." And yet this young woman, in a sense, is doing the "right" thing, according to a daughter's obedience to her mother.

But the "right" thing to do, in the eyes of society and family, is not always the right thing to do. Because the truth of God's Kingdom is not always evident or popular, neither to our society or our family. There might be commitments or relationships that we entered, for example, before we embraced faith, or when we were ill-advised or simply unwise—which God is now leading us to drop.

Today I pray for guidance, in His Spirit, to discern between what is truly right in His eyes, and what is just "the right thing to do," to please other people. I pray for the freedom to do His will, and to have the eyes to see His truth, because it is His truth that sets me free.

AUGUST 30

DEALING WITH REJECTION

"For my father and my mother have forsaken me, but the Lord has taken me in." (Ps 26/ 27:12)

The Psalms give expression to practically every human experience and emotion, from immense gratitude and joy, to the most difficult kinds of pain, like the one expressed here: Rejection.

Rejection can be an emotional wound from childhood, as the Psalmist mentions above, or it can come at other times in life, in smaller or greater doses: Being fired from a job, being turned down for a job or school of our choice, or being dumped by the person we love, or betrayed by a spouse, or not making the team, or generally not being accepted for who we are, etc.

Rejection can damage my life as few other things can, if I don't hand it over to God's unchanging love and light, as the Psalmist does above, in prayer. The wound of rejection, when left unhealed, can lead to all sorts of distortions in our journey: For example, unforgiveness, jealousy, self-pity. It can lead us to rebel, or to fabricate a personality, just to be accepted. Or, conversely, to reject everyone and anyone, just so we're not the first to be rejected. We may have the need always to be right, and become unable to accept constructive criticism, because of this inner insecurity.

In any event, today the Scriptures remind me that I am not alone in the very common human experience of rejection. Men and women of faith have cried out to the Lord in a similar experience, throughout the centuries, and He has not failed to be there, and to heal their wounds in His unchanging love and grace. Christ Himself was no stranger to this experience, after all, because *"He came unto His own, and His own received Him not."* (Jn 1:11) So let me remember today, if I deal with any rejection, great or small, that I find myself in quite illustrious company. Let me hand it over to Him, in prayer, shedding His healing light on an age-old matter.

AUGUST 31

A PUZZLING MASTER

"John answered, 'Master, we saw someone casting out demons in your name, and we tried to stop him, because he does not follow with us.' But Jesus said to him, 'Do not stop him; for whoever is not against you is for you.'" (Lk 9:49-50)

The "offense" felt by the disciples in this passage is not against the authority of our Lord, but against the authority of the disciples. They, apparently, had begun to misunderstand their authority as exclusive; that they, exclusively, were given the power of His name. But the Lord had also given this power to "someone" outside the chosen circle of disciples, for reasons He does not explain. He simply says, in no uncertain terms, "Do not stop him." And relax, because he is not against you.

How uncomfortable, how frustrating, is this passage for those of us embracing a "black and white" ecclesiology; for those of us who imagine that we can "master" the great mystery of the charismatic boundaries of "ecclesial reality." No, Jesus reminds me today, He alone is Master and Lord of all power and powers wielded in His name. And sometimes He puzzles and humbles us, by showering these powers on those who "do not follow with us." To Him I ascribe all glory and power today, to Him Who puzzles and humbles me, just when I think I have it all figured out.

SEPTEMBER 1

FIRST OF ALL, PRAY

"First of all, then, I urge that supplications, prayers, intercessions, and thanksgivings be made for everyone, for kings and all who are in authority, so that we may lead a quiet and peaceable life in all godliness and dignity. This is right and is acceptable in the sight of God our Savior, who desires everyone to be saved and to come to the knowledge of the truth." (1 Tim 2:1-4)

Today this is one of the most "counter-cultural" and also most neglected passages in the New Testament. And I mean, neglected by us Christians. It seems we consider it almost obligatory constantly to get angry, speak out, criticize, and discuss those in authority, despite the evident pointlessness of such discussions, which bring us much stress, discomfort, and occasionally disagreements with loved ones. Thus we don't lead a "quiet and peaceable life," as so sanely suggested here.

In any event, I never hear us speaking out and getting angry at the plain fact that we fall short of our primary obligation, to "first of all," as the Apostle stresses, make "supplications, prayers, intercessions, and thanksgivings" (as if "supplications" weren't enough!) for those in power. Yes, there is brief commemoration of civil and church authorities at our church-services, which most of us attend once or twice a week, if at all. But St. Paul is not talking about just that. He is talking also about our daily, private prayer. He believed in the power of daily prayer, as well as daily thanksgiving, for those in authority.

I spent many years neglecting this commandment, because I did not include the names of those in the highest positions of authority, in my country and in my Church, in my daily prayers. Not so long ago, however, after being struck by this passage, I began to include these people, and their immediate family, by name, in my prayers. I feel it subtly changed, and is still changing, my attitude toward the news and politics I read about here and there. I am grateful for the Apostle's reminder today, and begin this September with gratitude for everyone, the powerful and the rest of us. God bless and help and guide us all, under Him.

SEPTEMBER 2

THE RITE OF FORGIVENESS

"When they had finished breakfast, Jesus said to Simon Peter, 'Simon son of John, do you love me more than these?' He said to him, 'Yes, Lord; you know that I love you.' Jesus said to him, 'Feed my lambs.' A second time he said to him, 'Simon son of John, do you love me?' He said to him, 'Yes, Lord; you know that I love you.' Jesus said to him, 'Tend my sheep.' He said to him the third time, 'Simon son of John, do you love me?' Peter felt hurt because he said to him the third time, 'Do you love me?' And he said to him, 'Lord, you know everything; you know that I love you.' Jesus said to him, 'Feed my sheep. Very truly, I tell you, when you were younger, you used to fasten your own belt and to go wherever you wished. But when you grow old, you will stretch out your hands, and someone else will fasten a belt around you and take you where you do not wish to go.' (He said this to indicate the kind of death by which he would glorify God.) After this he said to him, 'Follow me.'" (Jn 21:15-19)

How very human, and humane, is this "rite of forgiveness." I mean, because here the guilty party, a grown man, never explicitly asks for forgiveness. Instead, what happens here is, our Lord cooks breakfast for everyone, including Peter, and then He lets Peter say what Christ knows already, that Peter does, indeed, love Him.

So there's more than one way to forgive, and ask forgiveness. That's all I'm thinking today. And glory be to my Lord's majestic, loving subtlety, because He lets me say I'm sorry, when I really am, in more ways than one.

SEPTEMBER 3

ASKING THE RIGHT QUESTIONS

"When the Pharisees heard that he had silenced the Sadducees, they gathered together, and one of them, a lawyer, asked him a question to test him. 'Teacher, which commandment in the law is the greatest?'" He (Jesus) said to him, 'You shall love the Lord your God with all your heart, and with all your soul, and with all your mind.' This is the greatest and first commandment. And a second is like it: You shall love your neighbor as yourself. On these two commandments hang all the law and the prophets.'" (Mt 22:36-40)

Christ is not "tolerant" with every single question posed to Him by His opponents. Sometimes He replies with a rebuke (Mt 22:29), and sometimes He refuses to reply at all (e.g., Lk 20:3-8).

But in this case, even though the Pharisees are insincere seekers, Jesus replies. Because the question in and of itself is an important one; a central one for those sincerely seeking to do God's will: Most importantly, He says, we are commanded to
     1. Love God;
     2. Love ourselves; and
     3. Love our neighbor.

The rest of God's law is ancillary to these three "loves."

When I take a bit of time today for self-examination, reviewing my actions, words, and thoughts, let me begin by asking myself the right questions, the central questions. These concern my love of God, of myself, and of my neighbor. Any other issues, the Lord reminds me, "hang" on these three.

SEPTEMBER 4

KEPT BY GRACE

"Help us, save us, have mercy on us, and keep us, O God, by Your grace." (Petition from a litany of the Byzantine Liturgy)

This brief text is repeated several times in almost every liturgical service of the Byzantine Rite. It is so simple, and yet so instructive, reminding me of two simple truths:

1. That it is grace by which I receive salvation; by which I receive mercy, and by which I am "kept" going, through all the ups and downs of everyday life. And,
2. This "grace" comes not from inside me, but from God. It is His uncreated energy, which He shares with those in communion with Him. So, we ask for it in prayer.

Today I begin my day with these words in mind, and repeat them often in my heart. I can repeat them often, because God is an energy-source that is never exhausted, never runs out. *"Help us, save us, have mercy on us, and keep us, O God, by Your grace."*

SEPTEMBER 5

A NEW COVENANT

"...you are a letter of Christ, prepared by us, written not with ink but with the Spirit of the living God, not on tablets of stone but on tablets of human hearts. Such is the confidence that we have through Christ toward God. Not that we are competent of ourselves to claim anything as coming from us; our competence is from God, who has made us competent to be ministers of a new covenant, not of letter but of spirit; for the letter kills, but the Spirit gives life." (2 Cor 3:3-6)

St. Paul reminds me here of the new "covenant," that is, the new arrangement between God and us, His people, made possible through Christ, in the Holy Spirit. The Apostle stresses that the Spirit of the "living God," as distinct from lifeless idols, and as distinct from the "letter" of some man-made ethical system or philosophy, is life-giving. The "letter kills" when it is devoid of the Spirit, because it makes external demands for obedience, without providing the power to carry it out. The Spirit "comes and abides in us," effecting inner change of human hearts.

Today I am grateful for this reminder, that I'm called first and foremost to seek communion with Him, in heartfelt prayer, rather than just go through the motions of external piety. It is inner change that is indeed possible and accessible to me, for it is brought about by the Lord, the Holy Spirit; a *"new self,"* created *"to be like God in true righteousness and holiness."* (Eph 4:24)

SEPTEMBER 6

GOING & DOING IN FAITH

"Now the Lord said to Abram, 'Go from your country and your kindred and your father's house to the land that I will show you. I will make of you a great nation, and I will bless you, and make your name great, so that you will be a blessing. I will bless those who bless you, and the one who curses you I will curse; and in you all the families of the earth shall be blessed.' So Abram went, as the Lord had told him; and Lot went with him. Abram was seventy-five years old when he departed from Haran." (Gen 12:1-4)

As it says in Hebrews, Abraham "obeyed and went, even though he did not know where he was going." (Heb 11:8) He leaves the seen for the unseen; the known for the unknown. That's faith. It means letting God do His will in my life, by accepting the responsibilities and people and places to which He has sent me, even though I can't understand, "Why me?"

So, "doing" God's will doesn't mean figuring it out. And faith in Him removes the anxieties of not knowing the "Why," as well as the "What Next." Let me renew my faith today, by re-connecting with God in prayer and re-focusing on Him. The Lord wants to "bless" me, so that I myself "will be a blessing," as He calls me and leads me "to the land" that He "will show me." Let me let Him do that today, as I get up and do the next right thing, in "meek" acceptance of His will. *"Blessed are the meek, for they will inherit the earth."* (Mt 5:5)

SEPTEMBER 7

SATAN THE ACCUSER

"One day the heavenly beings came to present themselves before the Lord, and Satan also came among them. The Lord said to Satan, 'Where have you come from?' Satan answered the Lord, 'From going to and fro on the earth, and from walking up and down on it.' The Lord said to Satan, 'Have you considered my servant Job? There is no one like him on the earth, a blameless and upright man who fears God and turns away from evil.' Then Satan answered the Lord, 'Does Job fear God for nothing? Have you not put a fence around him and his house and all that he has, on every side? You have blessed the work of his hands, and his possessions have increased in the land. But stretch out your hand now, and touch all that he has, and he will curse you to your face.'" (Job 1:6-11)

The name "Satan" means "accuser" or "adversary." God asks Satan whether he, having walked "to and fro on the earth," has noticed the especially good on the earth, namely, His servant Job. But Satan is blind to the good; he is stuck in his diabolical pattern of accusing, slandering, and "turning around" (διάβολος comes from διαβάλλω, to turn or throw over) any good he comes across.

While Satan's distorted "judgment" seeks to drag us down, God's true Justice brings us light, vision, and growth. This truth is revealed with particular clarity in His Son, to Whom the Father hands over all judgment (Jn 5:22). *"I came into this world for judgment,"* says Jesus, *"so that those who do not see may see, and those who do see may become blind."* (Jn 9:39)

Today let me beware of the kind of "judgment," both in the area of self-criticism or with regard to others, which seeks to drag down and stunt growth. Let me rather step into God's light, taking some time for prayer and reading of His word, that I "may see" myself as He sees me, and grow in His Self-giving, cross-carrying love.

SEPTEMBER 8

GOD'S SILENCE

"By Your Nativity, O Most Pure Virgin, Joachim and Anna are freed from the reproach of childlessness (ὀνειδισμοῦ ἀτεκνίας)..." (Kontakion or hymn of the Byzantine feast of the Nativity of the Mother of God)

Saints Joachim and Anna, the parents of the Most Pure Virgin Mary, were reproached and, one could say, "discriminated against," because for most of their marriage they had no children. They earnestly prayed for God to grant them children, yet He remained unresponsive for most of their lives.

Joachim and Anna's community saw their childlessness as a sign of God's displeasure, although the couple was virtuous and pious, leading a God-centered life. Thus human opinion presumed to be capable of reading a "sign," although it lacked the full story behind the "sign." And that full story was known only to God's mind. It was His plan for this couple that their prolonged "fruitlessness" and public humiliation was to be crowned late in life, producing the Blessed among Women.

So God's unresponsiveness can also be a "sign." In some area, in some respect, God might withhold His gifts, both in my life or in the lives of people I know. But His silence can also be a gift, leading me to growth, as does His word, when I accept it in faith. My acceptance of God's silence in my life teaches me patience, courage, humility, and compassion for others in a similar situation. Let me be attentive to God's silence today, and accept myself and others as we are, barren but for His grace.

SEPTEMBER 9

BEING REMINDED

"...You must make every effort to support your faith with goodness, and goodness with knowledge, and knowledge with self-control, and self-control with endurance, and endurance with godliness, and godliness with mutual affection, and mutual affection with love. For if these things are yours and are increasing among you, they keep you from being ineffective and unfruitful in the knowledge of our Lord Jesus Christ. ...Therefore I intend to keep on reminding you of these things, though you know them already and are established in the truth that has come to you." (2 Pet 1:5-8, 12)

This passage made me think today: Why the repetitiveness of the feasts and texts of the Church's liturgical calendar, which repeats itself year after year? Because my faith is supported by hearing/reading the same Scriptures, celebrating the same feasts, and being "re-minded" of the same saints and salvific events, over and over again. I need to be "re-minded," to have brought once again to my mind, which is ever-changing, the central stories and persons of Salvation History, most centrally of the Person of Jesus Christ, so that my own story and person have renewed direction and meaning. Together with practicing the virtues of faith, goodness, self-control, mutual affection, love, and so on, it is the knowledge and remembrance of the common Christian story, which lives on in the Body of Christ, that gives direction and meaning to my daily life.

Let me make a small effort today, once again to "re-mind" myself of "the truth that has come to me," as the Apostle Peter says here, so that my life is not "ineffective and unfruitful in the knowledge of our Lord Jesus Christ." Since my mind is ever-changing, from minute to minute, I can't build today on the liturgy or readings of last Sunday, which "I know already." I read a bit of Scripture today, once again, and discover it anew in my life.

SEPTEMBER 10

HE CARRIES EVERYTHING

"Long ago God spoke to the fathers in many and various ways by the prophets, but in these last days he has spoken to us by the Son, whom he appointed heir of all things, through whom he also created the ages. He is the radiance of God's glory and the exact imprint of God's very being, and he carries everything by his powerful word. When he had made purification for sins, he sat down at the right hand of the Majesty on high, having become as much superior to angels as the name he has inherited is more excellent than theirs." (Heb 1:1-4)

Indeed, God has spoken "to us." And He didn't only do so "long ago," nor only "by the prophets." He has spoken to us, and continues to speak to us, most directly, by the Son and our Lord Jesus Christ. Having become one of us, and taken on our humanity even unto our death and our hell, He "purified" all of it in Himself, and elevated us, our humanity, to a status "much superior to angels."

So this passage reminds me today of the radically-new possibilities opened up to me in communion with Christ, "the radiance of God's glory." He does not depart from this world, even as He sits "at the right hand of the Majesty," but continues to "carry everything," including me, as I am, "by His powerful word." Let me let Him carry me today, and speak to me, in my powerlessness and defects. These do not diminish Him, nor do they stop Him from carrying me, "by His powerful word."

SEPTEMBER 11

LET HIM DO THE SOWING

"Listen! A sower went out to sow. And as he sowed, some seed fell on the path, and the birds came and ate it up. Other seed fell on rocky ground, where it did not have much soil, and it sprang up quickly, since it had no depth of soil. And when the sun rose, it was scorched; and since it had no root, it withered away. Other seed fell among thorns, and the thorns grew up and choked it, and it yielded no grain. Other seed fell into good soil and brought forth grain, growing up and increasing and yielding thirty and sixty and a hundredfold..." (Mk 4:3-8)

In this parable, the Lord is talking about Himself (a "sower"), and His word (the "seed"), and all of us (various "soil") who hear it and then either embrace it or ignore it, in different ways.

I am thinking about this parable because of a conversation I heard yesterday: A woman said to her priest, "Father, I go to church and am very active in this parish; I attend a Bible Study class weekly; I read beneficial books and I have all these Apps on my phone, from daily scripture readings to inspirational speakers... But I have no peace, and I don't feel that I really pray to God." And her priest said to her, "Well, while you're doing all that, you probably don't let God get in a word edgewise."

I wasn't the one talking to this priest, but I realized that I needed to hear his very wise reply. It reminded me that Christ can often be "sowing" His word, that is, throwing it in my direction, but it may just be bouncing off of me, or languishing, or withering away, because I am not really tending to it, not keeping it, in the stillness, light, and regular watering that it requires for growth. Because I may be (perhaps inadvertently) smothering it with my own activities and words.

Today I remember the parable of the sower, and of Who the "sower" is. It is not my own saying or doing that begins and enables my growth. I must first be still, in Him, in order to receive, from Him, and then to speak, or act, in Him. *"Be still,"* He says to me, *"and know that I am God."* (Ps 45/46:10)

SEPTEMBER 12

THE LEAST AMONG US

"But while everyone was marveling at all the things he was doing, Jesus said to his disciples, 'Let these words sink into your ears: The Son of Man is about to be delivered into the hands of men.' But they did not understand this saying, and it was concealed from them, so that they might not perceive it. And they were afraid to ask him about this saying. An argument arose among them as to which of them was the greatest. But Jesus, knowing the reasoning of their hearts, took a child and put him by his side and said to them, 'Whoever receives this child in my name receives me, and whoever receives me receives him who sent me. For he who is least among you all is the one who is great.'" (Lk 9:43-48)

Jesus tries to point the disciples to His coming cross; that He is "about to be delivered into the hands of men." But the disciples quickly turn their attention to a question more interesting to them—a question about "them," not about Him: *Which of "them" is the greatest?* The disciples were thus self-preoccupied when Christ was about to become the "least" among everyone; when He was abandoned by the "greatest" of the apostles. This state of affairs doesn't seem to have changed much throughout Church history, as our preoccupation with our own status and authority scandalously continues, despite the light of His cross.

As we all prepare to accompany Him on His journey to Golgotha, let me let Him re-focus my attention on Him. Let me open my eyes and "see" what He is showing me, as He becomes entirely vulnerable, entirely "delivered into the hands of men." Let me "receive the Child" Who was laid in a manger in Bethlehem, and years later laid in a tomb, as His grief-stricken Mother watched. He does it all for me, He becomes the "least" among us, that I may have true life in Him, liberated from the deadening anxieties of self-preoccupation.

SEPTEMBER 13

CARRYING ONE ANOTHER'S BURDENS

"Bear one another's burdens, and in this way you will fulfill the law of Christ." (Ga 6:2)

The "burdens" of other people are not only their external misfortunes, but also their deep-seated defects of character: soft spots, blind spots, addictions, prejudices, delusions, self-centeredness, and so on. I am called to carry these burdens of other people, just like I, and others in my life, carry mine. Just like Christ carries mine and has them nailed to a cross.

I have this opportunity, to bear someone else's "burdens" and fulfill the law of Christ, the law of the Cross, whenever someone else's ego steps on my own. I am missing this opportunity if I'm focusing on my own burdens; if I'm constantly feeling hurt or neglected or needy. My burdens, perhaps ironically, are made lighter by carrying those of others. They aren't heavy, when I identify them as my own. "He isn't heavy," as someone once said, "he's my brother!"

SEPTEMBER 14

THE REJECTED STONE

"Jesus said to them, 'Did you never read in the Scriptures, 'The stone which the builders rejected, this became the chief corner stone; this came about from the Lord, and it is marvelous in our eyes?' Therefore I say to you, the kingdom of God will be taken away from you and given to a people, producing the fruit of it....'" (Mt 21:41-42)

I'm thinking about this somewhat sad passage today, when our New-Calendar friends are celebrating the great feast of the Exaltation of the Cross. Jesus is speaking of Himself as the "stone" rejected by the "builders" (cf. Psalm 117/118:22-23). By "builders" in this context He means the Pharisees and teachers of the Jews, who rejected Him and His way; the way of the cross.

But in our context we are all "builders," called to build our "house" on the firm foundation, on the "stone" or "rock" of the eternal Logos or Word of God: *"Everyone then who hears these words of mine and acts on them,"* He says, *"will be like a wise man who built his house on rock."* (Mt 7:24) Whether as individual persons, or as a family, or a community, or as a people, we are "builders" faced with a daily choice of our foundation. We can choose the Kingdom of God, where a crucified and risen Lord is King, or we can choose something else—some surrogate to prop us up, so to say. We can choose to build our own kingdom, as did the Pharisees, who preferred a Christ-less orthodoxy, their own orthodoxy, to a crucified Messiah.

In practical terms this means, among other things, that I choose, on a daily basis, to gratefully set my focus and reliance on a crucified and risen Lord. And I ask for the grace of His Spirit to carry with me His life-giving cross throughout my day.

SEPTEMBER 15

LIKE A LAMB THAT IS LED

"All we like sheep have gone astray; we have all turned to our own way, and the Lord has laid on him the iniquity of us all. He was oppressed, and he was afflicted, yet he did not open his mouth; like a lamb that is led to the slaughter, and like a sheep that before its shearers is silent, so he did not open his mouth. By a perversion of justice he was taken away. Who could have imagined his future? For he was cut off from the land of the living, stricken for the transgression of my people. They made his grave with the wicked and his tomb with the rich, although he had done no violence, and there was no deceit in his mouth." (Is 53:5-9)

Indeed, after we had "all turned to our own way," Christ came to be "led" through all the consequences of "our own way"; He is led "like a lamb to the slaughter," and "taken away" by our "perversion of justice."

Today I take pause to be quiet for a while, as I contemplate true Justice nailed to the cross. On that Friday, when the sun hid its light and God was silent, His Son "was cut off from the land of the living," in order to bring me new life, new light, and a new "way," in His justice. Let me open my heart to what He shows me today, and follow Him quietly on the way of the Cross.

SEPTEMBER 16

WHEN GOD RESTS

"Now there was a good and righteous man named Joseph, who, though a member of the council, had not agreed to their plan and action. He came from the Jewish town of Arimathea, and he was waiting expectantly for the kingdom of God. This man went to Pilate and asked for the body of Jesus. Then he took it down, wrapped it in a linen cloth, and laid it in a rock-hewn tomb where no one had ever been laid. It was the day of Preparation, and the sabbath was dawning. The women who had come with him from Galilee followed, and they saw the tomb and how his body was laid. Then they returned, and prepared spices and ointments. On the sabbath they rested according to the commandment." (Lk 23:50-56)

How full, how immense, is the "rest" of that Holy and Great Saturday. So much has happened, and much more is yet to happen, as the Lord sleeps in the tomb.

But for Joseph of Arimathea and the women in this scene, it was all over. Joseph "was" waiting expectantly for the kingdom of God, but now...? What now? It is hard to imagine the utter, grief-stricken loss for words of these people, who buried the One Who had raised others from the dead. And yet they still do what needs to be done for Him, according to custom and commandment. They do the next right thing, because there is nothing more they can do.

Today let me do the next right thing, even when things don't make sense; when God confuses me with unexpected loss, or His unexpected silences. Glory be to Him.

SEPTEMBER 17

TOUCH ME AND SEE

"While they were talking about this, Jesus himself stood among them and said to them, 'Peace be with you.' They were startled and terrified, and thought that they were seeing a ghost. He said to them, 'Why are you frightened, and why do doubts arise in your hearts? Look at my hands and my feet; see that it is I myself. Touch me and see; for a ghost does not have flesh and bones as you see that I have.' And when he had said this, he showed them his hands and his feet. While in their joy they were disbelieving and still wondering, he said to them, 'Have you anything here to eat?' They gave him a piece of broiled fish, and he took it and ate in their presence." (Lk 24:36-42)

So this is the first thing He says to those who had just abandoned Him, to those who were not there even for His burial: "Peace be with you." How humble, how Self-giving is my Lord in His triumph. "Touch me and see," He says, offering Himself to them, who hadn't believed other messengers of His resurrection. And then He lets them feed Him. Just as He asked a Samaritan woman to give Him to drink, opening Himself up to her, now He accepts fish from fishermen. How very human and meek is our Lord with us, when He's reconciling us with Him, and restoring our faith.

Today, on a sunny morning in Vienna, I thank my Lord for coming back to us, after we did everything wrong. He came back, clothed in "majesty," in our resurrected human body, redeemed, restored, and willing to be seen, touched, and fed by us. Let me let Him come back to me today, once again, even if I've done everything wrong. "The Lord is King," in His glorious and loving resurrection, "He is clothed in majesty."

SEPTEMBER 18

TWO KINDS OF RAGE

"Fools give full vent to their rage, but the wise bring calm in the end." (Prov 29:11)

...Because the "wise" can also have "rage." For example, a righteous "rage" against injustice, which is a desire to rectify the unjust. But the "wise," as distinct from "fools," do not "give full vent" to their rage; that is, they do not self-indulgently get caught up in the rage itself, for example, by ranting and raving about the injustice. Such self-indulgent rage does not help things, because it only seeks to underline one's own moral superiority.

The "wise" kind of rage focuses on restoring and healing what is wrong, in God's light. And God's light means: compassion, love, humility, self-giving. It does not, and indeed cannot, see injustice from a standpoint of moral superiority. In God's light we see things rather from a standpoint of shared responsibility, as "our problem." And it is this humbling and humbled wisdom that can draw the unjust back into God's love and communion, "bringing calm in the end."

SEPTEMBER 19

TIME TO REFOCUS

"Now after John was put in prison, Jesus came to Galilee, preaching the gospel of the kingdom of God, and saying, 'The time is fulfilled, and the kingdom of God is at hand (ἤγγικεν, has come near). Repent, and believe in the gospel.'" (Mk 1:14-15)

As I begin this day, I remember these very first words pronounced by the Lord, when He began preaching. It's time, He says, and the kingdom is "at hand," or "near." - Not in a galaxy far-far away, and not at some future date. The time has come for a "change of mind" ("metanoia" or repentance), that is, a change of focus.

Ever since these words of the God-Man resonated throughout the green landscape of Galilee, the time for re-focusing on His kingdom, from a self-centered to a God-centered life, is always now.

So let me refocus today, once again, on Him, and hear Christ's call to me, to embrace His kingdom, and His word, rather than my own. *"Behold, now is the accepted time; behold, now is the day of salvation."* (2 Cor 6:2)

SEPTEMBER 20

BEING BUILT TOGETHER

"Now, therefore, you are no longer strangers and foreigners, but fellow citizens with the saints and members of the household of God, having been built on the foundation of the apostles and prophets, Jesus Christ Himself being the chief cornerstone, in whom the whole building, being fitted together, grows into a holy temple in the Lord, in whom you also are being built together for a dwelling place of God in the Spirit." (Eph 2:19-22)

The Apostle reminds me today that I'm not alone; I'm not a "stranger" or "foreigner," wandering about with no purpose and no connections in a foreign land. I am "being built," little by little, along with other "members of the household of God," with whom I share a common language. My "fellow citizens" include the saints, the apostles and prophets, both of yesterday and today, with "Jesus Christ Himself being the chief cornerstone." And all of us in this "household of God" are held together, and are indeed "being built together," in the Spirit.

When I experience setbacks on my daily and hourly journey to God, like my own laziness and procrastination, I tend to lose sight of the positive fact that I am "being built," little by little, together with other cross-carriers, "for a dwelling place of God in the Spirit." The process of "being built" includes setbacks and difficulties—otherwise there would be no need for further "building." And I am reminded today that I'm not alone in this process, which occurs daily in me and others through spiritual progress, not spiritual perfection.

Today let me be willing to "be built" in the Holy Spirit, as I take up Christ's cross once again, which includes my own weaknesses, as well as those of others. I need not be discouraged in the place I am today, on my journey. Because that place is "the household of God," where I am not alone.

SEPTEMBER 21

THE NEW IN THE OLD

"A childless woman gives birth to the Theotokos, the nourisher of our life!" (End of Kontakion or hymn of the Nativity of the Mother of God)

Today we celebrate the Nativity of the Mother of God according to the Old(er) Calendar, so I'm once again thinking about Saints Joachim and Anna, Her elderly parents. They fervently prayed for a child for decades, but it was only very late in life that God granted them what they had been praying for, and a hitherto "childless woman gave birth to the Theotokos, the nourisher of our life."

Aside from the rare, biblical instances of elderly women giving birth, the later stages of life do present us with new opportunities, particularly with regard to our growth in God. While we might face the difficulties of forgetfulness, loneliness, depression, and various physical ailments, we also develop a willingness, in faith, to look death (and life) in the face. Our hearts open as they never opened before, in gratitude and humility before God and other people. I continuously observe this phenomenon, this very nourishing phenomenon of the open heart, in elderly people of faith.

Today, as we celebrate the birth of "the nourisher of our life," the Mother of God, to an elderly woman, I am gratefully reminded of the nourishing presence of elderly friends and relatives in my life. Glory be to God for revealing Himself in ever-new ways, in every stage of our lives.

SEPTEMBER 22

PEOPLE-PLEASING

"You were bought at a (high) price; do not become slaves of human beings." (1 Cor 7:23)

Here St. Paul is talking about the civic duties of slaves and freemen, in the context of his world, in which slavery was legal. But he uses this context to express the liberating "servitude" into which every Christian enters, having been "bought" with the complete self-giving of Jesus Christ, Who shed His blood on the cross for all of us. When I embrace Christ and live in Him, Who entirely embraced my humanity and infused it with His Spirit, the grace of His Spirit leads me according to His motivations and rules. This is one of the most exciting aspects of being a Christian: sharing in the freedom of the Spirit, made possible by sharing in the liberated humanity of the Body of Christ. He liberates me from the tyranny of people-pleasing.

I inevitably slip into people-pleasing whenever I cease to lead a God-centered life; when human opinion becomes my focus. When I am in "the disease to please," I am motivated by fear, personal gain, false obligation, the desire to be seen or accepted, and so on. All of this is "only human," and understandable outside God; without His Spirit. It is, I think, impossible to escape it without His help.

So today I ask, in prayer, to be led by Him; not to be left to my own devices. Because I know that He willingly gives of Himself when we ask, just as we willingly give our children what they ask, when they ask for the good: *"If you then, being evil, know how to give good gifts to your children, how much more will your heavenly Father give the Holy Spirit to those who ask Him?"* (Lk 11:13)

SEPTEMBER 23

PRAISE & GRATITUDE

"Praise the name of the Lord; give praise, O servants of the Lord..." (Ps 134/135: 1)

Giving praise, as distinct from asking for something, in prayer, is something I tend to neglect, when I am caught up in my usual concerns. Our liturgical services, however, consist largely of praise-filled texts and actions, although our ears tend to perk up more when we are asking for something, as in the litanies or "ektenies." It is a common human tendency, I suppose, to be more aware of what we need, than of what we already have, thanks to the Lord's abundant mercy and faith in us. So our prayers tend to look like shopping-lists of I need this and I need that, rather than praise-filled gratitude for His undying glory.

In order to be capable of praise-filled prayer, which fills my heart with humility, joy, and gratitude, I need to be aware of what I have. And this sometimes takes some work. I find it helpful to make a list of the many blessings, in the form of the experiences, situations, things, and people, in my life. The Lord, in His name, has carried me through many challenges and situations, both good and bad, lovingly leading me to growth. Above all He has given me Himself, most entirely, having elevated Himself on a cross, with outstretched hands, under Pontius Pilate. So today I thank Him, and praise His holy name: Praise the name of our Lord Jesus Christ, now and forever!

SEPTEMBER 24

THOSE WHO NEED A PHYSICIAN

"As he was walking along, he saw Levi son of Alphaeus sitting at the tax booth, and he said to him, 'Follow me.' And he got up and followed him. And as he sat at dinner in Levi's house, many tax collectors and sinners were also sitting with Jesus and his disciples—for there were many who followed him. When the scribes and Pharisees saw that he was eating with sinners and tax collectors, they said to his disciples, 'Why does he eat with tax collectors and sinners?' When Jesus heard this, he said to them, 'Those who are well have no need of a physician, but those who are sick; I have come to call not the righteous but sinners.'" (Mk 2:14-17)

So the scribes and Pharisees ask "Why?" This is not a well-meaning, earnest question. Hence the scribes and Pharisees are not posing it directly to Jesus, but rather to third parties, saying, Why does "he" eat with tax collectors and sinners? The question is not really seeking an answer. It is supposed to remain, firmly planted, in the minds of third parties. The scribes and Pharisees busy themselves with this kind of judgmental superficiality, while our Lord goes directly into the trenches, eating and drinking with those of us who really need Him.

Today I am so grateful for these liberating words, "I have come to call not the righteous"! Today, when in my church-world there is so much judgment "by association," so much judgment of one another, according to where and with whom one "was seen," according to external alliances, be they political, church-political, denominational, personal, or otherwise. As if Christ were merely an external alliance. No, He is the Physician of those who need one. And I remind myself today that I come to Him, and belong to Him, not as one who is "well," but as one not well, as one of "those who are sick." Today He says to me, "I have come to call not the righteous but sinners." Today let me have the ears to hear His call, amidst the chatter of those who "have no need of a physician."

SEPTEMBER 25

FINDING BY LOSING

"Then he began to teach them that the Son of Man must undergo great suffering, and be rejected by the elders, the chief priests, and the scribes, and be killed, and after three days rise again. He said all this quite openly. And Peter took him aside and began to rebuke him. But turning and looking at his disciples, he rebuked Peter and said, 'Get behind me, Satan! For you are setting your mind not on divine things but on human things.' He called the crowd with his disciples, and said to them, 'If any want to become my followers, let them deny themselves and take up their cross and follow me. For those who want to save their life will lose it, and those who lose their life for my sake, and for the sake of the gospel, will save it.'" (Mk 8:31-35)

Our Lord rebukes Peter for setting his mind "not on divine things but on human things." And by "divine things" He means the cross. While Peter wanted Jesus to do the "human thing," to "save" His life, the Lord had set His mind on giving it away, losing it.

Indeed, today I am called to "lose" myself in self-giving, because this is the path He shows me; It is the puzzling way of the cross, which does not make much sense, on the face of it. It is through giving away and losing that I find, I receive, and I save. I "save" or "make whole" my existence, my being, by coming out of my "self" and its bondage, connecting with God and others in self-offering. It is not in neediness or expectations of others that I am fulfilled, no. In fact that path, of neediness and expectations, brings me frustration and disappointment. So let me set my mind on "divine things" today and lose myself, that I may find. Because "those who lose their life for my sake, and for the sake of the gospel" my Lord promises me, "will save it."

SEPTEMBER 26

SAME SITUATION, DIFFERENT REACTION

"He causes his sun to rise on the evil and the good, and sends rain on the righteous and the unrighteous." (Mt 5:45)

This morning I woke up to the sound of heavy rain, and thought: How nice and soothing. It's raining! And then I thought of this passage from the Gospel, and how rain is a sign of God's love for both the righteous and the unrighteous.

But there have been mornings when I woke up to the sound of rain, and thought: Yuck. It's raining! How gloomy everything looks, and now I have to find my umbrella, and traffic will be bad, and so on.

My different reactions to the same weather remind me that external things—like the weather, or certain situations, or other people's behavior—these things are not actual reasons for my own reactions and state of mind. If I feel disturbed by something or someone, my "problem" is inside me. More specifically, I am missing that complementary action of God's grace, which helps me turn things around and see my world in His light.

On days like that, although I can't get myself back on track, I know that God can. I humbly ask Him for His grace, and hands things over to His will. "Thy will be done," I say, and "Thy kingdom come." This way, I at least don't misdirect my frustration and "bad mood" on other things or people, or on myself, in a destructive manner. He can, and does, open my eyes to see both the sun and the rain with gratitude, both as signs of His grace.

SEPTEMBER 27

THE FOOLISHNESS OF THE CROSS

"Has not God made foolish the wisdom of the world? For since, in the wisdom of God, the world did not know God through wisdom, God decided, through the foolishness of our proclamation, to save those who believe. For Jews demand signs and Greeks desire wisdom, but we proclaim Christ crucified, a stumbling block to Jews and foolishness to Gentiles, but to those who are the called, both Jews and Greeks, Christ the power of God and the wisdom of God." (1 Cor 1:20-24)

Jesus Christ, perfect Man and perfect God, was crucified in an imperfect world, at a specific time in our imperfect history, "under Pontius Pilate." This story of the Cross, which played out (and continues to be played out) in an imperfect, human setting, is a "stumbling block" and "foolishness" to many. From those perspectives it is a story of utter failure. And yet the life-giving Cross continues to be God's chosen path, the only path, to resurrection. It is the path He chose for me, and it is followed in a context of imperfection—my own imperfection, the imperfection of my community, and of my world. There is no cross in a perfect world.

Today as I contemplate the mystery of the Cross, as we celebrate the feast of the Elevation of the Cross according to the Old(er) Calendar, I contemplate the Cross of History—that imperfect context into which Christ willingly enters and in which He is crucified. It is in this context that we, as Church, do not even celebrate great feasts like this one, or like Christmas, together, because we bear, with Him and in Him, the Cross of History; the history of our weaknesses and divisions. This can indeed be seen as "foolishness" and a "stumbling block" to many. And yet we journey forward, in our weaknesses and imperfections, toward the light of the Resurrection.

Let me gratefully continue my imperfect, cross-carrying journey today, in "Christ the power of God and the wisdom of God," Who chose to make this journey as we do, in an imperfect world.

SEPTEMBER 28

DISRUPTED TRAVEL PLANS

"Since, then, we have a great high priest who has passed through the heavens, Jesus, the Son of God, let us hold fast to our confession. For we do not have a high priest who is unable to sympathize with our weaknesses, but we have one who in every respect has been tested as we are, yet without sin. Let us therefore approach the throne of grace with boldness, so that we may receive mercy and find grace to help in time of need." (Heb 4:14-16)

Yes, let us hold fast to our confession. I was beginning to reflect on this passage yesterday, when unexpectedly I got stuck at the airport in Moscow because of a visa-problem. And then I ended up in a little bed-and-breakfast near the airport, where the WiFi was not working. So I did not post any reflection yesterday, but now I am grateful for the disruption of my plans. I "hear" these words about our inimitable High Priest, Who is "not unable to sympathize (co-suffer) with our weaknesses," and Who "in every respect has been tested as we are,"—I hear these words more clearly, more gratefully, when things go against my plans, and I am "tested" in little or big ways. An unwelcome disruption to travel plans is, I think, a wonderful time to "hold fast to our confession," and to "find grace to help."

So here's the lesson I carry away from all this, for future reference. Let me pay close attention to the presence of Christ, when a border-guard asks me to step aside and come with him; Or when an airline-attendant tells me my flight is cancelled, delayed with no explanation, or that my luggage has not arrived. Let me "receive mercy," and pass it on, to the hotel-receptionist who tells me that the WiFi isn't working. Because we do, indeed, "have a great high priest who passed through the heavens," admittedly not in an airplane, with the preceding frustrations of our airports, but indeed having "been tested" at the hands of our darkness, frustration, betrayal, and abandonment. I thank Him today, for always being here, even at this airport.

SEPTEMBER 29

ALLEGORY & THE LANGUAGE OF LOVE

"Rejoice, star that shows forth the sun... Rejoice, heavenly ladder by which did God Himself descend..." (From the Akathist-Hymn to the Mother of God).

In various church-services of the Byzantine Rite, including the services in honor of the Mother of God, we have "allegorical" images. That is to say, we have poetical imagery called "allegory," which is "another" way of expressing reality.

The word "allegory" comes from the Greek words "allos" and "agorevein," which together mean "to explain/say in another way." The allegorical images of this hymnography take certain, central figures and moments of Salvation History, and cross-reference them to one another, or compare them to certain physical realities of our surroundings. For example, one takes the physical reality of a star and the sun, and "sees" them to signify the Mother of God and Her Son. This can be compared to poetry about love, in which one "sees" the face of the beloved in the sunset, or "hears" their whisper in the wind. All this can seem mildly ridiculous to outsiders; to those not in love.

But I don't have to be an outsider today, regarding liturgical allegory. Because, as a reminder of central figures/moments of Salvation History, which inspire me to focus on God, liturgical allegory is simply an aid to heartfelt prayer. It teaches me to see all things in His light and His truth. All things can "remind" me to re-focus on Him. So, at the risk of sounding mildly ridiculous, today when I observe the clear blue sky, for example, I can have it remind me of the liturgical color of the Mother of God, which is light blue. I can be reminded of Her "protection" of the world. I am reminded She is a part of my life, and there to help and protect me, as I ask Her to intercede for me, day to day.

SEPTEMBER 30

PASSING FROM DEATH TO LIFE

"Truly, truly, I say to you, he who hears my word and believes him who sent me, has eternal life; he does not come into judgment, but has passed from death to life. Truly, truly, I say to you, the hour is coming, and now is, when the dead will hear the voice of the Son of God, and those who hear will live. For as the Father has life in himself, so he has granted the Son also to have life in himself, and has given him authority to execute judgment, because he is the Son of man. Do not marvel at this; for the hour is coming when all who are in the tombs will hear his voice and come forth, those who have done good, to the resurrection of life, and those who have done evil, to the resurrection of judgment." (Jn 5:24-29)

The Lord reminds me today that His word is life-giving. And it is not just any kind of "life"-giving, but "eternal life"-giving. Because there is more than one form and level of "life," which is a gift we receive in order to develop it and grow it, to its unending potential, in the Source of Life Who is God. He alone has "life in Himself" and of Himself, so He alone can and does give us life, sharing with us His being.

Let me hear His voice once again today, and "come forth," responding to His call. He lets me "pass from death to life," again and again, teaching me responsive-ness and response-ability, whenever I slip back into various forms of death, which is fragmentation or separation within me, from His one ultimate purpose for me. This one, divine purpose is unity with Him and all creation. I learn in the here and now to get up and respond again, so that in the fulfilment, on the day of God's Final Judgment, I can come forth to "the resurrection of life." Today let me be among "those who hear," as I choose truly "to live" His kind of life, which includes Him in the ups and downs of my daily schedule.

OCTOBER 1

HER PROTECTION AND CARE

"Near the cross of Jesus stood his mother, his mother's sister, Mary the wife of Clopas, and Mary Magdalene. When Jesus saw his mother there, and the disciple whom he loved standing nearby, he said to her, 'Woman, here is your son,' and to the disciple, 'Here is your mother.' From that time on, this disciple took her into his home." (Jn 19:25-27)

In His final hour on the cross, Christ indicates to His mother that She is the mother of John, the beloved disciple, and to John Christ says that the disciple is Her son, who was to care for Her in Her old age.

According to a traditional interpretation of the Orthodox Church, She is also Mother to all disciples, to all followers of Christ. As members of the Body of Christ, communing with Him and in Him, we also enter into His relationships, becoming daughters and sons of His Mother and His Father. When I see an icon of the Mother of God, holding Her Child, I also see Her holding each and every one of us, who can run to Her protection and care with our cuts and bruises.

Today I remember the simple truth that I need the love, protection and care of others, just as others need mine. In the community of faithful, in the Body of Christ, the "others" include those already departed, who no longer need our protection and care, but are ready to provide it with their intercessions. This includes, most prominently, the Mother of God, whose motherly love is consistently there for me. Today let me ask for Her protection and care on my cross-carrying journey, because She does not abandon Her child on the cross.

OCTOBER 2

BY PRAYER AND FASTING

"And one of the crowd answered him, 'Teacher, I brought my son to you, for he has a dumb spirit; and wherever it seizes him, it dashes him down; and he foams and grinds his teeth and becomes rigid; and I asked your disciples to cast it out, and they were not able.' And he answered them, 'O faithless generation, how long am I to be with you? How long am I to bear with you? Bring him to me.' And they brought the boy to him; and when the spirit saw him, immediately it convulsed the boy, and he fell on the ground and rolled about, foaming at the mouth. And Jesus asked his father, 'How long has he had this?' And he said, 'From childhood. And it has often cast him into the fire and into the water, to destroy him; but if you can do anything, have pity on us and help us.' And Jesus said to him, 'If you can! All things are possible to him who believes.' Immediately the father of the child cried out and said, 'I believe; help my unbelief!' And when Jesus saw that a crowd came running together, he rebuked the unclean spirit, saying to it, 'You dumb and deaf spirit, I command you, come out of him, and never enter him again.' And after crying out and convulsing him terribly, it came out, and the boy was like a corpse; so that most of them said, 'He is dead.' But Jesus took him by the hand and lifted him up, and he arose." (Mk 9:17-27)

Jesus deals here with a "deaf and dumb spirit," who makes his victim, this boy, do self-destructive things. This kind of evil spirit reminds me of active, untreated addiction: When we are in the grips of it, we become, on the one hand, self-destructive, and on the other hand, we become "deaf and dumb," that is, unable to ask for, and receive, help. After healing this boy, our Lord says to His disciples that *"This kind cannot be driven out by anything but prayer and fasting."* (Mk 9:29) We can only be healed from our addictions by 1. Actively seeking God's help in prayer, and 2. Fasting, that is, total abstinence from our drug of choice.

How consoling, how helpful, is Christ's acceptance of the father's small bit of faith in this case. Our Lord knows that we are, on the most part, a "faithless generation," but He heals us anyway, time and again. If only we can come to believe, a little bit. Let me come to Him, with just a bit of faith, when either I or a loved one has lost all control, and is beyond the help of any human power. Our Lord is able and willing, even when we are not, to take us by the hand and lift us up. Because *"Jesus Christ is the same, yesterday and today and forever."* (Heb 13:8)

OCTOBER 3

DEMONS AND ANGELS

"The seventy (apostles) returned with joy, saying, 'Lord, in your name even the demons submit to us!' He said to them, 'I watched Satan fall from heaven like a flash of lightning. See, I have given you authority to tread on snakes and scorpions, and over all the power of the enemy; and nothing will hurt you. Nevertheless, do not rejoice at this, that the spirits submit to you, but rejoice that your names are written in heaven.' At that same hour Jesus rejoiced in the Holy Spirit and said, 'I thank you, Father, Lord of heaven and earth, because you have hidden these things from the wise and the intelligent and have revealed them to infants..." (Lk 10:17-21)

Here's a liberating fact: Evil does not exist as some objective force, floating about like a dark hole, on its own. Evil only exists within living, created beings, both visible and invisible, as the result of their free choice to reject the good. This fact is liberating, because it liberates us from falsely seeing evil as some "power" that we're up against. What we are up against is our own free choice to embrace good or reject it. We can also choose to be influenced in this choice through other living beings, both visible and invisible.

Any talk of demons or angels might prompt "the wise and intelligent" to smile, because this sounds like some medieval superstition or, well, infantile. As the Lord says in the above-cited passage, these things have indeed been "hidden from the wise and intelligent," and "revealed to infants." Note that in this context the Lord uses the concepts of wisdom and intelligence in a sarcastic sense, because it is neither "wise" nor "intelligent" to see evil as some objective, independent power. In fact it is the scariest kind of superstition, to believe in "Evil" with a big "E."

Today I gratefully remember that I do not live in a world where there is "Evil" with a big "E." I live in a world where there is only one higher power, to Whom I freely subject myself today: *"One God, the Father Almighty, Creator of heaven and earth, of all things visible and invisible."*

OCTOBER 4

FAITH SIMPLIFIES THINGS

"After these things the word of the Lord came to Abram in a vision, 'Do not be afraid, Abram, I am your shield; your reward shall be very great.' But Abram said, 'O Lord God, what will you give me, for I continue childless, and the heir of my house is Eliezer of Damascus?' And Abram said, 'You have given me no offspring, and so a slave born in my house is to be my heir.' But the word of the Lord came to him, 'This man shall not be your heir; no one but your very own issue shall be your heir.' He brought him outside and said, 'Look toward heaven and count the stars, if you are able to count them.' Then he said to him, 'So shall your descendants be.' And he believed the Lord; and it was reckoned to him as righteousness." (Gen 15:1-6)

How very perplexing, and yet simple, was Abraham's journey. His journey was perplexing because he so often did not understand the "how" and the "why" of what God told him and where God led him. In this passage, for example, Abraham is confronted with a situation he cannot understand; the worrisome fact of his lack of an heir. And then God shows Abraham the stars—yet another thing he doesn't understand. But Abraham makes things simple, by letting go of the voices in his own head, and having faith in God's word. He believes the Lord, and his faith aligns him with the Source of Righteousness, God. Abraham is thus "on the same page" with God, despite the remaining question-marks of his journey.

Today Abraham reminds me to embrace faith, when understanding fails me. When things make little "sense" from my perspective, amidst unfulfilled plans or unexpected turns of events, let me align myself to God's vision and God's will, regardless of how little I understand it. Let me simply accept today the people, things, and places He sends me, and hear God's voice say to me, as He said to Abraham: *"Do not be afraid. I am your shield."*

OCTOBER 5

TAKING HIS HAND

"But you, Israel, my servant, Jacob, whom I have chosen, you descendants of Abraham my friend, I took you from the ends of the earth, from its farthest corners I called you. I said, 'You are my servant'; I have chosen you and have not rejected you. 'So do not fear, for I am with you; do not be dismayed, for I am your God. I will strengthen you and help you; I will uphold you with my righteous right hand. All who rage against you will surely be ashamed and disgraced; those who oppose you will be as nothing and perish. Though you search for your enemies, you will not find them. Those who wage war against you will be as nothing at all. For I am the Lord your God who takes hold of your right hand and says to you, Do not fear; I will help you. Do not be afraid, Jacob, little Israel, do not fear, for I myself will help you,' declares the Lord, your Redeemer, the Holy One of Israel." (Is 41:8-14)

In this passage, God speaks to all of us, "descendants of Abraham," His friend. We are all "called," and "chosen," and "not rejected." Today it is the God of Abraham "who takes hold" of my "right hand" and says to me, "Do not fear, for I myself will help you." That's why we still read these words, spoken by the God of our fathers.

Let me hear God's undying promise, to disappear my "enemies," who do, indeed, become "as nothing at all" in light of His grace, when I let Him into my day, replacing fear with faith. Let me let Him do what He wants to do already, by trusting His call: "So do not fear, for I am with you; do not be dismayed, for I am your God." I take His "righteous right hand" into mine today, letting Him lead the way.

OCTOBER 6

IN SPIRIT AND TRUTH

"...But when the fullness of time had come, God sent his Son, born of a woman, born under the law, in order to redeem those who were under the law, so that we might receive adoption as children. And because you are children, God has sent the Spirit of his Son into your hearts, crying, "Abba! Father!" So you are no longer a slave but a child, and if a child then also an heir, through God." (Gal 4:4-7)

This passage from Galatians happens to be part of the epistle-reading for today, according to my Church's liturgical calendar. I am overwhelmed, as usual, by the very elevated, complicated Truth that I am called to contemplate and internalize, as a hearer/reader of Scripture, on a daily basis. This is no watered-down theology. Here the Apostle takes me through the very essence of Salvation History, reminding me of what it's all about: It's about the Spirit of God's Son being sent into my heart, making me His child.

Let me cry out to Him today, not as a slave to custom or law, but in the Spirit and Truth of His Son: *"Abba! Father! Who art in heaven..."* I am reminded today that all the texts, customs, and pious practices of my Church-Tradition are not there to make me a "slave" or robot of external motions. I am called to internalize them in my heart, in the Spirit of His Son. Without Him, without His Spirit, my external piety is but another form of slavery. Let me be free today, crying out in Spirit and Truth. Because, as Jesus says to the Samaritan woman, *"true worshipers will worship the Father in spirit and truth, for the Father seeks such as these to worship Him."* (Jn 4:23)

OCTOBER 7

SHE DID NOT UNDERSTAND

"...and when they (Mary and Joseph) did not find him, they returned to Jerusalem, seeking him. After three days they found him in the temple, sitting among the teachers, listening to them and asking them questions; and all who heard him were amazed at his understanding and his answers. And when they saw him they were astonished; and his mother said to him, 'Son, why have you treated us so? Behold, your father and I have been looking for you anxiously.' And he said to them, 'How is it that you sought me? Did you not know that I must be in my Father's house?' And they did not understand the saying which he spoke to them. And he went down with them and came to Nazareth, and was obedient to them; and his mother kept all these things in her heart." (Lk 2:45-51)

Today I'm reminded of the Mother of God "keeping all these things in Her heart." What "things"? The ones She did not understand. As in this instance, when the Most-Holy Virgin and Joseph spend not one, not two, but three days looking for the twelve-year-old Jesus "anxiously," only to find Him unapologetically sitting in His Father's house. The Mother of God "did not understand" what Her twelve-year-old has to say for Himself on this occasion, but the conversation ends here. I tend to imagine the silence on the way home as awkward. But really it is a picture of magnificent, human-divine restraint, humility, and loving obedience, amidst misunderstanding.

I need this reminder today, that it's sometimes best to say nothing. I got some disturbing church-news yesterday, and proceeded to comment, in a flurry of emails. Today let me let go, and keep things in my heart, by the intercessions of the Theotokos. May She cover and protect us all, in restraint, humility, and loving obedience, amidst misunderstanding.

OCTOBER 8

ON THE ROAD TO JERUSALEM

"Jesus said, 'Truly, I say to you, there is no one who has left house or brothers or sisters or mother or father or children or lands, for my sake and for the gospel, who will not receive a hundredfold now in this time, houses and brothers and sisters and mothers and children and lands, with persecutions, and in the age to come eternal life. But many that are first will be last, and the last first.' And they were on the road, going up to Jerusalem, and Jesus was walking ahead of them; and they were amazed, and those who followed were afraid. And taking the twelve again, he began to tell them what was to happen to him, saying, 'Behold, we are going up to Jerusalem; and the Son of man will be delivered to the chief priests and the scribes, and they will condemn him to death, and deliver him to the Gentiles; and they will mock him, and spit upon him, and scourge him, and kill him; and after three days he will rise.'" (Mk 10:29-34)

This is not the first time Jesus talks about the Cross, but it is as if the disciples do not hear Him. They are blocking out the word of the Cross, because they're afraid of it, as it says here, "and those who followed were afraid." But note that they do continue to follow, despite their fear. Our Lord Jesus Christ is that compelling, and that beloved, by the disciples, that they continue to follow Him, even when they can not, or will not, hear His words. Their love is stronger than their faith.

Today let me open up to Christ's compelling presence in my life, and follow Him even when I don't understand where we're going or why. Let me walk with Him "up to Jerusalem," detaching myself from other attachments, concerns, and issues. "Behold, we are going up to Jerusalem," He says to me today, "and the Son of Man will be delivered to the chief priests and the scribes, and they will condemn Him to death..." Let me not be afraid, but follow His lead.

OCTOBER 9

HE WHO IS COMING

"Now when Jesus came, he found that Lazarus had already been in the tomb four days. Bethany was near Jerusalem, about two miles off, and many of the Jews had come to Martha and Mary to console them concerning their brother. When Martha heard that Jesus was coming, she went and met him, while Mary sat in the house. Martha said to Jesus, 'Lord, if you had been here, my brother would not have died. And even now I know that whatever you ask from God, God will give you.' Jesus said to her, 'Your brother will rise again.' Martha said to him, 'I know that he will rise again in the resurrection at the last day.' Jesus said to her, 'I am the resurrection and the life; he who believes in me, though he die, yet shall he live, and whoever lives and believes in me shall never die. Do you believe this?' She said to him, 'Yes, Lord; I believe that you are the Christ, the Son of God, he who is coming (ἐρχόμενος) *into the world.'"* (Jn 11:17-27)

Christ refers to Himself many times in the Gospels as the one who (already) "has come" or "came" into the world (e.g., Mt 5:17; Mt 10:34; Lk 9:56; Jn 9:39; Jn 12:46, etc.). But the remarkable Martha refers to Him here as to one who still "is coming" into the world (ὁ εἰς τὸν κόσμον "ἐρχόμενος"). Because His Self-giving light, His glory, was not fully revealed to her, nor to the rest of us. At this point, our Lord is still "coming into the world."

Today let me embrace and re-affirm Martha's faith, in my Lord Who "is coming again," and again, into my world, revealing Himself "in glory," sometimes after prolonged absences, when I have the eyes to see, and the willingness to choose, His life over my death. *"I am the resurrection and the life...,"* He says to me today, and asks: *"Do you believe this?"* Yes, Lord, I say with Martha, despite the grief of the past few days, in the Lord's incomprehensible absence. *"I believe that you are the Christ, the Son of God, he who is coming into the world."*

OCTOBER 10
BUT TAKE COURAGE

"The hour is coming, indeed it has come, when you will be scattered, each one to his home, and you will leave me alone. Yet I am not alone because the Father is with me. I have said this to you, so that in me you may have peace. In the world you have tribulation (θλῖψιν ἔχετε). But take courage; I have conquered the world!" (Jn 16:32-33)

How very gentle, forgiving, and humble are these words of our Lord. He is about to be abandoned by us, by His very own, and delivered into the hands of His enemies. And yet He consoles us, so that, even in our weakness and failure in His final hours, in Him we "may have peace." He is about to face Judas's kiss, mockery, torture, and crucifixion, and yet He says to us: *"But take courage; I have conquered the world."*

So as Christ heads toward the Cross, He reminds me that in the world I have "tribulation." And a large part of this is my own falling short of His Self-giving, crucified love, when I am "scattered" and "leave" Him, time and again. But Jesus Christ conquers; He conquers all this, also in me. "I have said this to you," He reminds me today, "so that in me you may have peace." Glory be to Him.

OCTOBER 11

LEAVING IT TO GOD

"And it happened when he (Jesus) was in a certain city, that behold, a man who was full of leprosy saw Jesus; and he fell on his face and implored him, saying, 'Lord, if you are willing, you can make me clean.' Then he (Jesus) put out his hand and touched him, saying, 'I am willing; be cleansed.' Immediately the leprosy left him." (Lk 5:12-13)

The man "full of leprosy" has great faith; he is absolutely sure that the Lord "can" make him clean. He does not, however, presume that the Lord "wants" to. "If You are willing," he says, "You can make me clean," placing himself and his horrible disease quite literally at the Lord's feet. And Jesus does not reply, as perhaps some would expect, "But of COURSE I want to make you clean!" No, He simply says, I am willing (Θέλω); be cleansed. The time had come, according to God's will and wisdom, for this man to be free of his disease.

This may be difficult for me to accept, but the fact is, it is sometimes God's will that I endure various ailments or defects, physical and/or spiritual, and remain "unclean," as was the leper for a prolonged period of time. Through my own weaknesses, be they physical or spiritual, I learn compassion for others with similar weaknesses, as well as gratitude for little things. Today let me be grateful for whatever God sends me, and humbly ask Him to cleanse what needs cleansing, in His time. *"Lord, if You are willing, You can make me clean."*

OCTOBER 12

GO THEREFORE

"And Jesus came and said to them, 'All authority in heaven and on earth has been given to me. Go therefore and make disciples of all nations, baptizing them in the name of the Father and of the Son and of the Holy Spirit, teaching them to observe all that I have commanded you. And behold, I am with you always, to the end of the age.'" (Mt 28:18-20)

So—"go," He says. Because "all authority in heaven and on earth has been given to me." Also, most importantly, "I am with you always." He says this to us, because He knows we might procrastinate, crippled either by fear, or self-doubt, or simple laziness.

Today let me let the Lord's authority and presence lift me out of inactivity, that I may "go" and "do" in Him. Let me not get stuck in the dead-end of self-reliance, but embrace His help, which is always, always, on offer, "to the end of the age." Let me embrace His presence today, rather than block Him out, that I may share Him with others, any way I can.

OCTOBER 13

HE EMPTIED HIMSELF

"Have this mind among yourselves, which is yours in Christ Jesus, who, though he was in the form of God, did not count equality with God a thing to be exploited (ἁρπαγμός, seized booty), but emptied himself, taking the form of a servant, being born in the likeness of men. And being found in human form he humbled himself and became obedient (ὑπήκοος) unto death, even death on a cross..." (Php 2:5-8)

Here St. Paul tells us how we are to be "minded" (τοῦτο φρονεῖτε), as Christ was. We are not to use even our true prerogatives and talents as "a thing to be exploited," when these strengths of ours might lead us away from the self-giving path of the cross. Just as, for example, our Lord did not use His divine powers to "turn these stones into loaves of bread," just to prove Himself before a cynical doubter, the devil (Mt 4:3). Instead He makes Himself "empty" (ἑαυτὸν ἐκένωσεν).

This Self-emptying makes possible His "obedience" to the Father's will—and by "obedience" St. Paul does not mean a mindless following of instructions, no. The word "obedience" in English (from the Latin "ob," in the direction of, and "audire," listen) and in Greek (ὑπακούω, from "ὑπο," under, and ἀκούω, listen) means not only to "listen in," but to internalize deeply, comprehend, and, most importantly, to respond. This is a thoughtful and often painful process, as we see in Christ's prayer in Gethsemane, as well as His excruciating "Why?" from the Cross (Mt 27:46).

Today I ask God to help me be "empty," rather than full of myself, so I can "listen in" and truly respond to God and others.

OCTOBER 14

GRACE-FILLED FRIENDSHIP

"In those days Mary set out and went with haste to a Judean town in the hill country, where she entered the house of Zechariah and greeted Elizabeth. When Elizabeth heard Mary's greeting, the child leaped in her womb. And Elizabeth was filled with the Holy Spirit and exclaimed with a loud cry, "Blessed are you among women, and blessed is the fruit of your womb! And how (πόθεν, literally, from where) is this happening to me, that the mother of my Lord comes to me?..." (Lk 1:39-43)

This joyful meeting of two friends, the young Mary, the Most Blessed Virgin, and Her much older relative Elizabeth, mother of John the Baptist, occurs right after the Annunciation; right after Mary was paid a visit by the Archangel Gabriel and gave Her consent to become the Mother of God. She does not keep the news to Herself, but goes "with haste" to tell it (not to Joseph!) to another woman, Elizabeth. But Elizabeth, who is also expecting a child at this point, doesn't need to be told what has happened to Mary. She immediately knows, "filled with the Holy Spirit," and becomes the first woman to recognize Mary, her young friend, as the Blessed Among Women and as "mother of my Lord."

The Holy Spirit brings joy and mutual honor to this friendship. He brings the Most Blessed Virgin, on the one hand, to share "with haste" Her joy with Elizabeth; and He opens Elizabeth's heart to see Her young friend for who She is, and to rejoice with Her.

Today I am reminded to let the grace of the Holy Spirit into my friendships. It is His grace that makes me capable of sharing my joys and sorrows with my friends, and it is His grace that opens my heart to see and share theirs. And today I let the Mother of God, Full of Grace, be my model and guide in grace-filled friendship. *"Blessed are You among women,"* I gratefully say to Her today, because She comes "with haste" and is indeed "among" us, when we are open to Her grace-filled friendship.

OCTOBER 15

CLICKING WITH HIM

"We must no longer be infants (νήπιοι), tossed to and fro and blown about by every wind of teaching, by people's trickery, by their craftiness in methodical scheming. But speaking the truth in love, we must grow up in every way into him who is the head, into Christ..." (Eph 4:14-15)

Here the Apostle uses the word "infants" (νήπιοι), which is often used in the New Testament in a negative sense, signifying an immaturity and gullibility that is easily influenced and manipulated. It is not the same word used by the Lord, when He tells us to be like "children" (παιδία).

St. Paul's warning is particularly important today, in the age of the internet. We are confronted with various opinions and messages, be it in the form of advertising, news, or comments on social media, which mostly flow at us in a chaotic and coincidental manner. Almost imperceptibly we can find ourselves "tossed to and fro and blown about by every wind of teaching," clicking on contents that might be unnecessary, burdensome, or even damaging for our spiritual health. An indiscriminate absorption of all this information can negatively affect my capacity to "speak the truth in love."

Today let me begin my day by firmly establishing my focus on Christ, in prayer and quiet contemplation of His word. Let me strive to "grow up in every way into him who is the head," and let Him be the anchor of my thoughts, words, and "clicks."

OCTOBER 16

MAKE HIS PATHS STRAIGHT

"The beginning of the gospel of Jesus Christ, the Son of God. As it is written in the Prophets: 'Behold, I send my messenger before your face, who will prepare your way before you.' 'The voice of one crying in the wilderness: Prepare the way of the Lord; Make his paths straight.' John came baptizing in the wilderness and preaching a baptism of repentance for the remission of sins. Then all the land of Judea, and those from Jerusalem, went out to him and were all baptized by him in the Jordan River, confessing their sins." (Mk 1:1-4)

St. John the Baptist "prepares the way of the Lord"; He clears the "paths" or makes them "straight" for the One Who is coming, Jesus Christ. The "way" and the "paths" being talked about here are found in people's hearts. They are cluttered with "sin" that is a loss of focus, because sin, ἁμαρτία, literally means "missing the point." John calls the people to change focus, to "repent," and clear away the clutter of their sins by confessing them. By cleaning house in this way, by unburdening themselves of their sins, the people are made ready to hear the "gospel" or "good news" that is coming.

So everything begins with "the baptism of repentance," with a change of focus. This is a "baptism" to which I am called every day, because I lose focus, but also make a new beginning, every day. Let me keep watch over the "paths" that need to be kept straight in my heart, so that the Lord's voice can reach me. Let me maintain a humble openness to myself, to other human beings, and to Christ's voice in my life, by confessing my sins on a regular basis.

Today let me be open, in humble watchfulness, to the One Who is coming. He comes, bringing me change and growth every day, when I "make His paths straight" to the best of my ability.

OCTOBER 17

MOTHERHOOD

"On the third day there was a wedding at Cana in Galilee, and the mother of Jesus was there. Jesus also was invited to the wedding with his disciples. When the wine ran out, the mother of Jesus said to him, 'They have no wine.' And Jesus said to her, 'Woman, what does this have to do with me? My hour has not yet come.' His mother said to the servants, 'Do whatever he tells you.' Now there were six stone water jars there for the Jewish rites of purification, each holding twenty or thirty gallons. Jesus said to the servants, 'Fill the jars with water'..." (Jn 2:1-7)

Here our Lord says one thing, but does another. Because His Mother does what motherly love does so effectively: She ignores His words, letting them slide, and has full faith that He'll do the right thing. Thus in this very first of Christ's "signs" or miracles, done at Cana (Jn 2:11), He manifested not only His glory, but the glory of His Mother and Her unique and strange authority: the authority of a mom.

Today I note with gratitude the kind of love that doesn't pick at my every word, nor hold me to it. I thank God for my own, one-and-only mom, who loves me and has faith in me no matter what. I also thank Him for our glorious, Most-Holy Lady, the Theotokos and Ever-Virgin Mary, who shows us the grace of a love beyond words.

OCTOBER 18

NOT CONDEMNED

"For God so loved the world that he gave his only-begotten Son, that whoever believes in him should not perish but have everlasting life. For God sent the Son into the world, not to condemn the world, but that the world might be saved through him. He who believes in him is not condemned; he who does not believe is condemned already, because he has not believed in the name of the only Son of God. And this is the judgment, that the light has come into the world, and men loved darkness rather than light, because their deeds were evil. For every one who does evil hates the light, and does not come to the light, lest his deeds should be exposed. But he who does what is true (ὁποιῶν τὴν ἀλήθειαν) comes to the light, that it may be clearly seen that his deeds have been wrought in God." (Jn 3:16-21)

How liberating it is, to be one who "does what is true." When I am in "truth," doing the next right thing, being true to God, myself, and others, I am liberated from hiding all the time. One need not hide, or self-isolate, or have fear of people and their opinions, or of situations and their outcomes, when walking in God's light, small step after small step. Because faith replaces fear, self-loathing, and the kind of "judgment" that comes from darkness; the perpetual "thumbs down" toward everything and everyone, including myself.

Let me carry this word around with me today: The "condemnation" talked about here does not come from God, Who sent the Son into the world "not to condemn the world, but that the world might be saved through Him." Let me open up to Him, shedding His light on my entire being, the good and the bad. Because my good and my bad is taken on by His Son, Who is sent to bring me not a condemning "thumbs down," but the healing grace of salvation through Him.

OCTOBER 19

TREASURE THAT DOESN'T FAIL

"Sell your possessions, and give alms (ἐλεημοσύνην); provide yourselves with purses that do not grow old, with a treasure in the heavens that does not fail, where no thief approaches and no moth destroys. For where your treasure is, there will your heart be also." (Lk 12:33-34)

Give it away, the Lord says to me today. Give "alms" (a corruption of the Greek word "eleimosini," meaning "mercy" or "pity"). This includes my material possessions, but not exclusively and not even essentially. The kind of "alms" our Lord is talking about (eleimosini) involve a self-giving of the heart; an overflowing of the heart with mercy, pity, and compassion. This kind of giving is the opposite of self-pity, self-seeking, and self-isolation, and it provides me with true wealth "that does not fail."

Let me turn things around today, replacing dissatisfaction and neediness, which invariably "grow old," with self-giving mercy. Let me let God put my heart in a safe and light-filled place, where "no thief approaches," like fears and expectations of others, "and no moth destroys," like ingratitude and resentment. Let me ask what I can give today, perhaps in very small ways, rather than what I can get. I take my expectations down a notch today, extending mercy to myself and others, because my Lord offers to build with me an unseen treasure beyond my own expectations.

OCTOBER 20

MY OWN UNDERSTANDING vs. HIS

"Trust in the Lord with all your heart, and do not lean on your own understanding. In all your ways acknowledge him, and he will make straight your paths." (Prov 3:5-6)

So what does this mean in practical terms? Can I "simply" trust in the Lord and "not lean on my own understanding," when faced with daily choices and decisions? How does this work?

It works by "acknowledging Him in all my ways," that is to say, by acknowledging the paths the Lord is actually "making straight" before me, rather than the ones I might prefer or would like to imagine. Otherwise, if I "lean on my own understanding," I often find myself behaving like a person in a room with two doors, one wide open and one closed, who keeps staring at the closed one, wishing it would open.

Today let me "trust in the Lord with all my heart," acknowledging and accepting the paths He makes straight for me, be it in the people, places, or situations He sends my way.

OCTOBER 21

CALLED TO BE SAINTS TOGETHER

"Paul, called (κλητὸς) by the will of God to be an apostle of Christ Jesus, and our brother Sosthenes, to the church (ἐκκλησία) of God which is at Corinth, to those sanctified in Christ Jesus, called to be saints (κλητοῖς ἁγίοις) together with all those who in every place call on the name of our Lord Jesus Christ, both their Lord and ours: Grace to you and peace from God our Father and the Lord Jesus Christ." (1 Cor 1:1-3)

St. Paul himself is "called," as are the people to whom he writes—not only at Corinth in the first century—but "in every place" and throughout the ages, and today, wherever we are, who "call on the name of our Lord Jesus Christ." As "church" or "ekklesia" we are "the ones called forth" (the Greek word "ekklesia" comes from "ekkaleo," to call forth or call out), to be "saints" and "sanctified," which means dedicated to Him. It is in fellowship with others, both from the past and in our now, that we make our journey, through its ups and downs, of responding to our common call, to be and remain dedicated to Him.

Today let me renew my sense of belonging to this great community of the "called." Let me not lose sight of our primary purpose, to be "saints" together with all believers from the past and present, calling on the name of our Lord Jesus Christ, "both their Lord and ours." So I call to Him throughout my day, *"Lord, Jesus Christ, Son of God, have mercy on me, the sinner."*

OCTOBER 22

CHURCH DIVISIONS & POLITICS

"I appeal to you, brethren, by the name of our Lord Jesus Christ, that all of you agree and that there be no dissensions among you, but that you be united in the same mind and the same judgment. For it has been reported to me by Chloe's people that there is quarreling among you, my brethren. What I mean is that each one of you says, 'I belong to Paul,' or 'I belong to Apollos,' or 'I belong to Cephas,' or 'I belong to Christ.' Is Christ divided? Was Paul crucified for you? Or were you baptized in the name of Paul?" (1 Cor 1:10-13)

The "dissensions among you," St. Paul indicates to me today, come from placing human allegiances above the One "crucified for you." And further in this well-known first chapter of 1 Corinthians, the Apostle goes on to stress the centrality of the Cross and its unifying power, which "destroys the wisdom of the wise" and "makes foolish the wisdom of the world" (1 Cor 1:19-20), lifting us above the divisive phenomenon of human opinions. We are elevated by the humility and "weakness of God," which is "stronger than men" (1 Cor 1:25).

In any "dissensions" that arise among us, be it in church-politics or national politics, let me not depart from the unity of "the same mind and the same judgment" of the One and Only crucified for us. This means taking a step back into self-giving, when discussions among us turn into "quarreling among us" and tempt me to jump in, abandoning the Spirit of my cross-carrying journey. *"For the foolishness of God is wiser than men, and the weakness of God is stronger than men."* Glory be to Him.

OCTOBER 23

SEEKING THE LIVING AMONG THE DEAD

"But on the first day of the week, at early dawn, they (the women) went to the tomb, taking the spices which they had prepared. And they found the stone rolled away from the tomb, but when they went in they did not find the body. While they were perplexed about this, behold, two men stood by them in dazzling apparel; and as they were frightened and bowed their faces to the ground, the men said to them, 'Why do you seek the living among the dead? Remember how he told you, while he was still in Galilee, that the Son of man must be delivered into the hands of sinful men, and be crucified, and on the third day rise.' And they remembered his words, and returning from the tomb they told all this to the eleven and to all the rest. Now it was Mary Magdalene and Joanna and Mary the mother of James and the other women with them who told this to the apostles; but these words seemed to them an idle tale, and they did not believe them." (Lk 24:1-11)

What a confusing day this was, when the women rushed about the city, in apparently futile attempts to be helpful. The spices they prepared prove useless, and the words they relate to the apostles fall on deaf ears. The women in this picture are in the middle of great news and great change, and yet they are powerless to "do" anything about it. They seek the living among the dead—and among the deaf.

Today I am deeply consoled by this familiar picture of women appearing useless, and their words, their witness to change, falling on deaf ears among other followers of Christ. Because all the while, in this picture, there is One Who has already brought about the change of New Life, and He alone can "do" something about it. So let us not seek the living among the dead and the deaf, and trust in Him. *"Arise, O God, judge the earth; for You shall inherit all nations."* (Ps 81/82: 8)

OCTOBER 24

WORKS IN PROGRESS

"For the saving grace of God has appeared to all people, training us to renounce iniquity and worldly passions, and to live sober, upright, and godly lives in this world, awaiting our blessed hope, the appearing of the glory of our great God and Savior Jesus Christ, who gave himself for us to redeem us from all iniquity and to purify for himself a people of his own who are zealous for good deeds." (Titus 2:11-14)

Here the Apostle describes the dynamic adventure of our lives "in this world." On our cross-carrying journeys we embrace, and are "trained" by, the grace that has "already appeared," while awaiting the glory that is yet to appear—"the appearing of the glory of our great God and Savior Jesus Christ." So when I lead a God-centered life, I never stand in place, nor do I imagine that I have arrived at my destination, because the saving grace of God is ever "training" us like children (παιδεύουσα ἡμᾶς), like works in progress.

Today let me embrace what I "already" have, and strive for that which I do "not yet" have, among the "people of His own." I let Christ give me what He already has on offer, by opening up to Him in heartfelt prayer and surrender. He already "gave Himself for us," so let me hand myself and my concerns over to Him as well. And let me not be discouraged by the virtues and strengths I do "not yet" have, because I am His work in progress. Glory be to Him.

OCTOBER 25

HIS SUBTLE PROCESS

"And again he said, 'To what should I compare the kingdom of God? It is like yeast that a woman took and hid in three measures of flour until all of it was leavened.'" (Lk 13:20-21)

It takes just a little bit, which is at first barely noticeable, but eventually permeates all of life and transforms it. A little bit of what? Of God's "kingdom," which He subtly "hides" among us and within us, through the gentle and yet decisive hands of "a woman," His Church.

The "yeast" of God's kingdom is there, within me, and it "works" when I let it; when I don't disturb the "leavening" process. So let me clear away any disturbances today, like resentments toward myself or others, and take a few steps toward forgiveness, in any way that I can. Let me be attentive to God's subtle call in my heart, which grows stronger when I pay attention. "Thy kingdom come," I say to Him today, "Thy will be done," and please, help me to not get in the way.

OCTOBER 26

NEVER BE HUNGRY

"Jesus said to them, 'I am the bread of life. Whoever comes to me will never be hungry, and whoever believes in me will never be thirsty. But I said to you that you have seen me and yet do not believe. Everything that the Father gives me will come to me, and anyone who comes to me I will never drive away..." (Jn 6:35-37)

Such is His promise, and I know it's true, because He proves Himself, time and again, when I walk in Him and place my reliance on Him, rather than myself or someone/something else. When God is my focus, and I put Him first, I see things differently, by His grace, and feelings of insufficiency, neediness, disappointment, and unfulfilment are removed. I am no longer "hungry" or "thirsty," as the Bread of Life promises. Without Him, even too much is not enough, ever. And yet, He says to me today, "you have seen Me and do not believe." Because I tend to drift away, slipping again and again into self-reliance.

But I can come back this morning, as He reassures me: "Anyone who comes to Me," He says, "I will never drive away." So let me start afresh today, because I can. "Give us this day our daily bread," O Lord, that we not be hungry, or thirsty, with You in our midst.

OCTOBER 27

A RELIGION YOU COULD NOT HAVE GUESSED

"So Jesus said to them, 'Truly, truly, I say to you, unless you eat the flesh of the Son of man and drink his blood, you have no life in you; he who eats my flesh and drinks my blood has eternal life, and I will raise him up at the last day. For my flesh is food indeed, and my blood is drink indeed. He who eats my flesh and drinks my blood abides in me, and I in him. As the living Father sent me, and I live because of the Father, so he who eats me will live because of me. This is the bread which came down from heaven, not such as the fathers ate and died; he who eats this bread will live for ever.' This he said in the synagogue, as he taught at Capernaum. Many of his disciples, when they heard it, said, 'This is a hard saying; who can listen to it?'" (Jn 6:53-60)

And a few verses later, we learn that "after this, many of his disciples drew back and no longer followed him" (Jn 6:66). It is one of the many passages in the Gospels that makes me think of C. S. Lewis's famous comment: *"That is one of the reasons I believe in Christianity. It is a religion you could not have guessed."*

Indeed, our Lord is unpredictable and, at times, even outrageous. He calls me to unthinkable heights and unthinkable depths, of intimate connection with Him. He goes all the way, giving of Himself most entirely, that I may live not just happily, not just contentedly, but "for ever," and in Him, in the living God. Let me call upon His name today, and stay close to His unpredictable, life-giving word. Glory be to Him.

OCTOBER 28

A NEW PEACE

"...The man (the one healed at the pool of Bethesda) went away and told the Jews that it was Jesus who had healed him. And this was why the Jews persecuted Jesus, because he did this on the sabbath. But Jesus answered them, 'My Father is working still, and I am working.' This was why the Jews sought all the more to kill him, because he not only broke the sabbath but also called God his own Father, making himself equal with God." (Jn 5:15-18)

Here, in yet another incident within the ongoing "Sabbath controversy" between Jesus and the Pharisees, our Lord makes a shocking statement: *"My Father is working still (until now), and I am working."* Jesus is signaling a change in His Father's dealings with us, His people.

Previously, God had made His "rest" on the seventh day upon creation, as described in Genesis 2:1-3, a "sign" of the Old Mosaic Covenant between Him and us (Ex 31:13). We were blessed with the Fourth Commandment by "imitating" God and "resting" as He did upon His first creation. But now He reveals Himself as "working still," also on the Sabbath, because He is working, in His Son, on the new creation, which is to become the "New Covenant" in the blood of the Son (Lk 22:20); in the salvific works and workings of Christ crucified.

So now we are called to be "working" in Him, with Him, and like Him, Who offers us a new connection with Him, in "a new covenant in His blood" (1 Cor 11:25). Today I find new "rest" and new peace in the lightness of His redemptive Cross, according to His promise: *"Come to me, all who labor and are heavy laden, and I will give you rest. Take my yoke upon you, and learn from me; for I am meek and humble in heart, and you will find rest for your souls. For my yoke is easy, and my burden is light."* (Mt 11:28-30)

OCTOBER 29

CALLING A SAINT FOR HELP

"Now there was at Joppa a disciple named Tabitha, which means Dorcas (gazelle). She was full of good works and acts of charity. In those days she fell sick and died; and when they had washed her, they laid her in an upper room. Since Lydda was near Joppa, the disciples, hearing that Peter was there, sent two men to him entreating him, 'Please come to us without delay.' So Peter rose and went with them. And when he had come, they took him to the upper room. All the widows stood beside him weeping, and showing tunics and other garments which Dorcas made while she was with them. But Peter put them all outside and knelt down and prayed; then turning to the body he said, 'Tabitha, rise.' And she opened her eyes, and when she saw Peter she sat up. And he gave her his hand and lifted her up. Then calling the saints and widows he presented her alive. And it became known throughout all Joppa, and many believed in the Lord." (Acts 9:36-42)

Peter is not the only "saint" mentioned in this passage. But he is special. The other "saints" send for him, to "please come to us without delay," when tragedy strikes the community at Joppa. Why? Apparently, the community presumes that Peter can "do" something about the death of Tabitha. And he does. He prays to their and our common Lord, the One Source of sanctity, wonderful in His saints, and Tabitha rises from the dead.

Let me not hesitate to call upon the strongest among us, the saints of past and present, for help, when I need it. These people are not "sources" of sanctity, but have opened themselves up to God's grace more fully, more completely, and are thus powerful channels of His healing power. *"Wonderful is God in his saints: the God of Israel is he who will give power and strength to his people. Blessed be God."* (Ps 67:36)

OCTOBER 30

FINANCIAL CONCERNS & FAITH

"Someone in the crowd said to him, 'Teacher, tell my brother to divide the family inheritance with me.' But he said to him, 'Friend, who set me to be a judge or arbitrator (μεριστὴν, divider) over you?' And he said to them, 'Take care! Be on your guard against all kinds of covetousness (πάσης πλεονεξίας); for one's life does not consist in the abundance of possessions.'" (Lk 12:13-15)

Does this mean that our Lord is not willing to help us with financial worries? No. It means, He is not willing to contribute to "dividing" us through matters financial. Because money should not come between us, if our priorities are in order: First, we must maintain love and peace amongst ourselves and with Him, that we may have "life." We lose touch with "life" if the "abundance of possessions" becomes the primary object of our "yearning" or "coveting." Conversely, if my priorities are in the proper order, and I place my heart and my life in the hands of the Giver of Life, I also find peace with my financial situation, whatever it may be.

Today let me begin my day with putting God in the center of everything. I hand over to Him all my concerns, as I do the next right thing today, in my work and other responsibilities. "Give us this day our daily bread, and forgive us our trespasses," I say to Him today, "as we forgive those who trespass against us." That's what He teaches me to be concerned about today, as He continues to provide for me, in His light and His peace. Glory be to Him.

OCTOBER 31

ST. PAUL & HISTORICAL CONTEXT

"Look carefully then how you walk, not as the unwise but as the wise, making the most of the time, because the days are evil. Therefore do not be foolish, but understand what the will of the Lord is. And do not get drunk with wine, in which there is debauchery; but be filled in the Spirit, addressing one another in psalms and hymns and spiritual songs, singing and making melody to the Lord with all your heart, always and for everything giving thanks in the name of our Lord Jesus Christ to God the Father." (Eph 5:15-20)

In this well-known passage of Ephesians, before St. Paul goes on to instruct wives to be subjected to husbands (5:22ff), and slaves to obey their masters (6:5ff), the Apostle underlines an oft-overlooked aspect of what he is saying: historical context. Make the most, he says, "of the time,"—of the specific time in which these Christians are living, "because the days are evil." Therefore do not be foolish, but understand, within this specific time, what the will of the Lord is.

So today the Apostle calls me to "look carefully," and to walk "not as the unwise but as the wise," making the most of my own time. I am called to the joyous existence of "being filled in the Spirit," in His wisdom and in gratitude, "always and for everything giving thanks in the name of our Lord Jesus Christ to God the Father," in my own day. Today I give thanks for St. Paul, who speaks to me not as to a child, but as to an adult, capable of discerning, contextualizing, and exercising wisdom, in the freedom of the Spirit, rather than repetition of the letter. Glory be to Him, the life-giving Comforter of my here and now.

NOVEMBER 1

THE SENSE OF GOD'S PRESENCE

"Blessed are the people who know jubilation! O Lord, they walk in the light of your countenance, and in your name they rejoice all the day..." (Ps 88/89: 14/15-16)

Two things are mentioned here, which are closely connected:
1. Walking in God's "countenance" and
2. Rejoicing in His name "all the day."

When I call upon God's name, wherever and whenever throughout my day, I find myself consciously "walking in the light of His countenance"; that is, I sense God's presence amidst any situation, conversation, activity, or inactivity. And this sense brings me joyous "blessedness"; an assurance that all is good, even very good, in His hands.

Today let me call His name throughout my day; let me walk not in darkness, but in the light of His countenance. *"Lord Jesus Christ, Son of God, have mercy on me, the sinner."*

NOVEMBER 2

IT IS ALL GOOD

"It is good for me that I have been afflicted (Septuagint version: that you have humbled me, (ὅτι ἐταπείνωσάς με); that I might learn your statutes." (Ps 118/119: 71)

How blessed am I to have also this verse, this consoling word, in my spiritual "toolbox," to pick up and carry with me, whenever my own poor choices and sins rear their ugly head. …No, let me rephrase that: How blessed I am to have this verse to pick me up and carry me, whenever I am afflicted and beat down by my own afflictions. Because God carries me forward, "that I might learn." That's the great difference faith makes, God makes, in the human journey: He blesses both the ups and the downs with eternal meaning, with the grace of growth in His gifts of humility, wisdom, and compassionate light.

Today let me let God carry me onwards, shedding light on my cross-carrying journey. Let me place my sins and shortcomings where they belong, in His hands, where I can see them in His light, rather than hide them, or hide from them, in my own mind. "It is good for me that You have humbled me"; I say to Him today, "that I might learn from Your statutes."

NOVEMBER 3

SECRET REWARDS

"And when you pray, do not be like the hypocrites; for they love to stand and pray in the synagogues and at the street corners, so that they may be seen by others. Truly I tell you, they have received their reward. But when you pray, go into your room and shut the door and pray to your Father who is in secret; and your Father who sees in secret will reward you." (Mt 6:5-6)

It has often been noted that here the Lord is NOT telling us that we shouldn't pray publicly and in churches. What He is saying is, we shouldn't do it "like the hypocrites," for the purpose of being "seen by others." After all, Jesus Himself prayed publicly on many occasions, and also went many times to the temple, to which He referred as His "Father's house" (Jn 2:16).

But the Lord does remind me, in this passage and elsewhere, of the rewards of private, solitary prayer. He Himself repeatedly finds time for this kind of prayer, in the midst of His ministry to the multitudes, as in Mt 14:23: *"After he had dismissed them, he went up on a mountainside by himself to pray."*

And when Christ said, "go into your room and shut the door and pray to your Father who is in secret," the people listening to Him doubtlessly needed to hear this, as I do today. They may have limited themselves to "praying in the synagogues" and on public occasions like funerals and weddings, while neglecting private, alone-time with God. "Your Father who sees in secret," Christ reminds me, "will reward you."

Today let me find a bit of time for heartfelt, private prayer "to my Father who is in secret," and its secret rewards.

NOVEMBER 4

DON'T LIVE A COMPARATIVE LIFE

"Peter turned and saw that the disciple whom Jesus loved was following them...When Peter saw him, he asked, "Lord, what about him? Jesus answered, If I want him to remain alive until I return, what is that to you? You follow me." (John 21:20-22)

It is sometimes tempting to observe other peoples' lives and journeys, especially of our peers, and compare our own life with theirs. We also might wistfully observe the lives of celebrities, and feel somehow insufficient or less fortunate.

But today I'll remember what Christ said to Peter, and hear Him say it to me: *What is that to you? You follow Me.*

NOVEMBER 5

NOT JUST A KISS

"While he was still speaking, Judas, one of the twelve, arrived; with him was a large crowd with swords and clubs, from the chief priests and the elders of the people. Now the betrayer had given them a sign (σημεῖον), saying, 'The one I will kiss is the man; arrest him.' At once he came up to Jesus and said, 'Greetings, Rabbi!' and kissed him. Jesus said to him, 'Friend, do what you are here to do.' Then they came and laid hands on Jesus and arrested him." (Mt 26:47-50)

The obvious lesson of the infamous "kiss of Judas" lies in its perverted meaning. It is still a "kiss," the usual, instantly-recognizable "sign" of good will and/or friendship, but Judas uses the kiss, along with his "hello" ("Greetings, Rabbi!") as a "green light" for my Lord's executioners. This is a "kiss of death," first and foremost for Judas himself.

So my external motions, symbolic actions/words do not "guarantee" their usual meanings. I must be mindful that my heart's intention is aligned with the intended meaning of my external actions and words, be it in prayer and other forms of worship, or in my interaction with other people. Otherwise—and this is an unpleasant truth—I can do serious damage to myself and others. I can potentially slip into a habitual "fakeness" or posing, losing touch with my heart's actual state and ceasing to grow in true communion with God and others. This is why I am reminded, in the Byzantine Prayer Before Communion, *"...neither like Judas will I give You a kiss; but like the thief will I confess You: Remember me, O Lord in Your Kingdom."*

Today let me be mindful of my words and actions, that my "yes" be "yes" and my "no" be "no" (Mt 5:37). Ad let me take care to watch my heart, "cleaning house" on a daily basis, in honesty before God, myself, and others.

NOVEMBER 6

IN SPIRIT AND TRUTH

"The (Samaritan) woman said to him, 'Sir, I perceive that you are a prophet. Our fathers worshiped on this mountain; and you say that in Jerusalem is the place where men ought to worship.' Jesus said to her, 'Woman, believe me, the hour is coming when neither on this mountain nor in Jerusalem will you worship the Father. You worship what you do not know; we worship what we know, for salvation is from the Jews. But the hour is coming, and now is, when the true worshipers will worship the Father in spirit and truth, for such the Father seeks to worship him. God is spirit, and those who worship him must worship in spirit and truth.' The woman said to him, 'I know that Messiah is coming, he who is called Christ; when he comes, he will show us all things.' Jesus said to her, 'I who speak to you am he.'" (Jn 4:19-26)

We "know" what we worship, says our Lord, while you "do not know." And yet, the Father still seeks "true worshipers," because those who worship Him must worship not only in truth, but also in Spirit. The "knowledge" of truth is vital, but not enough. Because "God is Spirit."

Today let me carry this word with me, along with our Lord's promise to all of us: "Believe Me, the hour is coming when neither on this mountain nor in Jerusalem will you worship the Father." He makes this emphatic promise to a woman not "orthodox"; to a woman not "right" in so many ways. "The hour is coming, and now is," He says to me this morning, because "I who speak to you am He." Let me let Him in today, in His Spirit and His Truth, because the Father "seeks" me to do so. Glory be to Him, and to the Spirit and to the Truth, Who speaks to us so plainly, even when we are yet not "right" in so many ways.

NOVEMBER 7

PATIENCE

"In your patience possess/acquire your souls." (Lk 21:19)

What is patience? It is the power to wait. In Greek the word "patience," ὑπομονή, literally means a "remaining behind"; a holding out, while awaiting someone or something—regardless, I might add, whether one knows who/what that someone or something is.

I must "acquire" my soul, my very life, our Lord tells me, through patience. That is to say, I become alive to God, responsive to God, and am able to grow in Him, through a willingness to await whatever He sends next, amidst the ambivalences and "not yets" of my here and now. "Hence," writes the inimitable Hans Urs von Balthasar, "the importance of patience in the New Testament, which becomes the basic constituent of Christianity, more central even than humility: the power to wait, to persevere, to hold out, to endure to the end, not to transcend one's own limitations, not to force issues by playing the hero or the titan, but to practice the virtue that lies beyond heroism, the meekness of the lamb which is *led.*"

Today as I take up my work and interact with others, with all our ambivalences and limitations, let me carry with me our Lord's call to patience, in the Spirit of the Lamb Who was led.

NOVEMBER 8

THE ANONYMOUS ANGEL

"For an angel of peace, faithful guide and guardian of our souls and bodies, let us ask the Lord." (Litany of Supplication, Byzantine Liturgy)

This petition reminds me to ask for, rather than take for granted, the invisible, intelligent being called here "an angel of peace," a.k.a. my "guardian angel." I am thus reminded that this invisible "someone" is given to me by God, to look out for me, as it says in the Psalm: *"...for to his angels God has given command about you, that they guard you in all your ways."* (Ps 90/91: 11)

This "angel" is not only a "guardian of my soul and body," but also a "faithful guide," because he is God's "messenger" (ἄγγελος in Greek means "messenger"). He relates to me God's "messages," speaking to me in my conscience and in other ways, when I am open to "hearing" him. Now, we may often forget about our "faithful guides," and many people have trouble believing in their existence in the first place. Nonetheless, they look out for us and guide us, both invisibly and anonymously. As an "angel of peace," my guardian-angel doesn't cease to do what he does, even when he gets no credit for it. There are no celebrities among the "angels," who belong to the lowest "rank" of the invisible, bodiless powers. We don't even know the name of the angel who rolled back the stone of Christ's tomb and related that joyous news to the women, "He is not here; He is risen…" (Mt 28:6). For all we know, he may be somebody's guardian-angel today, quietly going about, making sure some unsuspecting truck-driver somewhere gets home safely to his wife and children.

Today let me be grateful to God, not only for His subtle guidance and "messages," which have so often nudged me in the right direction, but also for His "messengers," the angels. They selflessly, anonymously guide and guard our souls and bodies, even when we don't notice or thank them for it.

NOVEMBER 9

JESUS WEPT

"...When she (Martha) had said this, she went and called her sister Mary, saying quietly, 'The Teacher is here and is calling for you.' And when she heard it, she rose quickly and went to him. Now Jesus had not yet come to the village, but was still in the place where Martha had met him. When the Jews who were with her in the house, consoling her, saw Mary rise quickly and go out, they followed her, supposing that she was going to the tomb to weep there. Then Mary, when she came where Jesus was and saw him, fell at his feet, saying to him, 'Lord, if you had been here, my brother would not have died.' When Jesus saw her weeping, and the Jews who came with her also weeping, he was deeply moved in spirit and troubled; and he said, 'Where have you laid him?' They said to him, 'Lord, come and see.' Jesus wept. So the Jews said, 'See how he loved him!' But some of them said, 'Could not he who opened the eyes of the blind man have kept this man from dying?'" (Jn 11:28-37)

And that's precisely what I am wondering, when, so unexpectedly, I see the Lord "weep." He could have prevented this from happening in the first place! But instead He took His time, getting to Bethany... And even now, He tarries just outside the village, for some reason, and the story is dragging on and on, described by the Evangelist John in rather excruciating detail. Of course, we know about the light at the end of this story, but imagine the hours, then days, of the human beings involved here; of their waiting, hoping, then running out of time, and hope—while God stalls.

So God has His schedule, which does not always correspond to mine. At times this can bring frustration, fear, or even intense grief, as in the case of the death of a loved one. Things change, and often not at the precise time, or in the exact way, I would like. Thus God allows for this suffering, great or small, but always inherent to our being in time, that is, in changeability.

But note that He does enter into our suffering, with great compassion. How do I know that? Because "Jesus wept" with us. And God subjected His Son to the changeability and changes of our being in time, even unto our death, so that His Son could do for us what none of us could do for ourselves: Transfigure our suffering into light, and transfigure our death into life. This is the ultimate change He makes possible for me, in His cross and resurrection. Let me not fear change today, not the kind my Lord brings me, even if He takes His time.

NOVEMBER 10

FROM "TOLERANCE" TO ACCEPTANCE

"We who are strong ought to bear/tolerate (βαστάζειν) the failings of the weak, and not to please ourselves. Each of us must please our neighbor for the good purpose of building up the neighbor... May the God of steadfastness and encouragement grant you to live in harmony with one another, in accordance with Christ Jesus, so that together you may with one voice glorify the God and Father of our Lord Jesus Christ. Accept/receive (προσλαμβάνεσθε) one another, therefore, just as Christ has accepted you, for the glory of God." (Rom 15:1-2, 5-7)

So in this passage the Apostle calls us, first, to "bear" or tolerate (from the Latin "tolerare," meaning "to bear, endure"), but then he goes on to ask us to do even more: He says, "accept" one another, just as Christ accepted us, all of us, having "tolerated" or "carried" our entire humanity and its sins.

Today let me both "carry" and "accept" others, just as I am carried and accepted, as I am, by my crucified, buried, and resurrected Lord, "for the good purpose of building up" the other, whoever he or she may be throughout my day. Let me embrace the "good purpose" today, which the Apostle spells out for me: "so that we may with one voice glorify the God and Father of our Lord Jesus Christ." Amen!

NOVEMBER 11

BLESSED BROKENNESS

"And he took the bread, gave thanks and broke it, and gave it to them, saying, 'This is my body given for you; do this in remembrance of me.'" (Lk 22:19)

Just as He took the bread, broke it with His own, loving hands, and gave it to His disciples, so does He, the Bread of Life, continue to give Himself to us, in loving brokenness. And so does He also break me, having taken me and blessed me on a cross-carrying journey with and within His life-giving Body.

But there is more than one way to "brokenness." I can be broken without Him, in which case my brokenness leads to bitterness, resentment, and cynicism. But in His loving and life-creating hands, I am broken for new life, new growth, new service and self-giving, in His way. So let me turn my will and my life over into His hands today, because only He gives it back to me, transformed and blessed in His ever-new Gifts.

NOVEMBER 12

TEACHABILITY

"And it came to pass, that, as he was praying in a certain place, when he ceased, one of his disciples said unto him, Lord, teach us to pray, as John also taught his disciples." (Lk 11:1)

Evidently, in this passage our Lord "was praying in a certain place" in the presence of His disciples—who were not, however, praying with Him. For some reason, they were simply there (maybe just sitting around), and "when he ceased," one of them asked Him, "Lord, teach us to pray...." And Jesus famously proceeds to teach them the Our Father.

I don't know exactly how the Lord "was praying" in this "certain place," which prompted the disciple's request; whether Christ stood, kneeled, just sat quietly, whispered, or prayed aloud. Whatever He did, the disciples recognized that they did not, in contrast, know how to pray.

I note today the precious quality expressed in the request, "Lord, teach us..." It is teachability. It is the ability to recognize my need to be taught, and a desire to be taught, on my journey to salvation. If I have difficulty praying, or contemplating His word, or opening up to His grace in my work, or in my relationships with other people, let me ask Him, "Lord, teach me!" May I have the eyes to see and the ears to hear what God has to teach me today, be it through His word, and/or through the people, conversations, situations, difficulties or opportunities that come my way throughout this day.

NOVEMBER 13

THE TRUE LIGHT

"O Christ, the True Light, Who enlightens and sanctifies anyone who comes into the world: Let the light of Your countenance be signed upon us, that in it we may see the Unapproachable Light, and guide our steps in the doing of Your commandments, through the intercessions of Your most pure Mother, and of all Your saints. Amen." (Byzantine Prayer of the First Hour)

There are many kinds of "light." This morning I switched on the lamp in my room, while it was still dark outside. But now, two hours later, the lamp is useless, because the sun has risen and is shining all over the place. And yet, as useful and amazing as the gifts both of electric light and sunlight are, they cannot "enlighten and sanctify" me, as I "come into the world" today. For this I am given the greatest gift of all, sent to us by our Father—His Son, the True Light.

This morning I look to Him, as I pray before His holy image, that "His countenance be signed" upon me. I will see many images today, both good and bad, both online and in my immediate surroundings. But let me be "signed" only with His, that I may truly "see" others, myself, and everything else, in His gentle light and wisdom. Glory be to Him.

NOVEMBER 14

TRUE DISCIPLESHIP

"Then Jesus said to the Jews who had believed in him, 'If you continue in my word, you are truly my disciples; and you will know the truth, and the truth will make you free.' They answered him, 'We are descendants of Abraham and have never been slaves to anyone. What do you mean by saying, 'You will be made free'?' Jesus answered them, 'Very truly, I tell you, everyone who commits sin is a slave to sin. The slave does not have a permanent place in the household; the son has a place there forever." (Jn 8:31-35)

So it's not enough, to be "descendants of Abraham." It's not enough for true discipleship and true freedom, externally to belong to God's chosen people. Just as today it is not enough, for me externally to belong to the Church of the Fathers, merely repeating their words. I must "continue," as the Lord reminds us here, "in" His word, internalizing it in my own context, so that I may "know the truth," which makes us "truly His disciples." But if I smugly engage in what Fr. George Florovsky called "a theology of repetition," I am bound to "miss the mark," that is, commit "sin" or "amartia" in Greek, which means "missing the mark."

Today many of us are tempted to focus on our exclusivity as "Church," focusing on this one word, as if true discipleship depended on being "descendents of" our great Tradition. This focus tempts us to "miss the mark" of brotherly love, compassion, and conciliarity, enslaving us to perpetual disunity. So let me be reminded of another word of our Lord today, and let me "continue" in it, as He liberates me toward true discipleship: *"By this everyone will know that you are my disciples, if you love one another."* (Jn 13:35)

NOVEMBER 15

THE LOVE OF GOD

"Who shall separate us from the love of God? Shall tribulation, or distress, or persecution, or famine, or nakedness, or peril, or sword? As it is written, 'For your sake we are being killed all the day long; we are regarded as sheep to be slaughtered.' No, in all these things we are more than conquerors through him who loved us. For I am sure that neither death, nor life, nor angels, nor principalities, nor things present, nor things to come, nor powers, nor height, nor depth, nor anything else in all creation, will be able to separate us from the love of God in Christ Jesus our Lord." (Rom 8:35-39)

So let my focus be God-centered today, if human beings, however important and dear to me, or certain matters, close to my heart, fail to meet my expectations. Let me accept, in faith and love, the presence of God in Christ Jesus our Lord, amidst all the human words and behaviors, including my own, which fall short of "Him who loved us."

Today I take some time to re-connect with Him, in heartfelt prayer, because... Well, simply because I can. He is always there, always unchanging, in His undying love for all of us. "Who shall separate us from the love of God?" Glory be to Him.

NOVEMBER 16

ABIDE IN ME

"I am the true vine, and my Father is the vinedresser. Every branch of mine that bears no fruit, he takes away, and every branch that does bear fruit he prunes, that it may bear more fruit. You are already made clean by the word which I have spoken to you. Abide in me, and I in you. As the branch cannot bear fruit by itself, unless it abides in the vine, neither can you, unless you abide in me. I am the vine, you are the branches. He who abides in me, and I in him, he it is that bears much fruit, for apart from me you can do nothing." (Jn 15:1-5)

It's that simple. Because I can't share with others what I don't have myself. Without a daily connection with Christ, I am left with merely human words, behaviours, challenges, and interactions, which make no logical sense. And by "logical" I mean the kind of meaning that comes from Him, the eternal "Logos" of the Father. In Him, my every challenge, my every situation and interaction is subjected to a Great Vinedresser, Who "prunes" my entire being toward growth and beauty, which only He can bestow.

So let me "abide in Him" today, and let me be "made clean" by the word which He has spoken to us. He doesn't want me to be by myself, "as the branch cannot bear fruit by itself." Let me let You be in me today, O Lord, and I in You. *"Lord, Jesus Christ, Son of God,"* I say throughout this day, *"have mercy on me, a sinner."*

NOVEMBER 17

THE FUTILE WAYS OF OUR FATHERS

"You know that you were ransomed from the futile ways inherited from your fathers, not with perishable things such as silver or gold, but with the precious blood of Christ, like that of a lamb without blemish or spot. He was destined before the foundation of the world but was made manifest at the end of the times for your sake. Through him you have confidence in God, who raised him from the dead and gave him glory, so that your faith and hope are in God. Having purified your souls by your obedience to the truth for a sincere love of the brethren, love one another earnestly from the heart. You have been born anew, not of perishable seed but of imperishable, through the living and abiding word of God..." (1 Pet 1:18-23)

Indeed I have been "born anew, not of perishable seed but of imperishable." I am gratefully reminded of this today, when the "the futile ways inherited from our fathers" play out, succeeding, for the time being, to divide us and disrupt all efforts toward church-unity. It is not through the divisive words of men that we have been "born anew," but "through the living and abiding word of God."

So let me stay close to His word today, in "obedience to the truth for a sincere love of the brethren," whatever the "brethren" happen to be saying or doing. It is through Christ that we have "confidence in God, who raised him from the dead and gave him glory." Let us place our hope and faith where it belongs, in Him, Who alone is "without blemish or spot," that we may "love one another earnestly from the heart." O Lord, may Your word live and abide in us, now and forever. Amen.

NOVEMBER 18

CUT TO THE HEART

"...Now when they heard this they were cut to the heart, and said to Peter and the rest of the apostles, 'Brethren, what shall we do?' And Peter said to them, 'Repent, and be baptized every one of you in the name of Jesus Christ for the forgiveness of your sins; and you shall receive the gift of the Holy Spirit. For the promise is to you and to your children and to all that are far off, every one whom the Lord our God calls to him.'" (Acts 2:37-39)

Having heard St. Peter speak about Christ right after the descent of the Holy Spirit, the people were "cut" or "pierced" in the heart (κατενύγησαν τὴν καρδίαν). This experience makes the teachable, and they ask: What shall we do?

Today there are various experiences in my life that may "cut to the heart." Let me receive them as Spirit-filled messages, making me teachable—making me realize that, without His help, I simply don't know what to do. But I can ask, and be helped, *"For,"* as the apostle reminded us at Pentecost, *"the promise is to you and your children and to all that are far off, every one whom the Lord our God calls to him."* Let me call to Him today, as He calls to me, in the small and large "cuts" to my heart. *"A sacrifice to God is a broken spirit; a broken and contrite heart God will not despise."* (Ps 50/51:17)

NOVEMBER 19

NOT IN TALK, BUT IN POWER

"...Therefore I sent to you Timothy, my beloved and faithful child in the Lord, to remind you of my ways in Christ, as I teach them everywhere in every church. Some are arrogant, as though I were not coming to you. But I will come to you soon, if the Lord wills, and I will find out not the talk of these arrogant people but their power. For the kingdom of God does not consist in talk but in power." (1 Cor 4:17-20)

What "power" is St. Paul talking about, in this fatherly admonition to the Corinthians? He is referring to the power of the Holy Spirit, in which I am called to abide. His is the "kingdom" I am called to inhabit, not merely and not primarily by talking about it. Here the apostle is warning us against Spirit-less talk, be it about church-matters or other matters, because such talk is damaging and destructive, holding "power" not from above.

"Come and abide in us," I pray today, so that our "power," be it in silence or in words, may always be Yours, of the constructive and consoling kind. "For Thine is the kingdom, the power, and the glory, now and forever." Amen!

NOVEMBER 20

DAILY GRATITUDE

"Rejoice always, pray without ceasing, give thanks in all circumstances; for this is the will of God in Christ Jesus for you." (1 Thess 5:16-18)

I'm reflecting a bit on gratitude today, because it's almost Thanksgiving Day. Is "Giving thanks in all circumstances" (or simply "in everything," ἐν παντὶ) even possible, along with "rejoicing always" and "praying without ceasing," as the Apostle tells me to do in the above-cited verse? The three are intimately connected, but they do require a conscious effort on my part, on a daily basis. This "effort" is neither forced nor overwhelming, when I let God's loving discipline of joy, prayer, and gratitude into my day.

I find it helpful to list what I am grateful for this past day, when I write in my little, hard-covered notebook in the evening. I include this "gratitude" part along with the things I did well, and things I did poorly. And I find that gratitude changes the whole picture. Gratitude is a wonderful, God-given human capacity that gently removes the deep-seated disappointment or dissatisfaction I sometimes store up during the day (with situations, with myself, or others); It sheds a warm and humbling light on my day, however it went. Gratitude helps me be aware, on a daily basis, of God's continuous presence in my life, liberating me from self-reliant fears, self-centered expectations of others, and arrogant self-criticism. Finally, gratitude opens my heart to joy and prayer, which come hand-in-hand when I have this awareness of God's presence.

Today let me put gratitude in the center of my daily life. "For this," the Apostle reminds me, "is the will of God in Christ Jesus" for me.

NOVEMBER 21

PRAYER OF ENTRANCE

"Master and Lord our God, You have established in heaven the orders and hosts of angels and archangels for liturgical service (εἰς λειτουργίαν) to Your glory. Make our entrance be the entrance of the holy angels, concelebrating with us (συλλειτουργούντων ἡμῖν) and co-glorifying Your goodness." (Prayer of Small Entrance, Byzantine Divine Liturgy)

"Transitional" moments in liturgy, just like major "transitional" moments in life, are traditionally accompanied with intensified prayer. The prayer cited above is read by the priest at the so-called Small Entrance, which was originally at the very beginning of liturgy; when the people and clergy entered the church. In the prayer we ask God that our transition from the outside to the inside of the church, our "entrance" into the divine-human "work" of Liturgy, be in harmony with the "work" of the heavenly powers, the holy angels. On earth as it is in heaven. This unity of heaven and earth is an important leitmotif of Byzantine Liturgy.

I'm reflecting on this prayer today, when those of us on the Old(er) Calendar are celebrating the feast of St. Michael and all the heavenly powers, while those of us on the "New" Calendar are celebrating the Entrance of the Theotokos into the Temple. Both feasts remind me today of the importance of entering all of life's "transitional" moments with prayer, in harmony with God's will, on earth as it is in heaven. This includes small, daily transitions, like getting up from bed to begin the day, or going from home to church, or from home to work, or preparing for bed; as well as major "transitions," like moving to a new city, changing jobs, or, for some people, getting married, getting divorced, giving birth to a child, preparing for death, or whatever.

Today let me not fear any changes or transitions in life, but place them all in God's hands, in communion with those who did and continue to do His will, like the holy angels, and like the "more honorable than the cherubim," the Most Holy Theotokos. *"Thy will be done,"* I pray today, *"on earth as it is in heaven."*

NOVEMBER 22

COMMON PRAYERS

"You have given us these common prayers, offered in symphonic unity. You have promised to grant the requests of two or three gathered in Your name. Fulfill now the petitions of Your servants for our benefit, giving us the knowledge of Your truth in this world, and granting us eternal life in the world to come." (Priest's Prayer of the Third Antiphon, Byzantine Divine Liturgy)

Here's another gem from the little-known treasure that is the Liturgy. Before it begins today, let me reflect on the nature of "common" prayer, that is, liturgical prayer. Let me prepare to join in the actual prayer of the Eucharist, the Thanksgiving being offered in the "symphonic" (συμφώνους) and unified prayers of the Church, as the priest says in the above-cited Prayer of the Third Antiphon (chanted before the Small Entrance in the first part of Divine liturgy).

The common, liturgical prayer that I offer together with others inspires the private prayers that I offer alone—and vice-versa. I need both of these, both liturgical and private prayer, to maintain a healthy prayer-life. Let me nurture both, so that I approach the upcoming celebration of Thanksgiving in symphony with God, myself, and others.

NOVEMBER 23

SELF-GIVING ON THANKSGIVING

"...Lord, grant that I may seek rather to comfort than to be comforted—to understand, than to be understood—to love, than to be loved. For it is by self-forgetting that one finds. It is by forgiving that one is forgiven. It is by dying that one awakens to Eternal Life. Amen." ("Prayer of St. Francis")

Today let me turn things around, seeing what I can contribute to others this Thanksgiving, rather than to focus on what I can get out of the celebration. Let me tone down any neediness or pettiness, and be sensitive to the needs of others. Perhaps this might mean just helping with the dishes, or shutting up when an argument begins at the table. Or maybe I can invite some lonely person to join my table, because someone in my vicinity might be alone on Thanksgiving.

Let me give of myself today, in the way that I can, in gratitude for whatever I've been given. Have a Happy Thanksgiving!

NOVEMBER 24

THE HUMBLING CROSS OF DISUNITY

"For there must be also divisions among you, that they which are approved may be made manifest among you." (1 Cor 11:19)

Just yesterday I mentioned this passage to an Orthodox clergyman, one who has been working tirelessly for church-unity, both on the ecumenical and pan-Orthodox levels. I tend to think of him as one of those "which are approved." But when I mentioned this passage to him, the clergyman unexpectedly replied, "the 1 Corinthians passage makes me realize how abysmally I have failed." And when I asked, Why?, he said, "because I've been thinking: I haven't always focused on the goal..."

Humility! How refreshing and liberating it is, not to play the "blame game," or point fingers at others, as we bear our common cross of disunity and other human failings. Today let me take up this cross, as God's humbling gift; as His tap on my shoulder, reminding me of my own failings and loss of focus. Let me bear our humbling cross, rather than deepen our divisions through burdensome self-justification and self-righteousness. Today let the apostle's liberating, humbling call be heard in my heart: *"Bear one another's burdens, and so fulfill the law of Christ."* (Gal 6:2)

NOVEMBER 25

"BODY AWARENESS" vs. LIFE IN THE SPIRIT

"From now on, therefore, we regard (οἴδαμεν) no one according to the flesh (κατὰ σάρκα); even though we once regarded Christ according to the flesh, we regard him thus no longer. Therefore, if any one is in Christ, he is a new creation; the old has passed away, behold, the new has come. All this is from God, who through Christ reconciled us to himself and gave us the ministry of reconciliation..." (2 Cor 5:16-18)

Why has "the old" passed away? What, exactly, has changed? The coming of the Holy Spirit has changed everything, including the way we "regard" or "know" (οἴδαμεν) Christ, and the way we regard our own selves. When I embrace a life in the Holy Spirit, opening up to His abundant gifts, I am liberated from the burdens of excessive "body awareness" and its obsessions. *"For those who live according to the flesh set their minds on the things of the flesh, but those who live according to the Spirit set their minds on the things of the Spirit."* (Rom 8:5)

Does this mean I shouldn't care for my body, or disparage the material world altogether? No. It means that I embrace a new perspective on these things; a perspective of true life and true peace, which is a gift of the Holy Spirit. For example, rather than looking someone "up and down," and "according to the flesh," I am given to see beyond that, to see more than that, and not miss out on God's hidden gifts and messages in all things. He "reconciles us to Himself" through His way of seeing and knowing, because "all this is from God." So let me re-connect with Him today, opening up to His grace, as I care for my health, both in body and soul. *"To set the mind on the flesh is death, but to set the mind on the Spirit is life and peace."* (Rom 8:6) Glory be to Him.

NOVEMBER 26

THE HANGOVER

"Day to day pours forth speech, and night to night declares knowledge." (Ps 18/19:2)

This Psalm-verse talks about the connection between one day's "speech" and "knowledge" to the next day's "speech" and "knowledge." In practical terms this means that the words I say, hear, or read today, as well as the "knowledge" I receive today (through my words, experiences, encounters, actions—even my choices of food and drink, choice of bedtime, etc.) spill over into tomorrow. The "knowledge" I choose to accumulate today can either help my growth, moving me forward in God's wisdom, or it can take me a few steps back, like a crippling hangover.

Let me be mindful today, particularly in the evening, that I "process" everything I did, said, read, and thought this day, in a beneficial manner, in God's light. I find it helpful to take just a few minutes and jot down both what I did poorly (with a little "minus" sign next to those things) and what I did well (with a "plus" sign next to those). I also jot down what I'm grateful for, and several intentions about doing a bit better tomorrow. I have a little, hard-covered notebook for this purpose, which I carry around with me as a reminder.

I ask God today to help me acquire the kind of "speech" and "knowledge" that will help me build with Him, and in Him, tomorrow. I ask Him to help me help myself make healthy choices today: *"For You, Christ our God,"* as it says in the Prayer Before the Gospel, *"are the light of our souls and bodies."* To Him I give glory today, that I may get up to His greater glory tomorrow.

NOVEMBER 27

PROPER NOURISHMENT

"Blessed is the man who has not walked in the counsel of the ungodly… But his will is rather in the law of the Lord, and in His law will he meditate day and night." (Ps 1:1-2)

If I want my "will" to be "in the law of the Lord," I need to "meditate" in it. That is, I need to be nurtured by the Word of God, on a daily basis, rather than allow myself to be engrossed exclusively in that overabundance of words (either online or elsewhere), which is often either plain useless, or "the counsel of the ungodly." Because the words and information that I imbibe on a daily basis have an effect on me; they affect my "will" and can mold my desires and aspirations.

Let me remember today that I have a choice in this matter. I can abstain a bit from overindulging in useless stories or shows, and make healthier choices as to what I read or watch today. Because this is what I will carry around with me, in my heart, and this is what will affect the direction of my "will," for the rest of the day.

NOVEMBER 28

SHOCK & DISMAY

"Now the birth of Jesus the Messiah took place in this way. When his mother Mary had been engaged to Joseph, but before they lived together, she was found to be with child from the Holy Spirit. Her husband Joseph, being a righteous man and not wanting to expose her to public disgrace, planned to dismiss her quietly." (Mt 1:18-19)

As I prepare for the upcoming feast of the Lord's Nativity, let me reflect a bit on Joseph's surprisingly "quiet" reaction to Mary's as yet unexplained pregnancy. We see no shock or dismay in this righteous man, who was confronted with a situation that—let's say it like it is—looked very, very bad. And yet all Joseph wanted to do in this situation was:
1. protect Her from public disgrace, and
2. dismiss Her "quietly."

So this is a "righteous" reaction to the perceived sin of another human being. Today let me gratefully contemplate Joseph's humble and quiet discretion, lest I be tempted to display shock and dismay at any perceived amorality or sinful behaviour in my surroundings. My shock and my dismay is neither righteous nor helpful. In fact, when I am judgmental I become utterly incapable of being helpful; when I try to play God's role of Judge, I close myself off from His grace-filled mercy. I also display a lack of self-knowledge, but I'll elaborate on that point some other time.

During this Nativity Fast let me abstain from shock and dismay, that I can make my journey toward Bethlehem with a proper focus. Let me "make straight the paths of the Lord" in my own heart, that I may greet Him in the same way He is born, in quietness and humility.

NOVEMBER 29

RESTRAINT OF THE EYES

"My eyes are always on the Lord, for he will pull my feet out of the net." (Ps 24/25:15)

The eyes are a window through which all sorts of ideas, desires, emotions, or interests—not always healthy ones—can enter my mind and heart. This obvious fact is even more obvious during this "shopping season," when the storefronts and advertisements are all lit up with attractive Christmas lights and "bargains." But the eyes can be drawn, and choose to linger on, not only things, but people, to evaluate how they are dressed, how attractive they are (or not), what car they drive, and so on.

So I can become entangled, in my mind, in a sort of "net," which distracts me from my desired focus, from a God-centered, Spirit-centered life. This kind of "net" is what the Apostle calls "the mind of the flesh," which robs us of peace, leading to various forms of frustration, envy, lust, unhealthy spending or eating habits. *"To set the mind on the flesh is death,"* says St. Paul, *"but to set the mind on the Spirit is life and peace."* (Rom 8:6)

So today let me set my inner vision on the Lord, and ask that He help me restrain my eyes, according to His wisdom and His grace, liberating me from various, unwanted entanglements. Today *"My eyes are always on the Lord, for he will pull my feet out of the net."*

NOVEMBER 30

PREPARING FOR HIS COMING

"And may the Lord make you increase and abound in love for one another and for all, just as we do for you, so as to strengthen your hearts blameless in holiness before our God and Father at the coming of our Lord Jesus Christ with all his saints. Amen." (1 Thess 3:12-13)

The "coming" of our Lord Jesus Christ, for which we now prepare in a special manner (in the Nativity Fast or celebration of Advent), is something for which I am called to prepare constantly, on a daily basis. Because He is the One who is "coming again" (πάλιν ἐρχόμενον), and again, into my life and into my heart, when I remain open to Him, clearing away any obstacles I may build up on His path to me. I do this with His help, as the Apostle mentions above: He "strengthens our hearts blameless in holiness," making us "increase and abound in love for one another and for all."

Today, amidst any noise or obstacles on my journey of preparation, let me keep my focus on His help, in prayer. And let me not be discouraged, but re-focus, in repentance, when need be, as I make my way to Him. Because He can, and does, "strengthen my heart" so it can increase and abound in love for Him and for all.

DECEMBER 1

SPIRITUAL INFANCY

"And so, brothers and sisters, I could not speak to you as spiritual people, but rather as people of the flesh, as infants in Christ. I fed you with milk, not solid food, for you were not ready for solid food. Even now you are still not ready, for you are still of the flesh. For as long as there is jealousy and quarreling among you, are you not of the flesh, and behaving according to human inclinations? For when one says, 'I belong to Paul,' and another, 'I belong to Apollos,' are you not merely human?" (1 Cor 3:1-4)

The Apostle reminds me today of some of the pitfalls of spiritual infancy. This is an infantile behavior one might exhibit either when entirely new to faith, being newly-baptised, or many years after baptism, having rediscovered the faith of one's childhood with new zeal. One might be tempted, in this phase, to "quarrel" with others within the church-community about various matters of church discipline, like fasting rules or the details of liturgical celebration. St. Paul describes this "merely human" behavior as being "of the flesh"; "quarreling" on the basis of human alliances and "human inclinations." This reminds me of what Christ said to the Pharisees, after they criticized the Lord's disciples for "eating with defiled hands" and not "living according to the tradition of the elders." He says to them, *"You abandon the commandment of God and hold to human tradition."* (Mk 7:5-8)

During this period of the Nativity Fast, let me proceed with caution, watching that my own fasting, according to the tradition I embrace, be in His Spirit; in harmony with God's will, God's love, and God's mercy for me and others. *"A sacrifice unto God is a broken spirit,"* I remind myself today. *"A heart that is broken and humbled God will not despise."* (Ps 50/51:17)

DECEMBER 2

RIGHTEOUSNESS: IS IT WORTH IT?

"Blessed are those who hunger and thirst for righteousness, for they will be satisfied." (Mt 5:6)

Is it worth it, to invest time and energy in spiritual life, improving my conscious contact with God in prayer, contemplation, fasting, liturgy, self-examination, self-giving, and/or whatever other tools are available to me? It is perhaps easier to be motivated toward material goals, like going on a diet and jogging daily to be physically fit; or working hard at my job to make more money and attain more financial "security."

Yes, "righteousness" is worth it, the Lord reminds me today. I am "blessed" through hungering and thirsting for it, because this is an objective that "satisfies" or "fills" the hole in my heart. This hole can never entirely be filled, can never truly be satisfied, by material gain or betterment. I have tried it. But I found that when my focus is limited to material objectives, I am always not quite there; I am constantly dissatisfied and discontent to a greater or lesser degree. And this constant dissatisfaction cripples my unique usefulness to the human beings and world around me.

Today let me open my heart and hear the Lord's voice, motivating me to take time for Him and His righteousness. Let me take up the tools laid out before me this pre-Christmas season, in God's word and prayer, preparing for the vision of the upcoming feast as best I can. Because I will, indeed, be satisfied.

DECEMBER 3

MISTAKES AS ASSETS

"So let us not grow weary in doing what is good, for we will reap at the proper time, if we do not give up." (Gal 6:9)

Why would I "grow weary" in doing what is "good"? Because I experience setbacks; things do not always go as I expect, and I make mistakes, as do fellow-strugglers around me. Even when I focus on leading a God-centered life, and intend to "do what is good," my spiritual growth is not an overnight matter. The Apostle reminds me today not to be a spiritual infant, but to have patience with myself and others. There is growth, even through my mistakes, even if I am not always "reaping" as I would like.

Today I need not be discouraged or dragged down by any of yesterday's failings; for example, if I missed an opportunity to be helpful or just friendly to someone at the office, or if I wasted time or money, or blabbered thoughtlessly in conversations with friends, rather than listening to what they had to say. I can turn all these mistakes into assets, by taking note of them and handing them over to God's mercy, humbly asking Him for His wisdom and grace, to do a bit better today.

This morning I open myself up to His loving care of my spiritual garden, weeds and all, letting Him shed light and nourishment on my "work in progress." Because I "will reap at the proper time, if I do not give up."

DECEMBER 4

SHE IS LED

"The most pure Temple of the Savior; / the precious Chamber and Virgin; / the sacred Treasure of the glory of God, / is led (εἰσάγεται) today into the house of the Lord, / bringing grace with her in the Divine Spirit, / as the angels of God praise her: / "This woman is the abode of heaven." (Kontakion-Hymn of the Entrance of the Theotokos into the Temple)

The feast of the Entrance of the Mother of God into the Temple, celebrated today according to the Old(er) Calendar, is commonly called in Russian "Введение" or the "Leading In" of the Mother of God. Indeed, throughout Her life, the Blessed Among Women was led, by and in the Holy Spirit, on an immensely difficult, cross-carrying journey, which was ultimately to "pierce Her soul," as St. Symeon prophesied (Lk 2:35). Just as Her Son "was led like a lamb," according to the prophesy (Is 53:7), and just as ministers of the Church are led, being held under the arms by others, into the sanctuary at their ordinations.

Today as we celebrate this offering up of Her life to the care and guidance of the Holy Spirit, I am reminded of the immense cross She bore, for all of us. Already in early childhood, She is separated from Her beloved parents, who died when the Most Blessed Virgin was still very young. Later She was betrothed to Joseph, whom She probably barely knew (in any event, She did not confide in him about the Annunciation, leaving him quite unpleasantly bewildered about Her pregnancy). And throughout this difficult journey, She did not know precisely what it all meant, and where God was leading Her.

Today's feast, just like the upcoming feast of Christ's Nativity, is filled with light and triumph. It the light and triumph of the Cross, to which both the Most Blessed Virgin and Her beloved Child are to be led, willingly. May She, Full of Grace, protect and guide me on my own cross-carrying journey today, that I have the willingness to be led where God will. *"Rejoice, O Full of Grace. The Lord is with You,"* and through You, with us.

DECEMBER 5

WELCOMING HIM

"Then they came to Capernaum; and when he was in the house he asked them, 'What were you arguing about on the way?' But they were silent, for on the way they had argued with one another who was the greatest. He sat down, called the twelve, and said to them, 'Whoever wants to be first must be last of all and servant of all.' Then he took a little child and put it among them; and taking it in his arms, he said to them, 'Whoever welcomes one such child in my name welcomes me, and whoever welcomes me welcomes not me but the one who sent me.'" (Mk 9:33-37)

As Christ offers me this gentle lesson about greatness, He not only talks about service, about being "the last of all" and "the servant of all." He also talks about child-like simplicity, likening Himself to a little child. Greatness, in His eyes, is both in being of service, and in simply welcoming even the smallest of human beings.

Let me turn things around today, as I continue to prepare to welcome a child; the Child born in Bethlehem. Today let me take a step back from my neediness and expectations or demands of others, and see how I can be of service; and simply be welcoming. Because ultimately, the Nativity Fast and Advent are about preparing a welcome. That is, preparing the heart to soften and open to His coming.

I am helped in this process by other people, great and small, who come my way, when I put them first in any way I can. Today I ask God to clear away any rubble of neediness and expectations, and fill my heart with the grace of His Spirit, of service and simplicity.

DECEMBER 6

CLEANING THE HEART

"Blessed are the pure in heart: for they shall see God." (Mt 5:8)

So here is another gem from the motivational talk Jesus gave to all of us on the mountain. If you clean your spiritual house, He says, if you make an effort to clear away the burdensome junk that tends to pile up in your heart, like self-pity, envy, unhealthy wants and desires, self-centered fears, ingratitude, and so on—you shall "see God." Before I dismiss these words, as if they are only meant for some kind of super-humans in a galaxy far, far away, let me note how I, personally, am called to "see God."

God reveals Himself in many big and small ways in my life, if I have the eyes to see Him. He subtly shines through in my surroundings, relationships, responsibilities, and situations, when I pay attention to the wisdom and beauty He wants to show me on any given day. In more obvious ways, He reveals Himself on special occasions like the celebration of Divine Liturgy, and on great feasts, like the upcoming vision of His Nativity in Bethlehem.

Today let me take a bit of effort to "clean house," humbly admitting my faults, whatever they are, and clearing my inner vision of fears, worries, and cares, to take in the vision God wants to show me: Himself. As we sing in the Cherubic Hymn, *"Let us now lay aside all earthly cares that we may receive the King of all, escorted invisibly by the angelic orders. Alleluia."*

DECEMBER 7

SECONDARY ISSUES

"Woe to you, scribes and Pharisees, hypocrites! For you tithe mint and dill and cumin, and have neglected the weightier provisions of the law: justice and mercy and faithfulness; but these are the things you should have done without neglecting the others. You blind guides, who strain out a gnat and swallow a camel!" (Mt 23:23-24)

The scribes and Pharisees were meticulous about the smaller prescriptions of the law, like the prohibition, according to Leviticus 11, of eating any creature that "creeps along the ground." So they would strain their wine and other liquids, to make sure there was no "gnat" or other small insect in it. At the same time, they neglected the whole point of the law, which was "justice, mercy, and faithfulness." Christ is reminding them that they should be doing both: following the smaller, external rules, and embracing the "weightier," inner meaning of those rules.

It is sometimes difficult to discern, on a daily basis, what is primary and what is secondary. I may set out, for example, to "improve" my prayer-schedule or fasting discipline, say, during this period of the Nativity Fast. At the same time, I may be neglecting some bigger, outstanding problem in my heart, like being stand-offish and arrogant toward certain colleagues at work, or a member of my family. Or perhaps I am engaging in self-loathing, ungratefulness, and dissatisfaction with life as it is.

Now, the Lord is not telling me to neglect prayer and fasting. What He is, however, telling me, is that whatever external discipline I practice, I should all the time be focusing on the renewal of my heart in His Spirit; on my inner disposition to Him, myself, and others. Today let me ask for, and rely upon, His help and grace, keeping my heart open to Him and other "others" throughout my day.

DECEMBER 8

CRYING OUT TO HIM

"Lord, I have cried unto you: hear me; give ear unto my voice, when I cry unto you." (Ps 140/141: 1)

How does God become a real part of my life? This doesn't automatically happen, even if I seem to be doing the "right" things: I may be a model church-goer, sing in the church-choir, contribute to the bake sales, put up the candles, support the "right" kind of political causes, and so on. But none of this "automatically" makes God the transformative, grace-filling, all-encompassing Presence and Power in my everyday life—if I don't give up playing God myself. I must give up, and cry out to Him, and do so on a daily basis.

God becomes the God of my life when I stop fighting with people and situations, recognizing that I can't "handle" them; I can't "fix" them, or myself, according to my agenda. I give up and cry out to the Lord, and let Him in. And I don't tell Him what to do. I let God play His role, and discipline me, according to His loving, grace-filled will for me. Things "work out" when I do this, as God has reminded me several times, by sending me seemingly hopeless situations.

Today I once again give up, and cry out to Him. I ask God to build with me, according to His will, whatever that may be. I take the steps to do the next right thing, in humble and joyful dependence on His help. *"Lord, I have cried unto You. Hear me."*

DECEMBER 9

THOSE NOT FOLLOWING US

"John said to him, 'Teacher, we saw someone casting out demons in your name, and we tried to stop him, because he was not following us.' But Jesus said, 'Do not stop him; for no one who does a deed of power in my name will be able soon afterward to speak evil of me. Whoever is not against us is for us. For truly I tell you, whoever gives you a cup of water to drink because you bear the name of Christ will by no means lose his reward.'" (Mk 9:38-41)

Today Christ puts my mind to rest with regard to those outside His Church, who do good work in His name. I need not deny, nor be concerned about, "deeds of power" done in His name, happening through and among those who "are not following us." It is up to God to judge and to reward the good done in this world, not me. And He, apparently, is willing to reward every little "cup of water" given in His name.

Right now there are all sorts of events, celebrations, charities, exhibits, concerts, decorations, etc. going on around me in the name of "Christmas"; that is, in His name. Let me not be quick to disparage or judge how, or by whom, these things are done. It is up to Him to judge and to reward, as He sees fit.

As I continue my journey toward Bethlehem, let me accept that others also make this journey in different ways, in ways perhaps foreign to me. He led the Magi, "those who worshipped the stars" (οἱ τοῖς ἄστροις λατρεύοντες, звездам служащии), as we sing in the Nativity Troparion-Hymn, to come to Him in their own, unorthodox way, through a star. So today I leave it to Him to lead me, and others, to Bethlehem, as He sees fit. *O Lord, glory to You.*

DECEMBER 10

LIFTED UP IN HUMILITY

"And Mary said, 'My soul magnifies the Lord, and my spirit rejoices in God my Savior, for he has looked with favor on the humility of his servant. For, behold, from now on all generations will call me blessed; for the Mighty One has done great things for me, and holy is his name. His mercy is for those who fear him from generation to generation. He has shown strength with his arm; he has scattered the proud in the thoughts of their hearts. He has brought down the powerful from their thrones, and lifted up the humble; he has filled the hungry with good things, and sent the rich away empty...'" (Lk 1:46-53)

How delightfully unexpected this is. I mean that Mary, the All-Blessed Virgin, not usually a Woman of many words, suddenly burst into this profound and joyous proclamation of gratitude and praise. She rejoices in God's revelation to Her; of the triumph of humility over pride; of God's strength over human "power"; of true fulfilment over fleeting wealth.

We don't know that She actually saw "the powerful brought down from their thrones" in a literal way, however. She is contemplating a spiritual principle, of the way God works in our lives, bringing us down from our "thrones" if we are full of ourselves, and lifting us up when we recognize our powerlessness and rely on Him.

Today, as I continue to follow Her on our journey to Bethlehem, let me also be grateful. Let me be grateful for God's revelation to me, of my own powerlessness, in whatever ways it is shown to me; whether I mismanaged my time, or ran off at the mouth, or annoyed myself and others in some other way. Let me let God lift me up today, renewing me in His humility. *"For the Mighty One has done great things for me, and holy is His name."*

DECEMBER 11

TRUE LIGHT

"He was the true light that enlightens everyone coming into the world. He was in the world, and the world came into being through him; yet the world did not know him. He came to his own, and his own did not accept him. But to all who received him, who believed in his name, he gave power to become children of God, who were born, not of blood or of the will of the flesh or of the will of man, but of God." (Jn 1:9-13)

Indeed, His coming is the coming of "joy to the world"; of true light and true power. But it is easy to forget, among all the Christmas carols, Christmas lights, and egg nog, that in Bethlehem Christ begins a path of poverty and ultimate rejection by "His own"; a path of the Cross. Already at His birth, He lacks the basic necessities, like a normal house, a nurse or two, proper lighting, or bathroom with running water.

I am reminded today that, while our culture of "Christmas" seems to speak of abundance; an abundance of family laughter and gifts galore, it won't be that for many people. Just as it wasn't that for the Child born in Bethlehem. Many of us won't be able to afford the gifts our children wish for; and many of us might not have loved ones at all to share the feast with. In fact, the holiday may be a painful reminder of those we have lost, or those we never had in the first place.

Whatever the case may be for me this Christmas, I am reminded that my Lord is a Lord Who knows the worst-case scenario in this world. His "true light" comes on the path of the life-giving Cross, which He shared with us from day one of His divine-human life. As I prepare to receive Him, let me gratefully open up to His light and His power. It pours out abundantly on all of us, whether in poverty or wealth, in health or in sickness, among family or in loneliness. He is born to share all of it with us, giving us "power to become children of God,"—like the Child in a poorly-lit cave in Bethlehem.

DECEMBER 12

FRUITS vs. FATHERS

"John said to the crowds that came out to be baptized by him, 'You brood of vipers! Who warned you to flee from the wrath to come? Bear fruits worthy of repentance. Do not begin to say to yourselves, 'We have Abraham as our ancestor'; for I tell you, God is able from these stones to raise up children to Abraham. Even now the ax is lying at the root of the trees; every tree therefore that does not bear good fruit is cut down and thrown into the fire.' And the crowds asked him, 'What then should we do?' In reply he said to them, 'Whoever has two coats must share with anyone who has none; and whoever has food must do likewise.'" (Lk 3:7-11)

So as John the Baptist prepares us for the coming of Christ, one of the first things he tells us (after leading with "brood of vipers!" ☺) is, *"Do not begin to say to yourselves, We have Abraham as our ancestor."* Don't even "begin" to do that. Whatever long tradition of faith you come from, however Orthodox your ancestors were yesterday, you must "bear fruits worthy of repentance" in the here and now. This means sharing what I have, be it extra coats or food or something else, "with anyone who has none."

Today I will contemplate this message a bit more in my heart. It is indeed possible to be, like me, of Orthodox ancestry, officially to "belong" to an Orthodox tradition, an Orthodox nationality, and yet be one of "a brood of vipers." Let me hear this word today, offered to me by the Forerunner of Christ, and focus on what he is telling me to do: "Bear fruits worthy of repentance." Share what you have, he says, "with anyone who has none." Let me continue my journey of this Nativity Fast in the Spirit of self-giving and sharing, bearing fruits worthy of repentance.

DECEMBER 13

UNITY OF HEAVEN AND EARTH

"Let us who mystically represent the cherubim and sing the Thrice-holy Hymn to the life-giving Trinity, now lay aside all cares of life, that we may receive the King of all, escorted invisibly by ranks of angels. Alleluia, alleluia, alleluia."
(Cherubic Hymn, Byzantine Divine Liturgy)

Heaven and earth intermingling. That's what Christianity is all about. We experience and express this unity of heaven and earth in a particularly concentrated manner at Liturgy, when we liken ourselves to the heavenly powers and sing about them. Just as they sing about us, on the very first day of Christ's appearance among us, at His birth: *"Glory to God in the highest, and on earth peace among people of good will (ἐν ἀνθρώποις εὐδοκίας)."* (Lk 2:14)

It is He, the God-Man, Who unifies the earthly and the heavenly, in His incarnation. He brings all of it, and all of us, together in His human-divine Person. He overcomes my self-isolation, my tendency to close in on the self, in self-reliance and self-centeredness, and re-unites me with Creator and all creation, in Himself. This bringing together of all, this bringing back of the previously-separated, is ultimately what we are celebrating in His coming, on the upcoming feast of the Nativity. It is also what we celebrate at every Divine Liturgy: re-uniting in Him.

So today, once again, let me "lay aside all cares of life," unburdening myself of self-centeredness, and "receive the King of all, escorted invisibly by ranks of angels,"—and visibly by all of us. Glory be to Him.

DECEMBER 14

EXISTENTIAL ANGST

"In those days a decree went out from Emperor Augustus that all the world should be registered. This was the first registration and was taken while Quirinius was governor of Syria. All went to their own towns to be registered. Joseph also went from the town of Nazareth in Galilee to Judea, to the city of David called Bethlehem, because he was descended from the house and family of David. He went to be registered with Mary, to whom he was engaged and who was expecting a child. While they were there, the time came for her to deliver her child..." (Lk 2:1-6)

Today I'm looking at this passage from the Gospel, about a family in a most precarious situation. A Woman in the advanced stages of pregnancy is obliged to get up and travel from Nazareth to Bethlehem, a trip that must have been unexpected, and must have taken from four to seven days. And it wasn't exactly smooth-sailing when they got there, because there was no place for them to stay.

Unexpected, insecure situations like this one, when things don't seem to be going according to (my) plan, either for me or those I love, can fill me with deep anxiety. But that is to say, really, that life in general can fill me with anxiety, because life is commonly full of surprises, departing from my "script."

Today let me embrace what God is showing me through the unexpected, through the departures from my "script": that He is in control, not me. Let me ask for His will to be done, for His power to be shown, in my weaknesses and ambivalence. Today I open my heart to His grace and mercy, in a bit of heartfelt prayer. Only He can liberate me from the burdens of self-reliance, when I put myself and others in His hands, letting Him do what I can't do for myself or others. "Thy will be done," I say today; let it be done in my life, as it was done in the life of this Family that made the untimely trip to Bethlehem.

DECEMBER 15

HEARING HIS VOICE

"Therefore, as the Holy Spirit says, 'Today, if you hear his voice, do not harden your hearts as in the rebellion, as on the day of testing in the wilderness, where your ancestors put me to the test, though they had seen my works for forty years. Therefore I was angry with that generation, and I said, 'They always go astray in their hearts, and they have not known my ways.' As in my anger I swore, 'They will not enter my rest.' Take care, brothers, that none of you may have an evil, unbelieving heart that turns away from the living God. But exhort one another every day, as long as it is called 'today,' so that none of you may be hardened by the deceitfulness of sin." (Heb 3:7-13)

So the Apostle is exhorting me not to harden my heart "today," if I "hear His voice." This hardening of the heart is described here as "going astray" in the heart, by the "deceitfulness of sin." It prevents one from "entering His rest." There is much to be said about the Old Testament events described in this passage, how God's people hardened their hearts "on the day of testing in the wilderness." But let me reflect how this same thing can occur within me, on my own "day of testing," which is every day.

I can "go astray" in my heart today, if I accept various small or large distortions of reality, according to my own, limited vision of things. I can embrace envy on the basis of seeing only the negative in my life, and only the positive in someone else's. I can embrace fear on the basis of the news I read or watch, if I read and watch unenlightened by God's grace-filled word. I can embrace lust and greed, when perceiving people and things with a "carnal mind." And so on. This kind of "deceitfulness of sin" distorts my vision and robs me of peace. That is, it prevents me from "entering His rest," as the Apostle reminds me here.

Today let me take some time to hear God's voice, and let His light into my heart, that I may see myself and others as God does. *"Create in me a clean heart, O God; and renew a right spirit within me."* (Ps 50/51:10)

DECEMBER 16

HIS DISTURBING LIGHT

"In the time of King Herod, after Jesus was born in Bethlehem of Judea, wise men from the East came to Jerusalem, asking, 'Where is the child who has been born king of the Jews? For we observed his star at its rising, and have come to pay him homage.' When King Herod heard this, he was disturbed (ἐταράχθη), and all Jerusalem with him; and calling together all the chief priests and scribes of the people, he inquired of them where the Messiah was to be born. They told him, 'In Bethlehem of Judea; for so it has been written by the prophet..." (Mt. 2:1-5)

So the news of Christ's birth did not generate "great joy" in most of the people who heard about it. For Herod "and all Jerusalem with him" it was rather "disturbing," and unpleasantly so. How could this be? Wasn't this a religious society, aware of the Scriptures and prophecies, with religious authorities like the chief priests and scribes capable of understanding them? Yes. But this religious society was self-sufficient in its authorities and ways of doing things. The "interference" of the Holy Spirit, over Whom these authorities had no control, was not welcome in their midst.

Today as I continue the Nativity Fast, I am reminded to remain humbly open to any "disturbances" that may be caused by letting Christ into my day. Let me welcome His way of doing things, which is the way of the Cross. I may have to take a step back, letting go of neediness and self-seeking, being quietly useful to Him and others. I need not fear nor be "disturbed" by His way, because I know that His self-giving, in me, brings me "great light," according to the beautiful prophecy of Isaiah: *"The people who walk in darkness will see a great light; Those who live in a dark land, the light will shine on them."* (Is 9:2)

DECEMBER 17

WITNESSING TO HIM

"But you will receive power (δύναμιν) when the Holy Spirit comes on you; and you will be my witnesses (μάρτυρες) in Jerusalem, and in all Judea and Samaria, and to the ends of the earth." (Acts 1:8)

Here, the Lord shares two crucial bits of information with His disciples about "witnessing" to Him, or "martyrdom": 1. It begins with receiving the power of the Holy Spirit, and 2. It begins in their immediate surroundings, i. e., Jerusalem, and in all Judea and Samaria.

Today, when I am both blessed and horrified by news of Christian martyrdom in countries far away from me, I am reminded that the Lord calls all of us to be His "witnesses" much closer to home, in the here and now. He also reminds me that the "power" (δύναμις) to be His witness does not come from me, nor does it begin with my picking up a sign and marching with it angrily in the street. That just makes me an angry Christian with a sign. Being His witness begins with opening my heart, on a daily basis, to the gifts of the Holy Spirit, and sharing these gifts, in my daily routine and behaviour, in my immediate surroundings. It means walking with Him, and in Him, and not obscuring His light through my own agenda, fears, and anger.

So let me not be a mere spectator today of Christian "witness" or "martyrdom." Let me let His light into my heart, so that I can be His witness in the way He calls me to be: in and through the power of the Holy Spirit.

DECEMBER 18

SARCASM

"So also the chief priests, with the scribes and elders, mocked him, saying, 'He saved others; he cannot save himself. He is the King of Israel; let him come down now from the cross, and we will believe in him. He trusts in God; let God deliver him now, if he desires him. For he said, 'I am the Son of God.'" (Mt 27:41-43)

As Jesus Christ is slowly dying, nailed to a cross, these guys are having some very clever laughs. What a chilling example of the dark side of sarcasm.

In small doses, with proper motivation and at the proper time and place, sarcasm can enhance my conversation or speech, like a strong spice can enhance a meal. But it can also ruin the "meal" or an entire relationship, when overdone or misplaced. Jesus Himself used dry, ironic humor in small doses, for example: *"I have shown you many good works from the Father; for which of these do you stone me?"* (Jn 10:32)

Today I am reminded to use the God-given gifts of wit and humor with care and discretion. These gifts can relieve stress, build bridges, and "break the ice" in difficult conversations, when my heart is in the right "place." But these same gifts can also sabotage relationships: they can be used to keep relationships superficial, to avoid the vulnerability of sincere conversation, or to disguise aggression and hostility, if the latter have found a place in my heart. So, as with anything else that I do or say, let me examine my heart as to why I do or say it. Let any words or wit I use today be "spiced" with the light of His grace-filled Cross.

DECEMBER 19

HE COMES TO RESTORE

"Prepare, O Bethlehem, for Eden has been opened to all! / Adorn yourself, O Ephratha, for the tree of life blossoms forth from the Virgin in the cave! / Her womb is a spiritual paradise planted with the Divine Fruit: / If we eat of it, we shall live forever and not die like Adam. / Christ comes to restore the image which He made in the beginning!" (Byzantine Troparion-hymn of the Forefeast of the Nativity)

Christ comes, indeed, to "restore," to "make right" what goes "wrong" in our paradise. In our paradise, we tend to seek out "food" that isn't good for us; to nurture ourselves in unhealthy ways. Today our unhealthy "nourishment" is commonly useless information that we might choose to imbibe on a daily basis, through various news outlets and social media. This kind of information, if we immerse ourselves in it outside God's word and grace, commonly brings us painful self-awareness, either through fear (of calamities in the world, like terrorist attacks), or delusional comparison with other people's lives and fortunes, like the lives and fortunes of celebrities.

In reading up on the news I may have a good intention, because I want to better myself by knowing things. But if I constantly choose to seek this betterment outside God, with disregard for His word, I obscure His image in me, "the image He made in the beginning." I am left in burdensome communion with the self, with the merely human, as Eve did when she trusted the serpent's promise, that *"your eyes shall be opened, and you shall be as gods, knowing good and evil."* (Gen 3:5)

Christ brings me new vision and a new communion, with Himself, the Divine Fruit. He liberates me from the bondage of the merely-human through His light, that "blossoms forth from the Virgin in the cave." Today as I continue my journey to that cave in Bethlehem, let me take some time to sit in His light, in a bit of prayer and reading of His word. Let Him restore in me what I tend to lose when left to my own devices. *"Christ comes to restore the image which He made in the beginning."*

DECEMBER 20

GOD OF OUR FATHERS

"He has helped his servant Israel, in remembrance of his mercy; As he said to our fathers, to Abraham, and to his seed for ever." (Lk 1:54-55)

In the early days of Her pregnancy, the All-Holy Virgin Mary pronounced these words in Her famous "song of praise," when She "magnified" the Lord upon meeting Elizabeth. At this moment She, Full of Grace, praised God not only for Herself, but for all of Israel; for all the generations of "our fathers," who had awaited and longed for the coming of the One now in Her womb. She recognizes, awestruck in the Holy Spirit, that the Child She carries brings God's mercy not only to Her, but to all of God's people, to all of us.

In Christ, in His one Body, we all become sons and daughters of this Woman. When we receive Him, when we commune in Him, we share in His genealogy, which opens up to all nations and peoples in the incarnate, Only-Begotten Son of God.

However I have spent this Nativity Fast thus far, let me join in today, and take in the Light dawning in Bethlehem, for everyone without exception, including me. *"O God of our Fathers, Who always acts towards us according to Your meekness; take not Your mercy from us, but by their prayers guide our lives in peace."*

DECEMBER 21

CHRISTMAS GIFT-GIVING

"...O Lord, open my lips, and my mouth will declare your praise. For if you desired sacrifice, I would have given it; with whole burnt offerings you would not be pleased. The sacrifice acceptable to God is a broken spirit; a broken and contrite heart, O God, you will not despise. Do good to Zion in your good pleasure; and let the walls of Jerusalem be built. Then you will be pleased in a sacrifice of righteousness..." (Ps 50/51:15-19)

Giving gifts to one another on Christmas is a reminder of the self-giving of the Magi or "wise men from the East," who brought themselves and their gifts to Bethlehem, falling down before the Child and His Mother (Lk 2:11). The main sacrifice made by the Magi, I think, lies not only or even primarily in the price they paid for the expensive gifts of gold, frankincense, and myrrh. It lies rather in the great trouble they took to make the long trip to Bethlehem, to "search diligently for the young Child" (Lk 2:8), to fall down and worship Him as they did.

So let me remember the sacrifice of the Magi, as I go about my Christmas gift-giving, that I do it in the right Spirit; as a "sacrifice acceptable to God." I might be tempted to spend money I don't have, ultimately burdening myself and my family with debt and resentment; or I might burden myself with some other form of dishonesty, if my gift-giving is hypocritical, not aligned with the intentions in my heart. Let my gift-giving be constructive for my spiritual "house," letting "the walls of Jerusalem be built" rather than damaged by the holiday. As I continue my preparation for Christ's Nativity, let me put first things first, bringing to Him what is truly precious in His eyes, my "broken and contrite heart."

DECEMBER 22

STOP AND LISTEN

"While Jesus was teaching in the temple, he said, 'How can the scribes say that the Messiah is the son of David? David himself, by the Holy Spirit, declared, 'The Lord said to my Lord, Sit at my right hand, until I put your enemies under your feet.' David himself calls him Lord; so how can he be his son?' And the large crowd was listening to him with delight (ἡδέως)." (Mk. 12:35-37)

There is so much going on right now, with pre-Christmas preparations and end-of-the-year hustle and bustle, that I woke up this morning with my head full with a To Do List. It was hard to focus in prayer, after which I somewhat reluctantly opened my little Gospel-book, to do a bit of reading. And I came across the passage cited above, in which the Son of David calls me, in the subtle form of a question, to recognize His true Identity. As Jesus so humbly reveals Himself here as Lord, the crowd listens to His words "with delight."

Today I thank Him for His subtle, never pushy reminders of His lordship in my often-chaotic life. Let me let Him in today, as Lord of everything that happens to be going on in my day. Let me stop and listen "with delight" to my Lord's humble voice, reminding me that He is the One in control, putting His enemies "under His feet," not me. Glory be to Him, Who is quietly born in Bethlehem, to walk among us in meekness and humility.

DECEMBER 23

GREETING HIM IN HIS SPIRIT

"Brethren, even if anyone is caught in any trespass, you who are spiritual, restore such a one in a spirit of meekness; each one looking to yourself, so that you too will not be tempted. Carry each other's burdens, and in this way you will fulfill the law of Christ." (Gal 6:1-2)

Here it is again, the word one doesn't hear much anymore: meekness. It is a divine gift, a gentleness of the Holy Spirit, demonstrated in gentle behaviour when one is confronted with an opposite kind of behaviour. But I don't know if that sentence made any sense. What I mean is, "meekness" is a behaviour vis-à-vis confrontations and challenges. It is different from "humility," in that "humility" is first and foremost a state of being, while "meekness" is always a behaviour. It involves "carrying" other people's burdens/shortcomings rather than exacerbating them with annoyance, frustration, or condemnation. For example, if I am working on a project with my crew, and one of the crew messes it up, costing me time and money, I can choose to:
1. have a fit and tell him he is negligent and generally useless, or
2. I can take a deep, prayerful breath, sit down with him and help fix the mess-up, encouraging him to do better next time. Sadly I don't always choose 2. :/

In any event, as I begin another busy day of this holiday season, let me take pause and open up to His "Spirit of meekness." Let me unburden myself of unreasonable demands and expectations of others, taking up His light-filled cross, as I prepare to greet Him, Who is to be born in a lonely cave in Bethlehem. As He comes in meekness to begin His own cross-carrying journey, let me refocus from my will to His, greeting Him in His Spirit: *"Glory to God in the highest, and on earth peace among people of good will."*

DECEMBER 24

CHRISTMAS on DIFFERENT CALENDARS

"Today the Virgin gives birth to the Transcendent One, / And the earth offers a cave to the Unapproachable One! / Angels with shepherds glorify Him! / The wise men journey with a star! / Since for our sake the Eternal God was born as a Little Child!" (Byzantine Kontakion-Hymn of the Nativity)

I'll just come out and say it: I like seeing the Magi (or Wise Men) in Nativity scenes and Nativity icons, together with the shepherds and various animals in the cave. Even though, as pedants like me may remind you, the Magi clearly came later, entering a "house,"—not a cave—where they found Mother and Child and knelt down before Him (just read Matthew 2). But at the time of Christ's birth they actually still "journey with a star," as it says in the Kontakion quoted above. So the Magi and the shepherds celebrated "Christmas" at different times. And yet in our popular perception, in Nativity scenes and plays, and in present-day Byzantine tradition, we group them together, because they are participants in one "mystery," of greeting Him after He is born.

Today we also celebrate His Nativity at different times, for rather different reasons. As most of the Christian world enters the celebration of Christ's Nativity today, those of us on the Older Calendar do not. I'm thinking about this because I also belong to, and grew up in, a church-community that celebrates Christmas two weeks from now. From early childhood I've known the strange feeling of anticipating Christmas, while our neighbours' Christmas trees were already discarded on their front lawns or sidewalks.

Despite the awkward reality of different calendars, I am reminded today that we are, indeed, participants in one Mystery, of greeting Him upon His birth. While some of us still "journey with a star," continuing the Nativity Fast, I wish all of you who are greeting Him now a blessed feast. Whether you are with family, or lonely, or far away from home, may His birth in a lonely cave in the insignificant town of Bethlehem be a source of peace and joy and comfort in His Holy Spirit. Have a blessed Christmas, *"Since for our sake,"* for all of us, *"the Eternal God is born as a Little Child."*

DECEMBER 25

GO AND MEET HIM

"Christ is born; glorify him! Christ is from heaven; go and meet him! Christ is on earth; be exalted! O All the earth, sing unto the Lord, and people, sing with joy. For He is glorified." (Ode. 1, Byzantine Nativity Canon)

Once again, Christ is born in our hearts; Once again, He gives of Himself as "Bread for the whole world," as it says in the Byzantine Prayer of the Prothesis, or Preparation of the Gifts, a rite celebrated in the altar by the priest before Divine Liturgy begins. Christ's coming to us in "Beth-lehem," meaning in Hebrew "the house of bread," is thus celebrated and remembered at this "Prothesis Rite" before each Divine Liturgy, which is why an icon or fresco of the Nativity often adorns the Prothesis Table, on which the gifts of bread and wine are prepared for the Eucharist.

So "Christ is from heaven," and is now "on earth," accessible to us, to "go and meet Him." And we do this, we reply to His Self-giving, by giving of ourselves in the Eucharist. We bring our gifts of bread, wine, and ourselves, in body and soul, sharing in His Body and His Soul, at His table.

Let me not be left out today, in this celebration of the unity of heaven and earth, which He makes possible in His glorious Incarnation. Let me suit up and show up, whatever is happening in my life, or whatever calamities are happening in the world, or whichever Herods seek to kill the Child. He is born into it all, taking on our humanity, our pain, and our calamities, as One of us. Let me go and meet Him, as He has come to meet me. *"Christ is born; glorify Him!"*

DECEMBER 26

HAVING TIME FOR HIM

"Then Jesus said to him, 'Someone gave a great dinner and invited many. At the time for the dinner he sent his slave to say to those who had been invited, 'Come; for everything is ready now.' But they all alike began to make excuses. The first said to him, 'I have bought a piece of land, and I must go out and see it; please accept my regrets.' Another said, 'I have bought five yoke of oxen, and I am going to try them out; please accept my regrets.' Another said, 'I have just been married, and therefore I cannot come.' So the slave returned and reported this to his master. Then the owner of the house became angry and said to his slave, 'Go out at once into the streets and lanes of the town and bring in the poor, the crippled, the blind, and the lame...'" (Lk 14:16-21)

So, not everybody has time for the kind of fellowship, food, and entertainment God has on offer at His dinner party. Only the poor, the crippled, the blind, and the lame end up coming—the ones with all the time in the world, and nowhere better to go. The "invited" ones politely decline, because they "have" matters, like work and family and romance, which require their wholehearted attention.

Does one need to be poor, or crippled, or blind, or lame to hear God's call and "find time" for Him? Yes. It is necessary to be "poor in spirit," and have "a broken and humbled heart" (Ps 50/51:17). Perhaps ironically, sometimes the way to "a broken and humbled heart" is through a God-less dedication to work, family, or some relationship, romantic or otherwise. Without God in the picture, an intense dedication to a job or a relationship can leave me with a broken heart and emptiness. But this is my human condition without God in the first place, because I am not self-sufficient.

Today let me open up to God's fellowship, taking some time to be nurtured with His word. It is made so accessible to me in the God-Man Jesus Christ, Who comes into my world in Bethlehem, to dine with the poor, crippled, blind, and lame. Today, once again, I bring my brokenness and emptiness to His table, to be healed and filled with His grace. *"Taste and see that the Lord is good; blessed is the man who trusts in him."* (Ps 33/34:8)

DECEMBER 27

SHE IS OFFERED

"What shall we offer You, O Christ, Who for our sakes have appeared on earth as a man? Every creature made by You offers You thanks: the Angels offer a hymn; the heavens, a star; the Wise Men, gifts; the shepherds, their wonder; the earth, its cave; the wilderness, a manger, and we offer You a virgin Mother!// O Pre-eternal God, have mercy on us!" (Stichera from Byzantine Vespers of Nativity)

Indeed, She, the Holy Virgin, is offered. She is offered as the best "we" have to offer. And by "we" we mean "She," as one of us. Because She is the one who makes this decision, to offer Her life, Her entire being, body and soul, to the service of God's plan. She offers Herself up to the mystery of the Incarnation, from the moment She says "let it be" to the angel (Lk. 1:38). This decision, made by Her, meant a life of extreme trials, insecurity, and pain, particularly when "a sword" was to "pierce Her soul" at Her Son's crucifixion, as prophesied by St. Symeon (Lk 2:35).

Today we share in Mary's unique self-giving, as members of one Body of Christ, and we gratefully celebrate it, particularly on the great feast of our Lord's Nativity. Because it is through Her birth that we receive new life, new communion, and a new capacity to give, to create, and to grow in His grace. Let me stay close to Her now, in my thoughts and prayers, as we celebrate the feast, greeting Him, at the side of His Virgin Mother. For our sake She gives birth to a little Child, so that we don't remain barren and alone. "Today the Virgin gives birth to the transcendent One." Glorify Him!

DECEMBER 28

AIRPORTS & AFFRONTS

"But now you must get rid of all such things—anger, wrath, malice, slander, and abusive language from your mouth. Do not lie to one another, seeing that you have stripped off the old self with its practices and have clothed yourselves with the new self, which is being renewed in knowledge according to the image of its creator, in which there is no longer Greek and Jew, circumcised and uncircumcised, barbarian, Scythian, slave and free; but Christ is all and in all! As God's chosen ones, holy and beloved, clothe yourselves with compassion, kindness, humility, meekness, and patience." (Col 3:8-11)

Today this familiar passage hit me like a ton of bricks. Probably because I've spent much of the last 24 hours traveling, and still find myself at an airport because of a flight cancellation. So amidst the frustrations and occasional affronts of international travel, I am called to "a new self, which is being renewed in knowledge,"—a new kind of knowledge of the self and others, "according to the image of the Creator."

How wonderful, how powerful, to be reminded and challenged this way by the Word of God, in unexpected and chaotic situations. Let me let Him carry me amidst the small annoyances and unexpected conversations at boarding gates, airline service-centers, waiting halls with occasional very bad coffee. ☺ Let Him clothe me today, as He clothes all of us, as holy and beloved, wherever and whenever we let Him.

DECEMBER 29

SENSELESS TRAGEDY

"When Herod saw that he had been tricked by the wise men, he was infuriated, and he sent and killed all the children in and around Bethlehem who were two years old or under, according to the time that he had learned from the wise men. Then was fulfilled what had been spoken through the prophet Jeremiah: 'A voice was heard in Ramah, wailing and loud lamentation, Rachel weeping for her children; she refused to be consoled, because they are no more." (Mt 2:16-18)

There is such a thing as senseless tragedy in the Gospel, and justifiably inconsolable grief. The mothers and fathers who weeped for their massacred babies did not have any "explanation" for what had happened, nor did they have the hope of the resurrection. All they knew was that their children "are no more." Nobody was there to tell them that their children had died for the Saviour of the world. We know all that today, but they didn't. What they faced was the senselessness of a human will run riot; of Herod's insanity, which had the kind of power to order this brutal massacre.

The God-given freedom of the human will can have both horrible and wonderful consequences. And the whole picture only makes "sense" in the light of God's omniscience, justice, mercy, and ultimately—in His resurrection.

I am reminded of all this today, as I contemplate the massacre in Bethlehem, and other massacres and tragedies of today. Christ comes into my world in Bethlehem to take it all on, even unto death; a violent death at the hands of human wills run riot. He subjects Himself to all that in order to redeem it, and make it right, in the grace He brings and shares with us, of His light-giving resurrection. *"Help us, save us, have mercy on us, and keep us, O God, by Your grace."*

DECEMBER 30
IT GETS BETTER

"...And what more should I say? For time would fail me to tell of Gideon, Barak, Samson, Jephthah, of David and Samuel and the prophets—who through faith conquered kingdoms, administered justice, obtained promises, shut the mouths of lions, quenched raging fire... They were stoned to death, they were sawn in two, they were tempted, they were killed by the sword; they went about in skins of sheep and goats, destitute, persecuted, tormented. They, of whom the whole world was not worthy, wandered in deserts and mountains, and in caves and holes in the ground. Yet all these, though they were commended for their faith, did not receive what was promised, since God had foreseen something better so that they would not, apart from us, be made perfect." (Heb 11:32-33, 37-40)

No, they did not receive "what was promised"; they did not witness, in their time, the revelation of God's Son in the flesh, when He came and unified all of us, in His one Body. For reasons known only to God, the proper time for His salvific, unifying Incarnation came after the lifetimes of the great fathers mentioned here. And yet they believed in Him, and longed for Him, Whom they did not see.

Not everybody is given the gift of "seeing" Him, even today. There are people with severe spiritual or mental handicaps, or people who are perceived as inadequate in some other way; rejected by human opinion and perceived as "losers." For some people the "something better" that God has on offer will only come in the future life, for reasons known only to Him. And at times we ourselves may feel abandonment and darkness, as if He has left us, as if He "is" not.

Let me remember today, in faith, that it is God, not us, Who "makes perfect" that which in our world appears "destitute, persecuted, tormented." Let me be faithful to Him today, whether I see His light or don't. Glory be to Him, Who has "something better" in store for those who long, thirst, and hunger for Him today, rejected and inadequate in this world.

DECEMBER 31

MOVING FORWARD TOGETHER

"Let us hold unswervingly to the hope we profess, for he who promised is faithful. And let us consider how we may spur one another on toward love and good deeds, not giving up meeting together, as some are in the habit of doing, but encouraging one another—and all the more as you see the Day approaching." (Heb 10:23-25)

Why "celebrate" the New Year? This doesn't immediately make sense. Doesn't our movement through time, from one year to the next, one day to the next, and so on, "happen" anyway, regardless of how we feel about it? Yes. But is "life," as John Lennon says, "what happens to you when you're busy making other plans"? No. Not if you are a "practicing" Christian, anyway. And by "practicing" I mean "celebrating." Because we "celebrate" temporal transitions.

What does that mean? "Celebrating" a temporal transition, like the transition to a New Year, means we do this together. To "celebrate" (from the Latin "celebrare") means "to gather to honor." As Christians, we try to make our conscious "gatherings" as frequent as possible, "honoring" our movement through time, weekly from Sunday to Sunday, or even daily from evening to night, night to morning and so on, in the daily services, together, as frequently as possible. Our movement through time has common meaning, because it has common purpose, "the Day approaching," mentioned in Hebrews 6. We approach, together, with purpose, the ultimate fulfilment in God, in communion with His Son, powered daily by the grace of the Holy Spirit, which is poured out abundantly on us, in communion and community, on a daily basis.

So "let us consider how we may spur one another on toward love and good deeds...encouraging one another" in friendliness, courteousness, attentiveness to others, and avoidance of the stuff opposite of all that: neediness, too much talking about self, or hogging the potato chips. ☺ Onwards and forwards, everyone, and Happy upcoming New Year!

ABOUT THE AUTHOR

Dr. Sr. Vassa Larin, host of the popular, online program, "Coffee with Sister Vassa," is a scholar of Byzantine Liturgy and author of many publications, both scholarly and popular, on Eastern Orthodox spirituality and tradition.
Born in Nyack, New York in a devout, Russian Orthodox family, Sister Vassa is now based in Vienna, Austria.

For more on her internationally-acclaimed, online ministry, visit
coffeewithsistervassa.com.

Other books by Sister Vassa Larin:

Lent with Sister Vassa: Reflections for every day of Lent

*HealthyFast Lenten Guidebook:
Reflections and meal plans for every day of Lent*

*Reflections with Morning Coffee:
365 Daily Devotions for Busy People*

Tune in to Sister Vassa's inspirational, weekday audio-podcast, "Morning Coffee," and walk with zillions of our subscribers through the Church Year at:

patreon.com/sistervassa

www.ingramcontent.com/pod-product-compliance
Lightning Source LLC
LaVergne TN
LVHW011927070526
838202LV00054B/4519